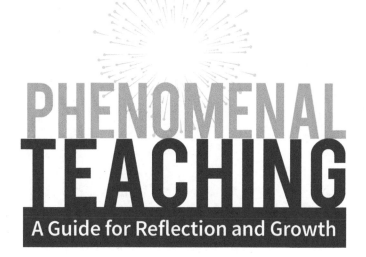

PHENOMENAL TEACHING

A Guide for Reflection and Growth

WENDY WARD HOFFER

Foreword by **JOHN HATTIE**

PHENOMENAL
TEACHING

A Guide for Reflection
and Growth

HEINEMANN
Portsmouth, NH

Heinemann
145 Maplewood Ave., Suite 300
Portsmouth, NH 03801
www.heinemann.com

Offices and agents throughout the world

The author and publisher wish to thank those who have generously given permission to reprint borrowed material:

Excerpts from Common Core State Standards © Copyright 2010. National Governors Association Center for Best Practices and Council of Chief State School Officers. All rights reserved.

Excerpt from *A Framework for K–12 Science Education: Practices, Crosscutting Concepts, and Core Ideas* by National Research Council. Copyright © 2012 by National Research Council. Published by The National Academies Press. Reprinted by permission.

List from "Ten Things the Mainstream Teacher Can Do Today to Improve Instruction for ELL Students" in *Strategies and Resources for the Mainstream Teachers of ELL* by Bracken Reed and Jennifer Railsback. Copyright © 2003. Published by Northwest Regional Education Library. Reprinted by permission.

Excerpt from *From a Nation at Risk to a Nation at Hope: Recommendations from the National Commission on Social, Emotional, & Academic Development* written and published by The Aspen Institute National Commission on Social, Emotional, and Academic Development. Copyright © 2018. Reprinted by permission.

Excerpt from "Wait Time: Slowing Down May Be a Way of Speeding Up!" by Mary Budd Rowe. From *Journal of Teacher Education* (vol. 37, issue 1). Copyright © 1986 by American Association of Colleges for Teacher Education (AACTE). Published by SAGE Publications on behalf of AACTE. Reprinted by permission.

ISBN: 978-0-325-09217-1
Library of Congress Control Number: 2020930633

Editor: Katherine Bryant
Production: Hilary Goff
Cover and interior designs: Suzanne Heiser
Photography: Laura Mahoney
Typesetter: Gina Poirier Design
Manufacturing: Steve Bernier

Printed in the United States of America on acid-free paper
4 5 6 7 8 9 10 BB 25 24 23 22 21
December 2021 Printing

For each and every teacher, with deep respect and deeper gratitude.

"To teach in a manner that respects and cares for the souls of our students is essential if we are to provide the necessary conditions where learning can most deeply and intimately begin."

—bell hooks (1994)

CONTENTS

1: STANCE 1

Chapter Question: What drives you?

2: PLAN 12

Chapter Question: How can we design learning experiences that cultivate students' understanding and agency?

3: COMMUNITY 49

Chapter Question: In what ways might we develop classroom communities that support the agency and understanding of every learner?

4: WORKSHOP 71

Chapter Question: In what ways might we facilitate learning experiences that support students grappling with challenging tasks in service of conceptual understanding?

5: THINKING STRATEGIES 101

Chapter Question: In what ways might we provide tools that increase learners' agency and understanding?

6: DISCOURSE 131

Chapter Question: In what ways might we scaffold productive, engaged academic conversations?

7: ASSESSMENT 161

Chapter Question: In what ways might we monitor and support progress?

FOREWORD

I have visited classrooms with Wendy where these *Phenomenal Teaching* ideas are being implemented. The success of these approaches was visible in the language of the students who welcomed the struggle of thinking, saw learning as hard work, knew the power and had the skills of collaboration, and demonstrated great respect in being critical evaluators of their own and others' ideas. Ashley, one lab host teacher we observed, "engineered" these things to happen; it was not by accident or osmosis. She did not dominate the learning, and she taught the skills that allowed students to become their own teachers.

This book captures the methods, the thrill, the skill, and the evaluation of this form of teaching. This work is based on identifying where there is excellence, and then scaling this up. Too often, we look for failure and remediate—here, we are beginning with assets and growing from there.

I find it fascinating that when we ask adults about who their best teachers were and why, they tend to report two major attributes: great teachers turn students on to their passion, and great teachers see strengths and successes in students that the learners had not previously seen in themselves. These attributes can be developed through the methods and messages described in these chapters. For students, this leads to a sense of wonder, of excitement, of seeing errors as opportunities for learning, of making class an inviting place where they want to be.

The analogy of a rope is used to identify the six key strands of the Public Education & Business Coalition Teaching Framework. We need to recall that the strength of the rope is not in the strength of any or all of the strands, but in the overlapping of the many strands. Using these approaches together, we can teach students strategies for learning, the pleasure of discovering ideas, the skills for relating these ideas, and the delight in transferring their learning to new situations—the actions of agency and understanding.

Given my penchant for wanting evidence of impact, and that I have seen the impact of the strands woven throughout this book in action, this is a phenomenal book. Enjoy.

—John Hattie

ACKNOWLEDGMENTS

Fortune smiled on me when I landed in the lap of the Denver-based Public Education & Business Coalition (PEBC) in 2004. I am indebted to PEBC's thought leaders, Ellin Oliver Keene, Susan Zimmerman, Stephanie Harvey, Anne Goudvis, Debbie Miller, Cris Tovani, Patrick Allen, Lori Conrad, and Samantha Bennett, and all of the long-time lab hosts and staff developers who preceded me and set the standard for excellence, as well as the brilliant thought partners with whom I enjoy the privilege of collaborating.

PEBC's original Continuum of Growth in Research-Based Instructional Best Practices, of which this work is an outgrowth, was initiated by Paula Miller and Stevi Quate, supported by the work of the UCD Evaluation Center, and midwifed for some time by Suzanne Plaut, to whom I am indebted.

The Framework stands on the shoulders of generations of Denver-area PEBC Lab Hosts and Lab Host Fellows who model phenomenal teaching and inform our thinking, many of whom permitted the gathering of ideas, artifacts, and stories from their classrooms to animate this book, including Patrick Allen, RheaLynn Anderson, Jenny Ardourel, Tiffany Askins, Val Beckler, Leslie Blauman, Jenn Brauner, Ashley Bromstrup, Veronica Carrejo, Jeff Cazier, Lesli Cochran, Michelle DuMoulin, Jana Durbin, Jennifer Engbretson, Josh Feiger, Lindsay Folker, Rachel Gardner, Keri Gordon, Carrie Halbasch, Gabrielle Hovinen, Bill Huber, Karlee Hunt, Christine Jasmann, Shawna Jensen, Michelle Joy, Sue Kempton, Kate Klaver, Mary Korte, Jennifer Krause, Beth Lakin, Margo Lane, Candace Lewis, Jeff Lewis, Susan Logan, Chris Martin, Suzanne Martin, Deb Maruyama, Missy Matthews, Kathleen McHugh, Susan McIver, Ryan McKillop, Ana Mettler, Caitlin Moore, Andrea Overton, Jessica Piwko, Rachel Rosenberg, Jamie Salterelli, Allison Sampish, Kathy Sampson, Erika Schenk, Tracey Shaw, Shannon Umberger, Alisa Wills-Keely, Angel Wolf, Angela Zehner, and Cheryl Zimmermann.

The current iteration of the PEBC Teaching Framework was fostered by my close thought partner Annie Patterson, facilitator of PEBC's lab network, as well as by the consistently insightful input of our Professional Learning Team. In addition, the Framework's evolution has been supported by members of our think tank, Lori Conrad, Parker Griggs, Emily Kotnis, Karen Lowenstein, Nancy Meredith, Stevi Quate, Rachele McCawley Robertson, Sue Sava, Tracy Wagers, and Laurie Wretling, as well as benefited from the insight of all PEBC's staff developers over the years, including Sarah Berger, Jenn Brauner, Linda Fiorella, Missy Matthews, Kirsten Myers-Blake, Suzanne Nisely, Emily Quinty, Carla Randall, Tracey Shaw, Kristen Venable, Sue Wilson, and more.

I appreciate client schools and districts too numerous to mention who welcome me and my colleagues in to see your work, hear your thinking, listen and respond to ideas, embrace challenges, collaborate on planning and instruction, reflect on your craft. We are thankful for your trust and for all that you teach us.

This book would never be were it not for PEBC and all those who have fostered and supported the organization at various periods in our history, including but not limited to Mindy Armbruster, Tom Brinegar, Craig DeLeone, Mariah Dickson, Rose Hagood, Leanna Harris, Joyce Joyce, Melissa Kircher, Traci Lacheta, Jon Lehmann, Kim McGrigg, Natalie Newton, Brooke O'Drobinak, Renee Ostuni, Lori Pidick, Suzanne Plaut, Denise Powell, Ashley Ruhl, Sue Sava, Jon Sisk, Diane Sweeney, Barb Volpe, and Rosann Ward. Your impact on teachers and students reaches further than you might ever know.

In bringing this book to life, I am indebted to Annie Patterson, Dana Sorenson, Heather Kuzma, Michelle Morris Jones, Moker Klaus-Quinlan, Kristie Krier, Scott Murphy, and Sathya Wandzek, who shared their notes, ideas, classroom observations, student work samples, book recommendations, references, photographs, and insight to strengthen the narrative, as well as chipped in to provide editing support. Thank you for trusting me to tell our story.

Many thanks to Dawn Carrico, Keri Gordon, Michelle Joy, and their students and families at Traylor Elementary School as well as Scott Wolf, Jennifer Engbretson, Ryan McKillop, and their students and families at North High School for welcoming us in to take photographs of them in action. Countless thanks to Rachel Rosenberg and her students and their families at Hallett Academy. I appreciate Laura Mahony for her excellent rapport with students, which results in beautiful photography. Many thanks to Katherine Bryant at Heinemann for her thoughtful feedback, which made this book stronger, to Hilary Goff for ushering this book through the publication process, and to all the Heinemann colleagues who helped to put this together.

Most importantly, I am deeply grateful to all my family and friends who supported me, distracted me, and humored me throughout this project, especially my phenomenal children, who invite me to sing, play, laugh, and remain humble; and to Wallace, eye of the whirlwind, who reminds me that all is well. God carries.

"If we create a culture where every teacher believes they need to improve not because they aren't good enough but because they can be even better, there's no limit to what we can achieve."

—Dylan Wiliam (quoted in Phillips 2018)

"Phenomenal." This is how education researcher John Hattie described Ashley Bromstrup's teaching on his October 2016 visit to Denver. He observed Ashley facilitating her third graders as they wrestled to make sense of a complex math task. They discussed strategies, explained thinking, analyzed solutions, shared creative ideas using academic language, disagreed respectfully, and gave and received peer feedback nonstop for ninety minutes.

Ashley's fine craft as a twenty-first-century educator was molded by years of personal effort and intensive professional development. Ashley now shares her expertise by serving as a lab host to visitors from around the country, who attend structured visits to her classroom to observe her and her students at work.

When we enter the classroom of a phenomenal teacher, we enter a world of wonder. We see learners hard at work, and hear them speaking eloquently about their understanding, moving purposefully and respectfully; sometimes we have to look around to find the teacher, perhaps bent over a table chatting quietly with a group while the rest of the students manage themselves. It appears as magic. And yet writing guru Don Murray (1987) reminds us, "Writing isn't magic, but then magic isn't magic either. Magicians know their craft, and writers must also know their craft." Similarly, magical teachers, who appear to cast spells over children and conjure excellence from raw material year after year, know exactly what they are doing. This is a book about those teachers, the magical, phenomenal ones, and about you and how you can be among them.

Phenomenal Teaching

The truth is, you and your students are already phenomenal. We are here to believe in and support you in bringing your potential into reality in your classroom every day. When we design learning experiences that honor thinking and invite creativity, wonderful and amazing results can't help but blossom in our classrooms. Wherever you are now, no matter how many years of experience you do or don't have, regardless of how optimistic or discouraged you may feel, this book is offered as a resource and a guide to invite your continuing reflection and growth.

In this book, we will walk together step by step to consider the ways in which the complex craft of teaching can produce results for each and every learner. This is not a book of theories—it is based on the experiences of reflective, humble, striving exemplars who work hard in their classrooms every day to bring educational research to life in service of their best hopes for children. You will meet them, hear their thinking, reflect on your own, and find pages filled with ideas to try in your own classroom tomorrow.

PHENOMENAL YOU

Tell about your best day teaching. What worked? Why? What did you learn about your students and yourself?

Backstory

Since 1983, the Public Education & Business Coalition (PEBC) has convened teachers to explore how we most effectively implement research-based instructional practices in order to effectively teach for understanding. Our approach has always celebrated independent thinking and fostered agency for teachers and students of all backgrounds.

After nearly thirty years of learning alongside teachers, PEBC synthesized our best understanding of effective instruction into a seven-point Continuum of Growth in Research-Based Instructional Best Practices (2012), a framework outlining teacher development. A team of experienced staff developers and lab hosts (teachers implementing effective instruction at high levels and prepared to open their doors to visitors curious to observe and discuss instruction) have spent most of the past decade developing, field-testing, and refining this tool in classrooms across the nation.

We are now ready to present a comprehensive picture of our pedagogical expertise: six time-tested, research-based instructional approaches that educators at all levels can adapt to their own context to effectively strengthen students' confidence and competence as problem solvers and makers of meaning. This Teaching Framework is not an evaluation tool but rather an invitation for reflection and a road map for your and your colleagues' continuing growth. You can find the full Framework in the Appendix of this book.

These featured approaches are not new, and yet they are not outdated. They do not rely on instructional technology or specific curricula, nor are they targeting certain populations of learners. We foster growth in Cupertino, the highest-achieving district in the nation, and effectively support teachers and their students in some of Denver's high-needs urban schools, as well as work with teachers in rural South Dakota to implement this pedagogy. Teaching for agency and understanding works for everyone. So, start where you are, use what you have, teach whomever comes through your door. You can foster a classroom where phenomenal learners—you included—thrive.

Welcome to *Phenomenal Teaching*

Chapter 1, "Stance," explores the critical foundation for all effective teaching—our purpose, as well as our beliefs about our students, our content, and ourselves. These established, each subsequent chapter introduces you to one of six strands of the Teaching Framework.

Picture phenomenal teaching as a rope that tethers our work to our best hopes for learners; that rope is comprised of six strands, or instructional approaches, which form the conceptual backbone of this framework; each strand is made up of certain subcomponents, called here elements. Each chapter takes one key practice or strand, element by element, starting with research, providing a variety of examples across grade levels and content areas, and then offering an array of strategies for implementation. In addition to presenting content in a variety of formats, each chapter also offers ample invitations for you to engage and reflect.

ENGAGE

Although a typical book on education might come across more as a lecture, this book is designed as a professional development workshop. In each chapter, you will find multiple opportunities to draw upon your background knowledge, to synthesize research, to reflect on vignettes and examples, and generally to talk back to the text. In addition, there are a number of graphic organizers to invite thinking and planning. At the close of each chapter is a different, specific invitation for reflection: all of these prompts, cues, and questions are presented not only to get you thinking but also to model some of the ways in which we might invite learners of all ages to engage with material as agentic students on a quest to understand. Steal any formats that work for you, ditch those that don't, and replace them with your own wonderful ideas. The purpose behind the design of this book is to create a thought playground where you can build your own sense of agency as a teacher-learner while considering new approaches to drawing forth your own students' highest and best.

WRITE IN THIS BOOK

This Introduction already offered you two chances to respond to the text. Did you? If not, I understand; to stop and write slows your pace, and also this book is all clean and new, and you might not be ready to mark it up. But I truly invite you to write all over it—annotate, underline, ask, respond. You will learn more, have a record of your thinking, and, plus, it will be more fun. Of course, you can write anywhere, but blue brackets and blue text boxes are specifically designed to invite your responses. Please allow yourself the gift of time to ponder and chat with colleagues about these ideas, then give yourself the space to reflect and jot a few notes right here, as a log of your insight. I promise this is worth the time. (Read more in Chapter 4 on the value of reflection.)

How do you feel about being asked to write in a book? Sketch a quick emoji of how that idea strikes you.

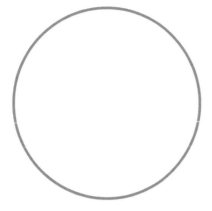

COLLABORATE

Although you can explore and experiment with this book independently, it might be more fun to partner with a colleague, coach, or team for conversation as you read and to test-drive some new approaches together. If you are collaborating, here are some ways to milk this book:

- discuss the anticipation questions before reading each chapter
- present your own real-life examples of each approach
- share and compare your own thinking about the teacher vignettes
- talk through the varied graphic organizers and your responses
- discuss the chapter reflections after reading
- conduct action research: agree on a new approach to all try, and then report back.

What sounds good?

You are phenomenal. Your choosing to read this book and reflect on your craft is testament to your commitment to our future. I am truly grateful for your dedication to your own and your learners' growth. Thank you.

REFLECTION

As you embark on this learning journey, what do you hope you will gain? What do you fear that you might encounter?

1 STANCE

ANTICIPATION QUESTIONS

• How would you describe your stance as a teacher?

• What are your closest-held beliefs about teaching and learning?

• As a teacher, what is your purpose?

**Teacher Voice:
The Power of Beliefs**

"Whether consciously or unconsciously, we make our beliefs public every day. They come through in the ways we design our classrooms for student independence, in the ways we plan our lessons for engagement, even in the ways we talk with our students. When we take the time to reflect on our beliefs, we can bring them to life by empowering students with the strategies to accomplish their goals. This changes the way we teach, allows students to take off and fly."

—ANNIE PATTERSON

Inferring Stance

"She hates me," a reluctant social studies learner told me of his history teacher, "and she thinks I'm stupid." I tried to pry this belief from his mind with reason and rationalizations, but he would not be moved. I went to watch. He sat in the back. She lectured. She did not call on anyone. At the end of class, she listed off the names of people with missing assignments who had to stay in for lunch. His name was on the list. I got the picture: by his twelve-year-old logic, anyone who would take away his recess must certainly hate him, and a person who never stops talking must think their audience is stupid. He read her stance (rightly or wrongly) from her behavior. His behavior coalesced to match her beliefs: pretty soon, he was failing that class. It was a steep climb out of that hole.

REFLECTION: INFERRING STANCE

Tell the story of a time when you read an unsupportive stance from a person in a position of authority. What did you infer? Why? How did that affect your performance or learning?

Beliefs

Consciously or unconsciously, our beliefs inform our behavior; our behavior, in turn, shows the world what we believe.

As teachers, our beliefs have far-reaching influence on the lives of the learners we strive to serve. I remember reading in grad school about the now-illegal research Robert Rosenthal and Lenore Jacobson described in their 1968 book *Pygmalion in the Classroom*: teachers were told at the beginning of a school year that one actually typical group of students was highly gifted while another actually typical group of students had subpar potential. By the end of the year, as you may know, the students met their teachers' expectations, a self-fulfilling prophecy. More recent studies demonstrate the power of teacher beliefs on student learning outcomes: Sian Beilock and her colleagues (2010) at the University of Chicago studied the effect of teachers' math anxiety on their students and found,

> By the school year's end, however, the more anxious teachers were about math, the more likely girls (but not boys) were to endorse the commonly held stereotype that "boys are good at math, and girls are good at reading" and the lower these girls' math achievement. Indeed, by the end of the school year, girls who endorsed this stereotype had significantly worse math achievement than girls who did not and than boys overall.

Each of us can also look to our own experience for additional proof: someone's belief in you—or lack thereof—surely influenced who you have become. To provide the best possible learning opportunities for children, we need to identify our own beliefs and notice how our actions reflect them—or how to adjust so that they do.

Take some time to consider where you sit on the belief spectra in Figure 1.1. I invite you to jot some thinking after marking your position on each line.

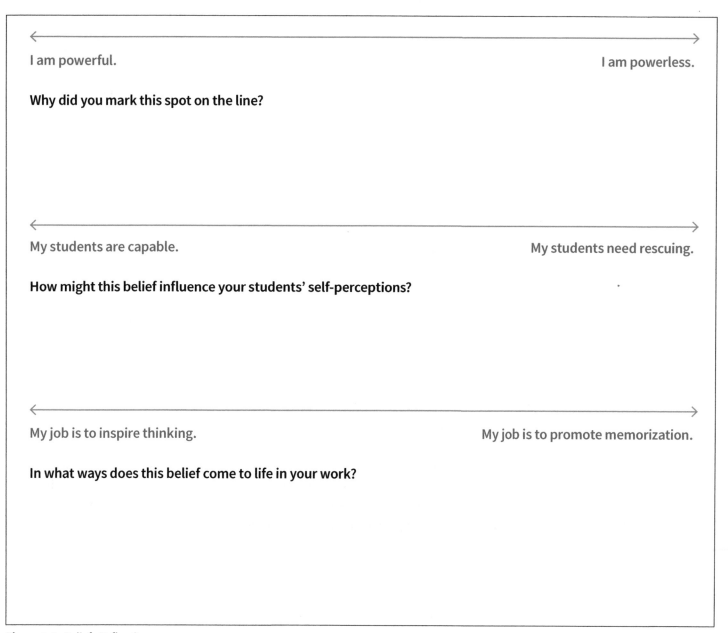

←——→

I am powerful.   I am powerless.

Why did you mark this spot on the line?

←——→

My students are capable.   My students need rescuing.

How might this belief influence your students' self-perceptions?

←——→

My job is to inspire thinking.   My job is to promote memorization.

In what ways does this belief come to life in your work?

Figure 1.1 Beliefs Reflection

BELIEFS ABOUT OURSELVES

We teach who we are. I firmly believe this. What virtuous qualities would you yourself like to invite learners to embrace? How can you model them in your classroom? Figure 1.2 is a list of productive beliefs demonstrated by many of the phenomenal teachers described in this book. Which ring true for you? What might you add? How do you envision bringing these beliefs to life in a classroom? (If you are not sure yet, come back later, as you progress through the book.)

"Every student deserves the chance and has the right to explore his or her glorious potential. Helping our students to believe in themselves when perhaps no one else does and working with them to cultivate hope where seemingly there is none are two of the greatest gifts educators can offer to our youth."

—*Vicki Zakrzewski (2017)*

Belief	Might Be Modeled By . . .
I am powerful.	Speaking out to address racist comments.
I am kind.	Providing extra snacks for those in need.
I have high expectations.	
I am a lifelong learner.	
I am a hard worker.	

Figure 1.2 Productive Beliefs About Ourselves

BELIEFS ABOUT LEARNERS

As described in the previous examples, our beliefs about our students make a deep impact on their experience in school today, as well as their future success. Look at Figure 1.3. Which of these beliefs match stances you take or would like to take with learners? Add to this list, and think about how you might demonstrate those beliefs.

Belief	Might Be Modeled By . . .
You are important.	
You are welcome here.	
You bring background knowledge to share.	
You need to do the hard work of learning.	

Figure 1.3 Productive Beliefs About Students

PHENOMENAL TEACHING

BELIEFS ABOUT TEACHING AND LEARNING

Paulo Freire (1970) criticized the banking model of education—that knowledge can be deposited, stored, and withdrawn as needed at a later date—as requiring students to be passive recipients rather than active thinkers engaged in claiming their education. Progressive education today stands on another set of beliefs about the inherent strengths and abilities of learners. Read the beliefs in Figure 1.4. How do these resonate with you? What is missing? How might you show them in your instruction?

Belief	Might Be Modeled By . . .
Learners' questions and ideas are important.	
Teachers are facilitators.	
Content is a vehicle to practice thinking and understanding.	
The purpose of school is to foster learners' independence.	

Figure 1.4 Productive Beliefs About Teaching and Learning

REFLECTION: ACTUALIZING BELIEFS

If you are not yet fully sure how you might fill in the right-hand columns in Figures 1.2–1.4, that is alright. This book is all about exploring some concrete ways you might bring your beliefs and best intentions for every learner to life in your instruction, so read on. But first, what questions do you have?

Purpose: Agency and Understanding

This book defines teacher success as raising learners to possess two gifts: agency and understanding, two shoes that will get you where you need to go. Lace up agency, and you have an individual who believes in their own power and possibilities, who faces obstacles with courage and confidence, who perseveres with poise through challenge and change. Tie

Teacher Voice: Results of Acting on Our Beliefs

"Working with PEBC has made me more confident in what I believe in as a teacher. I think that students should be able to learn for themselves and learn in their own way. I have grown more confident in implementing these strategies within my classroom. I've seen the benefits in my students' motivation, as well as the amount that they're keeping up with—and they like—their learning. The kids have been maintaining their knowledge more than in years past when I'd just been doing kind of the old school approach where they're just taking notes and regurgitating that information. Now they're actually coming up with their own ideas rather than my ideas.

"Students see the benefits of what I am doing in my classroom because they are seeing that they are learning more, whether that's on our weekly quizzes or even on our monthly progress monitoring. The kids are becoming more motivated because they are seeing that growth within themselves."

—*Andrew Jones, Berry Creek Middle School*

"If nothing else, children should leave school with a sense that if they act, and act strategically, they can accomplish their goals. As teachers, then, we try to maximize children's feelings of agency. There are really three parts to this: the belief that the environment can be affected, the belief that one has what it takes to affect it, and the understanding that that is what literacy is about. Developing in children a sense of agency is not an educational frill or some mushy-headed liberal idea. Children who doubt their competence set low goals and choose easy tasks, and they plan poorly."

—*Peter Johnston (2004)*

understanding onto the other foot, and you have someone who knows—or who knows how to know—a lifelong learner competent at grappling with challenging content and making meaning for themselves. With agency and understanding, all things are possible.

AGENCY

Agency is essentially a belief in one's own efficacy, one's ability to control his or her own life. Agency is an orientation toward the past, present, and future that reflects free choice, optimism, conscious influences, and uniqueness (Bandura 2001). It is a can-do attitude, a willingness to work with hard, dogged perseverance on a quest. Educational researcher Manja Klemenčič (2014) describes it this way:

> By exercising their agency, students exert influence on their educational trajectories, their future lives and their immediate and larger social surroundings. . . . Yet, through their agency they also contribute to the development of others, development of knowledge and to economic and social development.

Numerous factors beyond learners' control—socioeconomic status, cultural capital, family of origin, health condition, and more—contribute to one's sense of agency. Still, history is rich with tales of those who rose from humble beginnings to accomplish great tasks. Alexander Hamilton, Oprah Winfrey, Mohandas Gandhi, and LeBron James all shared confidence in their own capacity to influence their futures and that of our world. We can raise children to believe in themselves too.

To this end, we can design learning experiences that put students in the driver's seat, that invite them to bring their authentic selves and to strive in wonderful and unique ways for their own visions of success.

REFLECTION: AGENCY ALIVE

Describe someone you know who has a strong sense of agency. How does their agency come to life?

UNDERSTANDING

Understanding is the construction of meaning, meaning that can be remembered and reapplied in new situations. Although we aspire to raise students who understand a great many things, the collective of human content knowledge is so vast that an even greater gift to our children is knowing *how* to understand. Jay McTighe and Elliott Seif (2014) explain,

> The world is increasingly interconnected and rapidly changing, offering new potentials and problems. Search engines, computers and smartphones give most people increased and immediate access to huge amounts of information. E-mail, Twitter, Facebook and soon-to-be invented technologies enable instantaneous communication with people throughout the globe. The highly complex job market, with its array of novel and changing careers, calls for creative, innovative individuals who can think critically and apply their learning to new situations while functioning as continuous, lifelong learners.

McTighe, along with Grant Wiggins, defined the six facets of understanding as the abilities to explain, interpret, apply, demonstrate perspective, display empathy, and have self-knowledge (Wiggins and McTighe 2005). Given the vast landscapes of our learners' future, our goal is to cultivate graduates who not only grapple with important ideas but also have the ability to tackle unfamiliar topics with an eye on understanding.

REFLECTION: DEFINE UNDERSTANDING

What does understanding look and sound like in your content area(s)?

How Do We Get There from Here?

What does it look like to build students' agency and understanding amidst shifting standards, changing assessments, waves of mandated curricula, and evolving educational policies? If, against that backdrop, we believe in fostering the unique promise inherent in each child, how might our classrooms look and sound? If we are devoted to celebrating the thinking and creativity of every individual, what might we do?

This book will offer an overview of six teacher superpowers that, when taken together, can make all the difference for student learning. We will examine these approaches in Chapters 2–7, and all are summarized in the Appendix.

◆ **Plan (Chapter 2)**
How can we design learning experiences that cultivate students' understanding and agency? In this chapter, we will consider both yearlong and unit-level planning.

◆ **Community (Chapter 3)**
In what ways might we develop classroom communities that support the agency and understanding of every learner? This chapter is all about supporting collective and individual efficacy, as well as productive identities in our classroom.

◆ **Workshop (Chapter 4)**
In what ways might we facilitate learning experiences that support students grappling with challenging tasks in service of conceptual understanding? Here we will explore how workshop model teaching scaffolds students' success as independent thinkers and problem solvers.

◆ **Thinking Strategies (Chapter 5)**
In what ways might we provide tools that increase learners' agency and understanding? This chapter describes the thinking strategies and how effective teachers can bring them to life in service of learners' understanding.

◆ **Discourse (Chapter 6)**
In what ways might we scaffold productive, engaged academic conversations? In this chapter, we will explore how to cultivate students' speaking and listening across learning experiences.

◆ **Assessment (Chapter 7)**
In what ways might we monitor and support progress? Assessment for learning, as a tool in students' hands, is the key idea of this chapter.

PHENOMENAL TEACHING

These practices, each powerful in their own right, work together to create an environment that fosters productive learning for students of all backgrounds. Remove one, and the others will stand, yet more weakly. Strengthen one, and all are fortified.

Believe in Yourself

Have you seen the movie *The Great Debaters*? It is based on the true story of Wiley College professor Melvin Tolson, who coached the debate team of his small, African American college in a tiny town in Texas in 1935. So great was Tolson's faith in his students that he wrote letters to colleges all over the nation inviting them to debate Wiley's team. Eventually, due to Tolson's persistent letters and his students' hard work, Harvard University's championship team accepted the challenge, hosted a debate with Wiley, and lost. Tolson believed in his students, took a stance of faith in their great potential, and behaved accordingly.

What we believe about ourselves, our students, and the processes of teaching and learning informs how we behave. When we take as our purpose the development of learners' agency in service of their own understanding, we plan carefully, develop community, facilitate workshops, teach thinking strategies, scaffold discourse, and enact ongoing assessment.

You are already making a difference in the lives of your students. And yet I applaud your courage in opening this book, seeking to do more. As you read on, take charge. I am not here to tell you what to do, just to share what has brought success to other aspiring teachers dedicated to developing learners' agency and understanding. Read critically; think hard about each facet: Does it make sense for you? How might it work in your own setting? In what ways might you need to adjust the ideas presented to best meet learners' needs? How might you begin? Take on small challenges in a manageable time frame. Enlist collaboration and the support of colleagues. Pause often to reflect: How did that go? What might you try next? Learning takes time. Be patient with yourself. You can do this.

REFLECTION: TEACHER EFFICACY

In what ways do you feel efficacious as a teacher now? In what ways might you like to grow? Which of the six strands previously described seem to offer the greatest promise to that end?

"Yeah, But . . ."

- ### "What about the test?"

  You are about to read about teachers whose students consistently outdo state and district averages on standardized assessments of student achievement, though those students may come from historically underperforming groups. These learners succeed not because their teachers conscientiously cover every micro-standard listed in government-generated documents but because their teachers prioritize and honor student thinking and build learners' confidence so that they can grapple with unfamiliar content and make meaning.

- ### "What about my scope and sequence, my curriculum?"

  These pedagogical approaches can serve to support teachers in implementing most curricula. I say "most" because if the primary goals are mere memorization and regurgitation rather than critical thinking, you might have picked up the wrong book. Yet this work is well aligned with the Common Core and related standards that prioritize learners' thinking and comprehension: demonstrating independence; building content knowledge; responding to demands of audience, task, purpose, and discipline; comprehending and critiquing; valuing evidence; using technology strategically; and understanding other perspectives and cultures.

- ### "Am I allowed . . . ?"

  Yes. You are. A lot of teachers ask us this, as if someone else had a better understanding than you do of what is best for the learners in your care. Yes, you are allowed to make instructional decisions in service of your highest and best hopes for students. Now, you may not get to toss out the standards or rewrite the test, but you do get to infuse the route to those ends with rich invitations for thinking. Staff developer Sathya Wandzek advises, "Take a risk. It may not work quite like you expect, but you'll never know until you try."

STANCE REFLECTION

• What new thinking do you have about your and your colleagues' teaching beliefs?

• Which beliefs are you curious about learning to enact more fully?

• In what ways are agency and understanding alive and well in your classroom and school?

• In what ways might you enrich learners' agency and understanding?

• What do you envision might be different for you and your students as a result of your having worked through this book?

REFLECTION ON CHAPTER QUESTION: WHAT DRIVES YOU?

Invitation: Write a tweet about what drives you. Here are a couple of sentence stems, if you'd like to use one or both:

• As a teacher, I am driven by my beliefs that . . .

• My purpose is . . .

If you like, share your tweet on Twitter and tag me @wendywardhoffer.

2 PLAN

CHAPTER QUESTION: **HOW CAN WE DESIGN LEARNING EXPERIENCES THAT CULTIVATE STUDENTS' UNDERSTANDING AND AGENCY?**

Teacher Voice: Planning for Understanding

"I start with what makes the learning meaningful. Why do the standards matter? Why does this text matter? What would engage students to make them want to do the work? That requires time to dig in, questions to make this topic compelling. I think through that and how to connect all the pieces, how to balance choice for kids: When and where do they need choice? And when do they need a collective experience? I go for engagement."

—JENN BRAUNER

ANTICIPATION QUESTIONS

- What are your current strategies for planning?

- How do you use the resources provided by your school or district to support your planning?

- In what ways do you prioritize thinking and understanding?

- How do your plans foster learner agency?

Planning in the Real World

When my son was three, he was done watching his older sister cruise around on her red bike while he tilted back and forth between his training wheels on his tiny two-wheeler. "Take them off, Mama," he told me. And so I did. He grabbed the bike and headed down the sidewalk, not looking back. He jumped onto the seat, but then leapt off after pushing the pedals a couple of turns. He realized he had not yet mastered this balancing. "Teach me, Mama," he said, now open to my coaching. I thought about how to break this learning process into manageable steps for him, laid out a plan in my mind, and explained how we were going to do this. He let me hold the handlebars with him as we made slow laps in a nearby church parking lot. Then I transitioned to holding onto the back of his seat while jogging around that same lot. Soon, he was ready to try it alone. We set small goals—ride to the tree, ride to the white car, ride in a circle—and he practiced each of those several times before moving on to the next. He was road ready in a matter of days.

REFLECTION: PLANNING IN THE REAL WORLD

Tell the story of a time when you planned a learning experience wisely. What happened? What supported learners' success? What did you learn?

What: Plan for Agency and Understanding

"Believe in the children, fight foolishness, and learn who our children are and the legacies they bring," education expert Lisa Delpit (2012) implores us in *"Multiplication Is for White People."* The foolishness she is referring to is wasting teachers' time keeping track of noninstructional tasks in regimented, teacher-proof curricula. As a result of this foolishness, educator Zaretta Hammond (2015) explains in *Culturally Responsive Teaching and the Brain*, too many culturally and linguistically diverse learners become dependent—let teachers carry the cognitive load and wait passively for learning to come to them, limiting their opportunities to experience the neuroplasticity that inspires growth. This dependency is the opposite of the agency we seek to foster.

Planning for agency and understanding involves designing purposeful and meaningful learning experiences that invite students to use their good minds to solve worthy problems. This is a complex endeavor that takes us beyond teacher's guides and online resources. This planning requires us to ask big questions about why we are doing what we are doing, what learners really need, and how we can nudge them toward the important goals of confidence and competence. When our purpose is to draw forth the wonderful thinking of all students in our care, we need to plan tasks that motivate and engage learners, providing appropriate amounts of guidance and structure while letting students' curiosity lead.

If we are striving to cultivate student agency, we also need to be agentic: to own the work of designing rich learning experiences, to see commercially produced curricula as resources and guidelines, but to begin our planning with our students in mind: Who are they? What do they need? From here, we build the bridge between learners and our learning intentions through inquiry, rich tasks, and an abundance of enticing invitations.

This chapter is focused on big picture planning, which has implications for daily planning, though that will be explored in greater depth in Chapter 4, "Workshop." Take a few moments in Figure 2.1 to reflect on some aspects of teaching for agency and understanding.

Planning for Agency and Understanding *Is . . .*	Planning for Agency and Understanding *Is Not . . .*	Your Thinking . . .
Keeping learners' needs, interests, and strengths at the front of our minds	Doing what we did last year	
Providing interesting, meaningful, challenging work, perhaps drawn or modified from commercial curricula	Making up everything from scratch	
Embedding intentional instruction of process skills within content-rich learning experiences	Assigning tasks and hoping kids already know the requisite skills	
Scaffolding learners' independence throughout a purposeful series of tasks	Distributing a packet of topic-related activities for learners to complete alone	

Figure 2.1 Clarification Corner

Why Plan?

"Meticulous planning will enable everything you do to appear spontaneous," said Mark Caine (quoted in Hutchinson 2016). When we know what we are doing, have thought it through, and have considered the possible hiccups or fireworks, we are best prepared to facilitate a seamless learning experience. High-level planning takes time, thought, and experience, and yet the payoffs in terms of efficiency, engagement, and excellence are well worth the effort.

Research by John Hattie and colleagues identifies teacher clarity—the assurance that both teachers and students alike are poised to answer, "What am I learning? Why am I learning it?

How will I know when I have learned it?"—as a strongly effective aspect of teaching (Hattie 2009). As John T. Almarode (2017) explains, "When teachers know why students are learning what they are learning, they can better design learning experiences that are authentic and relevant to learners. Finally, when teachers know what success looks like, they can show learners what success looks like, design opportunities for students to make their own thinking and learning visible, and gather evidence about where to go next in the teaching and learning. All this, because of teacher clarity." Hence, when we know what we are after, we can then invite learner ownership and agency of both our process and the shared goals.

"Think of the grade-level standards as building materials. As a construction supervisor, we wouldn't simply drop off materials and tools at a worksite and have the workers 'go at it.' Instead, we would begin with a blueprint—an overall vision of the desired building to guide its construction," explain Grant Wiggins and Jay McTighe, authors of the classic text *Understanding by Design* (2005), in their recent article "From Common Core Standards to Curriculum: Five Big Ideas" (McTighe and Wiggins 2012). We know this, and yet, at times, we can rely heavily on curricular resources, last year, and raw hope.

The National Research Council's (2012) *Educating for Life and Work* synthesizes a plethora of research on deeper learning, the sort of learning that allows students to take what they gain in one situation and apply it in novel contexts, a behavior that defines understanding. The authors write, "The product of deeper learning is transferable knowledge, including content knowledge in a domain, and knowledge of how, why, and when to apply this knowledge to answer

"The enemy (of teaching) is clutter."

**—Thomas Newkirk
(quoted in George 2018)**

questions and solve problems" (National Research Council 2012). Toward these ends of building both knowledge and twenty-first-century skills, research recommends the following instructional approaches:

- Use multiple and varied representations of concepts and tasks, with support mapping across the varied representations.
- Encourage elaboration, questioning, and explanation.
- Engage learners in challenging tasks, with guidance to reflect on their own learning and understanding.
- Teach with examples, cases, and phenomena.
- Connect topics to students' personal lives and interests.
- Use formative assessment to make goals clear to students, continuously monitor, provide feedback, and involve students in self- and peer assessment.

All of these require careful planning.

REFLECTION ON RESEARCH

- How does this research connect with your thinking about instructional design?

- What information is inspiring?

- What is intimidating?

- What questions linger?

How: The Elements of Planning

In examining the transferable elements of planning at every grade level and across the content areas, we find three key areas we need to juggle artfully: purpose, people, and process. *Purpose* asks us to know what students are learning, why, and why it matters. *People* invites us to know learners' context and to respond in an ongoing manner to their needs and readiness. *Process* is all about how we pursue our learning—attending to discipline-specific practices through rich experiences punctuated with intentional language development activities and supported by a broad array of resources.

These are the elements of planning we will explore in the balance of this chapter:

Purpose

- Clarity: What is the purpose?
- Life-worthiness: Why does this matter for learners?
- Content and process: What and how are we learning?

People

- Context: Who are the learners?
- Responsiveness: What will these learners need?
- Inquiry: How will learners' curiosity, voice, and choice be incorporated?

Process

- Learning experiences: How will learners develop and demonstrate understanding?
- Language development: How will learners develop academic vocabulary and discourse skills?
- Resources: What will best support learning?

Let's take these one at a time, knowing that each is integral to the design of a productive year or unit and that emphasis on refining one will surely influence the implementation of the others. Throughout the rest of this chapter (and in the following chapters), you'll see the PEBC Framework (see Chapter 1) for each element we discuss. Where along the continuum for each element do you see yourself?

PURPOSE

Have you watched the video "Know Your Why"? In this, inspirational comedian Michael Jr. (2015) finds a high school choir director in his audience and invites that man to sing a few bars of "Amazing Grace," which he does beautifully. Next, the speaker asks the man to sing again, this time, "The version as if your uncle just got out of jail, and you were shot in the back when you was a kid . . . let me see the 'hood' version." This time, the singer's voice is so rich and impressive that he has the audience on their feet and receives a thunderous round of applause. "When you know your *why*," concludes Michael Jr., "your *what* becomes more impactful because you are walking towards or in your purpose." This is true not only for singers, but also for teachers, for all of us: when we know why we are doing what we are doing, our work truly sings.

Clarity

I recently had the opportunity to plan with a fourth-grade team interested in aligning their U.S. History curriculum. Across the year, the team had traditionally taught five units, the first of which was on Native Americans. When I asked the teachers about the learning goals of that unit, one shared that she always has students create models of native dwellings, exploring materials use; a second teacher explained that she asks students to learn the regions of the United States and which native nations lived where prior to Colonial times; a third teacher described how this unit is really about subsistence lifestyles; and a fourth teacher, the newest to the team, confessed, "I really don't teach that unit because I am not sure what it is supposed to be about."

Clarity—knowing what we are about and what we are after—is critical to the success of every learning experience. To be able to explain why we are doing what we are doing and how each task aligns with our targets ensures efficiency and lays a foundation for success. Let us consider how identifying understandings and questions, and being transparent about them, can enhance teacher and learner clarity. (See Figure 2.2 for the PEBC Framework for Clarity.)

	First Steps	Next Steps	Advancing	Peak Performance
Clarity (also see Chapter 7, Assessment)	Attend to standards and standardized assessments. Design assessment(s).	Prioritize a small number of important content and process standards. Design demonstrations of understanding and success criteria aligned with learning intentions.	Align targets, tasks, and assessments with essential questions and enduring understandings; communicate these clearly with learners. Identify evidence of learners' understanding that can be gathered before, during, and after unit of study.	Learners demonstrate understanding, can articulate their own growth toward targets, and advocate for their learning needs.

Figure 2.2 Plan: Clarity

PHENOMENAL TEACHING

Understandings

Learning targets, objectives, goals, intentions . . . educators have come up with many names for what we intend for learners to understand. These press our teaching beyond assigning a bunch of stuff about a topic, keeping kids busy and out of trouble, to instead heading learners toward a target on purpose. The big ideas of a discipline offer us a conceptual framework to demonstrate how that content is interconnected to enduring understanding. Wiggins and McTighe (2005) coined the phrase "enduring understandings" to describe those important, significant concepts we target in our instruction. For example, we may decide that we are studying Native Americans to appreciate that many thriving nations existed on this continent before the Europeans arrived. Once we establish our enduring understanding, we can make wise choices about which learning experiences and tasks actually support students' access to that idea.

To continue with this example, which activities might best serve the goal: building native dwellings, memorizing regions, or learning about subsistence lifestyles? Or might there be other studies to better bring home this enduring understanding? More on learning experiences will be discussed below.

When determining enduring understandings to guide a unit, we zoom out and ask ourselves, "What here is really important? What few key concepts do we expect learners to understand and hold on to?" The clarity of these answers can help us sift and sort through all of the materials and ideas in front of us to streamline our unit design.

For example, here are some learning targets developed for a high school language arts unit by teacher Alisa Wills-Keely:

> **Determining what's most important**—I can articulate how I make decisions about what is important in a text context and how my decisions enhance my overall comprehension of the text.
>
> **Synthesis**—I can monitor the overall meaning and themes in a text as I read and maintain an awareness of the ways text elements fit together to create overall meaning or a theme.

Literary devices—I can explain how an author uses literary devices and discuss the impact the device has on the reader.

Textual analysis—I can closely read for textual evidence and patterns to determine the author's impact.

Argument/point of view—I can closely read for an author's and/or character's point of view to reveal the purpose/argument and impact.

REFLECTION: ASK YOURSELF

For your current or next unit, what is it you intend for learners to come to understand? What will that understanding look like?

Questions

Cris Tovani (2011) invites us to explore *provocative questions* that help learners to care and see the meaning behind their work. Planning gurus Wiggins and McTighe (2005) advise us to seek *essential questions* that take us to the heart of our discipline, that we can revisit throughout our studies and consider with new insight. By any name, open-ended, rich, generative questions with no one obvious answer and many angles for consideration drive us deep into our work. A great question is one that we can answer, based on our background knowledge, at the opening of a learning sequence, and then revisit with layers of new thinking as our understanding progresses.

Some teachers appreciate working with broader questions, while others feel more confident pursuing narrow ones. In either case, the quality of a question is determined by how deeply it can evoke us to think and seek understanding.

Figure 2.3 proposes some examples of enduring understandings and essential questions. What else might you add to flesh out these ideas? And what understandings and questions will you plan for your upcoming units?

Transparency

Once we gain clarity on our unit- or yearlong understanding(s) and questions, we need to share them with our students: chew on them together, revisit them, and explore how we are synthesizing our new learning with prior knowledge, how our thinking has grown and changed. This lens for reflection can recur to guide us through the upward spiral of a learning experience. (See Figure 2.4.)

Topic	Understandings	Questions
Cells	Life begets life.	
Geography		What is the relationship between agriculture and global warming?
Poetry	Poetry is for thinking.	
Graphing		How can we use math to predict the future?
Music	Music creates moods.	
History		

Figure 2.3 Enduring Understandings and Essential Questions: Add Your Ideas

What about the curriculum?

Everyone is ready to tell teachers what to do. Although prepared resources and pacing guides can be excellent references, their authors do not know us, our students, or what actually needs to happen next to galvanize understanding. We can be critical consumers, clear on our purpose, and select from these resources the best tasks for learners that will develop, and provide evidence of, understanding.

Commercially produced curricula often provide us with clear goals, and distinct tasks as well as scripts instructing us how to implement those tasks. We best leverage those resources by recognizing that we have choice: the purpose—or targets—require some fidelity. We may or may not agree that the proposed products are worthy demonstrations of understanding and might choose to modify them. The processes, too, may or may not be worthy. If we take an inquiry stance, we need to shake loose some of these structures and make space for learners' questions to lead. (See Figure 2.4.)

Purpose (Goals)	Products (Evidence of Understanding)	Process (Activities, Materials, Groupings)
Why?	What?	How?
Nonnegotiable	Negotiable	Flexible

Figure 2.4 Sifting Curricula

Life-Worthiness

Sitting with a group of third-grade math teachers pondering their next unit on multiplication, I asked the question, "So what? How does multiplication make us powerful?" From there, we launched into some brainstorming on the real-world application of multiplication. We thought about their school, their classroom furnishings, what it would take to calculate the number of tables and chairs and such needed in a new school. Then, one teacher reminded us that their humanities unit was currently focusing on Pakistan, and we began to wonder about providing furniture for a new school there, doing the math to figure how many of each sort of furnishings would be needed and at what cost . . . pretty quickly, we were looking online to find an agency building schools in Pakistan that we could contact and offer to help.

This is just one example of finding the life-worthiness (a term coined by author David Perkins) of a topic. Learners deserve to explore content that is, as staff developer Kirsten Myers-Blake explains, "transferable to forever." (See Figure 2.5 for the PEBC Teaching Framework for Life-Worthiness.)

	First Steps	Next Steps	Advancing	Peak Performance
Life-Worthiness	Seek connections between content and life outside the classroom.	Establish relevance of current learning.	Engage with content that has meaning beyond the classroom and will support learners as scholars, citizens, and humans.	Learners know the relationship between their learning and their lives at large.

Figure 2.5 Plan: Life-Worthiness

The Relevance Question: Why Should I Care?

I recently observed a high school physics lesson in which the teacher was lecturing about Charles' law, explaining the relationship between heat, pressure, and volume of a gas with an equation on a black-and-white PowerPoint slide. An excited student chipped in to say that this reminded him of hot air balloons. The teacher immediately squelched that connection, waving away the comment with "We are getting off track." Deflating.

Most of what we are expected to teach and learn in school is actually quite relevant to the real world. That's how it got into our curricula in the first place. And yet, years of machination seem to have robbed some skills listed in the standards from their authentic use. One might be asked to study math as naked numbers, commas as a thing unto themselves, when instead calculating to solve an authentic problem or punctuating to make a finer point becomes dazzlingly more interesting. How can we shore up the life-worthiness of our content?

When we think about how what we're teaching has value outside the classroom and where and how students might use it, we are often pointed toward a rich inquiry that can elevate the learning targets. I will share a few examples and then invite you to consider some of your own in Figure 2.6.

* Study *Cry, the Beloved Country* to make a determination about the source of goodness.

* Study heredity and inheritance to make an argument about the ethics of cloning.

* Study the U.S. Constitution to defend a claim about immigration policy.

* Study exponential growth to understand public health problems and propose solutions.

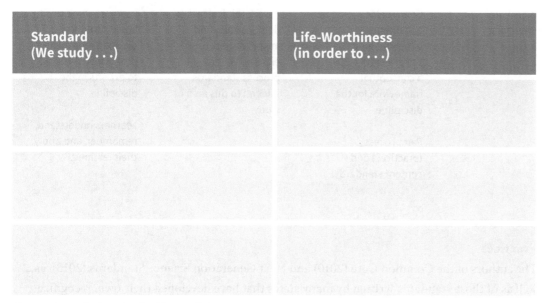

Standard (We study . . .)	Life-Worthiness (in order to . . .)

Figure 2.6 Make Standards Life-Worthy

Content and Process

Standards provide us with some focus and direction for our efforts. Knowing standards well—both content and processes or practices—can increase instructional efficiency. The National Research Council (2000) also found that students benefit from learning within conceptual frameworks, sometimes referred to as the big ideas of the discipline.

Learners' identities and agency are strengthened when they have opportunities to learn content as an expert in the field might come to understand: study bugs by lying beside them in the grass, learn geography by examining and comparing maps, grasp literature by immersing themselves in the work of exemplary poets. In these ways, we invite learners not only to *know*, but also to gain deeper appreciation for *how* to know.

Familiarity with all layers—the content, those bigger ideas, and the processes of coming to understand through discipline-authentic ways of knowing—allows a teacher to leverage each lesson to address all three in some measure. This may sound like a tall order, and yet it is quite manageable with a bit of attention and practice. (See Figure 2.7 for the PEBC Teaching Framework for Content and Process.)

Content

Once you know the content standards you are expected to address, dive in! Find out what brilliant examples or real-life phenomena make this topic interesting. Advanced Placement Biology teacher Erika Schenk livened up a dry unit of heredity by engaging learners in a case study on supernumerary (or extra) nipples. Fifth-grade teacher Tami Thompson invited students to explore natural disasters as a means to understand earth's forces. We can enliven every unit when we find interesting and related events, phenomena, and examples that pique learners' curiosity.

	First Steps	Next Steps	Advancing	Peak Performance
Content and Process	Be familiar with the content and standards.	Connect facts, events, and phenomena to overarching principles; provide a conceptual framework for the discipline. Pair process (practices) and content standards.	Model, think aloud, demonstrate, and invite learners to experience the process standards integral to this area of study.	Learners come to know about the discipline through processes authentic to experts in the discipline. Learners understand, remember, and apply their learning.

Figure 2.7 Plan: Content and Process

Practices

The authors of the Common Core (2010) and Next Generation Science Standards (2013), as well as of those standards written by many states that have developed their own, recognize that whatever specific topic of study we may be exploring, there are transferrable practices we can invite learners to experience and master to come to know content in a manner parallel to that of professionals in the field. We need to intentionally and often invite learners to experience these practices.

What relationships do you see among these process standards? Which are you already addressing directly? Which might you work on next? Annotate the list in Figure 2.8.

Thinking Strategies

The thinking strategies, which will be explored in depth in Chapter 5, offer us a meta-list of processes that can be introduced across the curriculum as tools to scaffold learners' understanding. These strategies closely link to or support the content-area process standards listed in Figure 2.8. Consider this list. What connections do you see between these and the processes and practices in Figure 2.8? Show your thinking by drawing connections where you see relationships:

- background knowledge
- questioning
- inferring
- sensory imagery
- determining importance
- synthesizing
- monitoring for meaning.

Common Core State Standards for Reading (Condensed)	Common Core State Standards for Mathematical Practice	Next Generation Science Standards: Science and Engineering Practices
1. Read closely to determine what the text says.	1. Make sense of problems and persevere in solving them.	1. Asking questions (for science) and defining problems (for engineering)
2. Determine central ideas or themes of a text and analyze their development; summarize the key supporting details and ideas.	2. Reason abstractly and quantitatively.	2. Developing and using models
3. Analyze how and why individuals, events, or ideas develop and interact over the course of a text.	3. Construct viable arguments and critique the reasoning of others.	3. Planning and carrying out investigations
4. Interpret words and phrases as they are used in a text.	4. Model with mathematics.	4. Analyzing and interpreting data
5. Analyze the structure of texts, including how the parts contribute to the whole.	5. Use appropriate tools strategically.	5. Using mathematics and computational thinking
6. Assess how point of view or purpose shapes the content and style of a text.	6. Attend to precision.	6. Constructing explanations (for science) and designing solutions (for engineering)
7. Integrate and evaluate content presented in diverse media and formats.	7. Look for and make use of structure.	7. Engaging in argument from evidence
8. Delineate and evaluate the argument.	8. Look for and express regularity in repeated reasoning.	8. Obtaining, evaluating, and communicating information
9. Analyze how two or more texts address similar themes or topics.		
10. Read and comprehend.		

Figure 2.8 Comparing Processes and Practices

PEOPLE

Clear on our purpose, we consider our people: Who are these learners? How can we build a bridge into this content in ways that invite students to grow as thinkers, solvers, and agents in their own learning? What are their interests, readiness, contexts (past and present), and cultural and language backgrounds, as well as prior experiences with schooling? We benefit from knowing who our students are and ensuring that they see themselves in our curriculum, and we respond to them appropriately.

Context

"What does it mean to see students? Seeing students requires teachers to recognize them as valuable contributors to the classroom space, as opposed to social, cultural, and academic burdens on the so-called master in the room—the teacher," explains Crystal Belle (2019), director of teacher education at Rutgers University–Newark.

To understand how best to teach anyone, we must first really see and know their context. Our culture is full of biases and stereotypes, and as teachers we must be vigilant to the ways in which these influence our own behavior and instruction, making the unconscious conscious and humbly welcoming learning and growth. We all need to work to decolonize curricula, which Cambridge University lecturer Priyamvada Gopal (2017) describes as "shaped by a long colonial history in which straight white upper-class men are at the top of the social order" and in "most disciplines give disproportionate prominence to the experiences, concerns and achievements of this one group." When we bring the experiences of people of diverse backgrounds to the center, not the margins, of our instruction and celebrate human achievements and understanding around the globe, we are teaching equity and justice.

In addition to ensuring that our content represents the diversity of humanity, we best serve learners when we embrace their own heritage and cultural contexts as a starting point for our studies. When students can truly see themselves in the work we are doing, when learners are welcomed to offer what they already know, to make connections between their ancestral strengths as well as their own needs and interests, their learning serves to strengthen their identities and agency, creating conditions for success. (See Figure 2.9 for the PEBC Teaching Framework for Context.)

	First Steps	Next Steps	Advancing	Peak Performance
Context	Be aware of learners' cultures, interests, and language backgrounds, as well as prior knowledge.	Select or refine content and materials to connect to learners' knowledge and heritage, individually and collectively.	Build on learners' language skills, cultural backgrounds, interests, and readiness in planning differentiated instruction.	Learners can explain the relevance of their learning in their own cultural contexts and beyond.

Figure 2.9 Plan: Context

Into the Classroom

Knowing Students

When we know learners well, we can celebrate their background knowledge and unique insights, as did first-grade teacher Susan McIver. In the moments of the following dialogue, a recently arrived student from Japan with limited English skills chimed in on their class discussion about *Inky's Amazing Escape*, a story that includes an octopus eating a clam.

Susan narrates, "Inky is getting the clam with the sucker. He uses his suckers to pull the clam open and eat the meat. I don't think he eats the shell. The shell falls away, and he eats the meat."

A student adds on, animatedly acting out the scenario with her arms, "I envisioned Inky and the clam. He opened the clam, and he ate that meat."

Susan turns to a previously confused student. "So now what are you understanding?"

"Octopus eat the meat, and that's new schema," he explains.

"He had to pull hard to open it. In Japan, I am eating clam meat. Slow open," adds her Japanese student.

Susan enthusiastically embraces this comment. "So you have opened clams before?"

The shy girl nods.

"She has schema that we don't have, from her time in Japan. Did you hear that? It's hard to open!"

Build Bridges

When learners see the work in our classrooms as someone else's ideas for someone else's purpose, they quickly lose interest. When students feel welcome and connected and appreciate the ways in which their learning today will support and benefit their families tomorrow, they are poised to embrace school. We can build bridges for students in so many ways—by representing the world's diversity, by displaying an understanding of their home communities visually in our classrooms, by including them in our conversations and invitations, by sustaining awareness of related current events, by intentionally making connections between our curricula and learners' heritage, or simply by demonstrating an openness to all learners' insights and unique experiences.

Ten Ways to Improve Instruction for Culturally and Linguistically Diverse (CLD) Students

(adapted from Reed and Railsback, *Strategies and Resources for Mainstream Teachers of English Language Learners* [2003], 31–32)

1. Enunciate clearly, but do not raise your voice. Avoid idioms, slang words, and colloquial expressions that CLD students would not understand.

2. Whenever possible, support your words with visuals and gestures. Point directly to objects, dramatize concepts, and display pictures when appropriate. Visuals, gestures, and smiles help CLD students create meaning from a new environment.

3. Write clearly, legibly, and in print—CLD students may have difficulty reading cursive.

4. Develop and maintain regular routines. Use clear and consistent signals for classroom instructions.

5. Repeat information and review frequently. If a student does not understand, a teacher should try rephrasing or paraphrasing in shorter sentences and simpler syntax. Check often for understanding, but do not ask, "Do you understand?" Instead, have students demonstrate their learning in order to show comprehension.

6. Present new information in the context of known information.

7. Announce the lesson's objectives and activities, and list instructions step-by-step in small "chunks."

8. Present information using a variety of methods and delivery formats.

9. Provide frequent summations of the salient points of a lesson, and always emphasize key vocabulary words.

10. Recognize student success overtly and frequently. But, also be aware that in some cultures, overt individual praise is considered inappropriate and can therefore be embarrassing or confusing to the student.

CONSIDER HOW YOU MIGHT HONOR LEARNERS' CONTEXT AS YOU PLAN

- In what ways might you celebrate the heritage of your students within your classroom and instruction?

- How might you make connections between content and learners' cultural backgrounds and current lives?

- What materials can you have on hand to demonstrate your awareness of and appreciation for diversity?

- How can you ensure equity of access to higher-level challenges for all learners?

Responsiveness

Knowing what our students know and can do before designing a unit or a lesson helps us plan where to begin, when to slow down, and what needs to be scaffolded.

Hans Barber, Executive Director of Instruction in Cupertino Union School District, described how intentional planning fostered teachers' growth. "They are not so focused on the what and the how as they are on the who. This perspective on planning forced teachers to think, 'What do my kids need, and what am I doing that meets that need?' They had to open their eyes and recognize, 'I have been doing that for so long, but why am I doing that? Did it work?' We had to start to think intentionally about how to plan for all types of kids." (See Figure 2.10 for the PEBC Teaching Framework for Responsiveness.)

	First Steps	Next Steps	Advancing	Peak Performance
Responsiveness	Consider learners' prior assessment data.	Gather formative assessment data throughout planning and instruction.	Use data to hone priorities for instruction and adjust as needed. Plan differentiated instruction with flexible groupings and scaffolds, based on data.	Learners self-assess, set and refine goals, and reflect on their growing understanding.

Figure 2.10 Plan: Responsiveness

Formative Assessments

To meet learners where they are, we need to know what they already know. Sometimes last year's teacher is a valuable source in explaining learners' background knowledge, and yet the students themselves are our best resource in understanding what truly stuck with them. For this reason, early formative assessment ensures that we launch every unit in an engaging and accessible way.

More on formative assessment will be addressed in Chapter 7, "Assessment," but for now let us consider sources of data that might help us understand learners' strengths and needs and allow us to be responsive in our planning. Data can come from a broad variety of sources. Look at the list in Figure 2.11. Which do you use? Which might you try gathering? Which seem not applicable in your context as sources of data? What might you add?

Sources of Data	Already Use	Want to Try	Not Applicable
Learners' class work			
Conferring notes			
Student-brainstormed lists			
Class discussions			
Learner surveys			
Parent surveys			
Homework			
Exit tickets			

Figure 2.11 Sources of Data

Student Focus Group Interview

Although one-on-one time with learners is at a premium, small focus group interviews can be a great source of data to inform your planning. Try this: over, say, one lunch, gather a small, mixed group of learners before planning an upcoming unit. Ask those students to respond not just from their own perspectives but as representatives of the larger group. Spend a few minutes explaining the main topic(s) that unit will address, inviting learners' input:

- "What does this remind you of that you have studied in the past?"
- "In what ways does this unit sound life-worthy?"
- "What sounds boring?"
- "Which project ideas do you like best?"
- "What other suggestions might you have?"

Even the opportunity to give input can have a powerful effect on those students' motivation and engagement—and that of their peers who will hear about this discussion later. Everyone loves to have voice and choice.

Plan with Data

Once you have gathered data through assessments and conversations, you have some great input for your planning. What did you learn about students' needs? Interests? Readiness? How will you respond? Figure 2.12 shows some ideas; add your own.

Needs	Interests	Readiness
• Pre-teach essential skills. • Develop tasks that honor multimodal presentation. • Offer small-group instruction. • • •	• Provide choice. • Create interest groups. • Develop opportunities to share expertise and insight. • • •	• Develop tasks with "low floor and high ceiling." • Offer resources to scaffold independence. • • •

Figure 2.12 Planning from Students' Needs, Interests, and Readiness

Inquiry

"If a student can figure something out for him- or herself," explains educator Peter Johnston (2004) in *Choice Words*, "explicitly providing the information preempts the student's opportunity to build a sense of agency and independence . . . when you figure something out for yourself, there is a certain thrill in the figuring. After a few successful experiences, you might start thinking that figuring out is something that you can actually do. Maybe you are even a figuring-out kind of person."

Inquiry is all about inviting learners to pursue authentic questions—theirs or ours—to experience learning as a process of uncovering and discovery. When we take a stance of inquiry, we pursue an investigation unsure of what we will find out, but clear about our questions and intentions. Inquiry engages learners, creates connections with new knowledge and prior experience, and offers the conditions for deep understanding. (See Figure 2.13 for the PEBC Teaching Framework for Inquiry.)

	First Steps	Next Steps	Advancing	Peak Performance
Inquiry	Pose invitational, open-ended questions. Model a stance of curiosity and interest.	Invite authentic questions. Offer choice and variety. Anticipate adjustments to resources and targets in response to learners' interests, needs, and understanding.	Provide time, space, and structure for exploring topics of interest, sharing learning, and the unexpected.	Learners demonstrate curiosity, autonomy, and agency by asking their own questions and investigating beyond the content provided.

Figure 2.13 Plan: Inquiry

Curiosity

When we are curious, we are engaged; we want to know. A study in the United Kingdom found that four-year-old girls—the most curious of all children—ask, on average, 390 questions per day, while nine-year-old boys ask 120 (*Telegraph* staff 2013). From there, our outward curiosity is said to decline; learners ask fewer and fewer questions, typically, as they progress through school. And yet, when we step back and look at most everything that has ever been accomplished by humankind, often it began with a question: What's on the other side of that ocean? How might we cure polio? Can we survive in outer space? Questions are a tribute to curiosity, even if we can't answer them in the moment.

In addition to posing your own provocative questions to guide your unit, as described previously, make space for learners' questions: What are they wondering about the topic at hand? These curiosities, even if not pursued directly during school learning time, can serve to engage students' interest in the work. Some questions might be answered by research, some might be a matter of opinion, and some may remain unanswerable all our lives, but being curious means our minds are turned on, no matter what we are wondering.

REFLECTION: BE CURIOUS

- What are all the things you are wondering—or could be wondering—right now? Let your curiosity ooze out onto this page. Can you ask ten questions? Twenty? Give yourself five whole minutes to wonder, and see what happens.

- Now look back over your questions. Is there one you'd like to pursue and answer? How did it feel to be curious on purpose?

Productive Questioning

Inquiry is not just asking questions for questions' sake but rather asking things we'd like to find out. We support learners' inquiry when we:

- Model curiosity. We talk about our own questions and how they drive our thinking.
- Teach learners to ask good questions. We model and practice open-ended, generative, thoughtful questions.
- Teach learners to seek answers. We discuss many sources of resolution and teach learners to pursue each as appropriate.
- Provide time and space for inquiry. We provide flexibility for learners to pursue their own curiosities and share back to the group.
- Keep questions alive in the classroom. We record and revisit questions throughout a unit, determining which we have answered and how, and which continue to drive our understanding.

As we plan a unit, we can dedicate time to considering what we are wondering, to recording those wonderings, and then allow time to circle back. In addition, we can provide space for learners' self-determination. For example, during Jamie Salterelli and Jeff Lewis' fourth-grade classes' unit on Colorado History, the classes together explored important topics like the Louisiana Purchase and Manifest Destiny before learners launched into exploration with partners of topics of their choice, such as Zebulon Pike (of Pike's Peak). Planning a whole-group investigation where students experience and practice research and thinking skills, followed by independent, scaffolded inquiry work, can effectively set the stage for learners' success. (See Figure 2.14.)

How Much Freedom?

The notion of inquiry can be scary because it means letting go of some—but not all—control. Inquiry is about balancing time and space for learners' thinking and questions while also attending to the standards and other responsibilities of our courses. Inquiry exists on a continuum, from totally teacher centered to totally student centered, and there is a time and a place for each. What is important is that we recognize and seek opportunities, when feasible, to allow students more ownership of their learning, either the content, the process, or both.

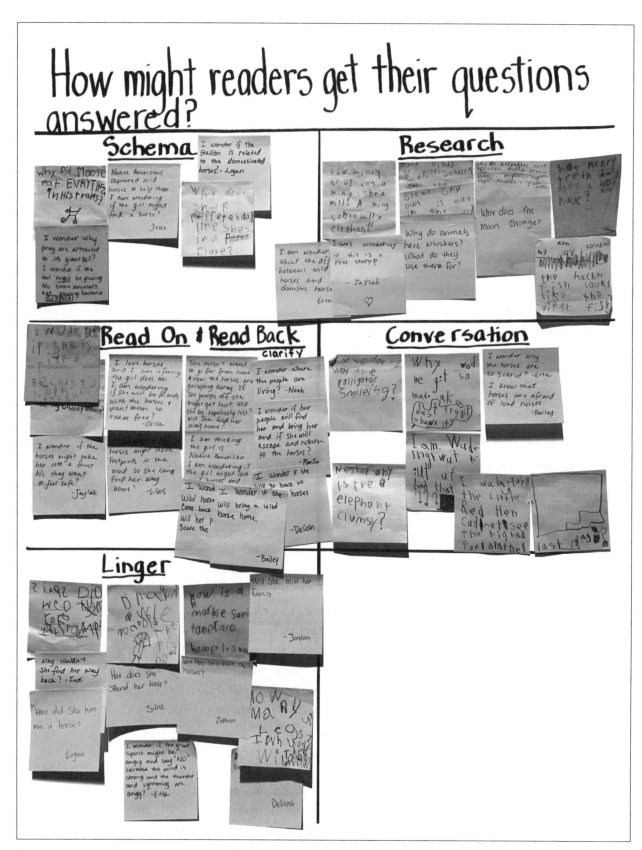

Figure 2.14 Mary Korte and Ana Mettler's primary students ask questions as readers and then consider where they might find answers: in their schema (background knowledge), with additional research, by reading on or reading back, through conversation, or perhaps simply by lingering with that curiosity.

PROCESS

Clear on what we are teaching and who we are teaching, we ask ourselves, "How will learners come to know?" What learning experiences, language development opportunities, and resources will galvanize learners' agency and understanding throughout our studies? Careful planning can not only strengthen the bridge we are building to connect learners with learning objectives but also cultivate students' identities as thinkers and owners of their own learning.

Learning Experiences

Ellin Oliver Keene frequently notes in her presentations that students need to focus on fewer concepts of great import taught in an in-depth manner over a long period of time with an opportunity to apply the concepts in a variety of texts, contexts, and content areas. As we focus on fewer enduring understandings and as we consider all the possible learning we could incorporate into a unit, we pay attention to both the authenticity of each task and its cognitive demand. (See Figure 2.15 for the PEBC Teaching Framework for Learning Experiences.)

	First Steps	Next Steps	Advancing	Peak Performance
Learning Experiences	Prepare learning activities.	Design cognitively challenging tasks that invite learners to explore important content through discipline-authentic processes.	Engage learners with open-ended, differentiated challenges that invite struggle in service of conceptual understanding. Create opportunities for learners to authentically "uncover" and synthesize key ideas.	Learners understand the discipline, both as a body of knowledge and a process of making meaning. Learners understand, remember, and reapply their learning.

Figure 2.15 Plan: Learning Experiences

Authenticity

As described previously, learners gain understanding of a discipline as a way of knowing when we engage them with discipline-authentic processes. When designing a math unit, we might ask what people really do with this stuff. Do they fill out worksheets or solve actual problems in the real world? And what kind? When designing a book study, we might ask how sophisticated readers truly engage with a text. Do they try to think of a better title for the piece and remember the names of the tertiary characters, or do they talk about the author's message and the meaning they derived? Those real things that real people outside of a school setting do with this sort of information can offer us a window into the sorts of things we can ask learners to do.

In this quest for authenticity, we might consider which artifacts, examples, or experiences could offer a trail of clues to help learners understand a concept, rather than feel we need to tell them directly. We might look at statistics of voters over time and ask learners to evaluate whether the electoral college system is fair. When exploring the problem of electronic waste, we might examine maps and shipping patterns to conclude about its social justice issues. In these two examples, we ask learners to think as social scientists and draw their own conclusions.

REFLECTION: PLAN FOR AUTHENTICITY

How might you develop an authentic opportunity for your learners to uncover a concept?

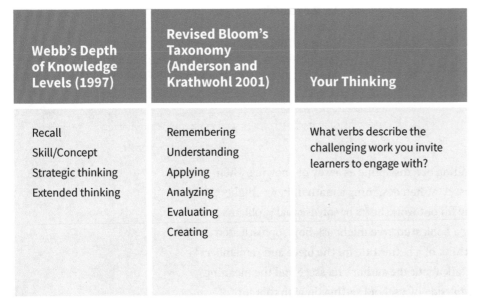

I used to think that delivering content by "telling" was ~~more~~ effective because less would get "lost in translation", ~~being the most~~

Now I think having students work to discover/experiment/communicate leads to deeper understanding. So I will be more thoughtful about lesson design.

Figure 2.16 A teacher reflects on the value of inviting learners to make meaning for themselves.

Webb's Depth of Knowledge Levels (1997)	Revised Bloom's Taxonomy (Anderson and Krathwohl 2001)	Your Thinking
Recall	Remembering	What verbs describe the challenging work you invite learners to engage with?
Skill/Concept	Understanding	
Strategic thinking	Applying	
Extended thinking	Analyzing	
	Evaluating	
	Creating	

Figure 2.17 Levels of Cognitive Demand

Cognitive Demand

Authenticity in and of itself can create cognitive demand—opportunities for learners to make connections and think conceptually, beyond simply memorizing or applying a known procedure. Bloom's taxonomy and, more recently, Webb's work on cognitive demand remind us that a more complex task intentionally invites learners to stretch their thinking, which will, in turn, generate richer understanding. Each system, listed in Figure 2.17 from the least to the most complex thinking, describes a hierarchy. How would you characterize the complex thinking of your discipline?

Thinking about verbs can nudge us to reconsider the nature of the tasks we invite learners to explore. To adjust familiar tasks or develop new ones, we can ask ourselves a few questions:

- In what ways might learners grapple with raw data or primary sources?
- What might experts in the field do along these lines?
- What would understanding really look like?

Figure 2.18 shows some examples. What ideas might you add?

Topic	Instead of . . .	Learners might . . .	Which would require them to . . .
Geography	Reading about global agricultural trends and their economic impacts	Examine a series of maps and data tables and draw inferences about how agriculture is changing.	• Read maps. • Interpret data. • Infer meaning. • Argue with evidence.
Math	Memorizing one algorithm for multiplication	Learn several approaches, select the one that works best for them, and explain why.	• Understand multiplication. • Compare methods. • Argue with evidence.
Language arts	Writing a literary analysis describing the events in a text	Write a fictional story about characters from two different texts meeting up and engaging in a conversation.	• Understand characters. • Empathize with perspectives. • Be creative. • Write dialogue.
Science	Completing an experiment by following prescribed instructions to create a known result	Develop, conduct, and document an investigation to test a novel idea.	• Ask a testable question. • Design an experiment. • Record data. • Interpret data.
(Your idea)			

Figure 2.18 Increasing Cognitive Demand

Cognitive demand can be highly engaging when done well, or disengaging if learners feel unprepared or lack confidence or interest. So when we raise the cognitive demand of student work, we need to be certain that it is purposeful and interesting and that we provide the necessary scaffolds toward learners' independence. These are easily offered through workshop instruction, described in greater detail in Chapter 4.

Language Development

More than ever, language development is a critical area to address in our planning. To succeed, learners need access to the language demands of our schools in general and our disciplines specifically. (See Figure 2.19 for the PEBC Teaching Framework for Language Development.) To this end, we can provide intentional scaffolds for academic language development, including access to:

* discipline-specific vocabulary, such as *onomatopoeia, mitosis,* or *perpendicular*

* discourse patterns and phrases, such as "I respectfully disagree with you," or "Let us critique this argument . . ." (Discourse is addressed more deeply in Chapter 6.)

* modes of written and oral language specific to a content area, such as written proofs or debates.

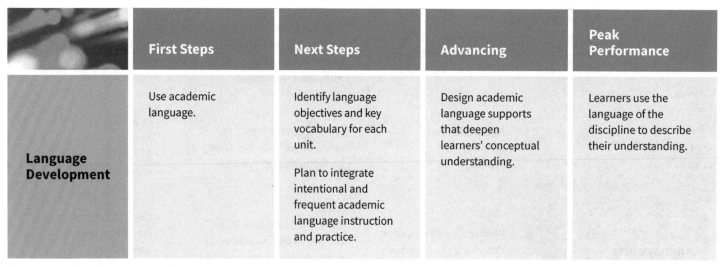

	First Steps	Next Steps	Advancing	Peak Performance
Language Development	Use academic language.	Identify language objectives and key vocabulary for each unit. Plan to integrate intentional and frequent academic language instruction and practice.	Design academic language supports that deepen learners' conceptual understanding.	Learners use the language of the discipline to describe their understanding.

Figure 2.19 Plan: Language Development

Vocabulary Instruction Resources

* Janet Allen, *Words, Words, Words*

* Isabel L. Beck, Margaret G. McKeown, and Linda Kucan, *Bringing Words to Life: Robust Vocabulary Instruction*

* Jane D. Hill and Kathleen M. Flynn, *Classroom Instruction That Works for English Language Learners*

* Robert Marzano and Debra Pickering, *Building Academic Vocabulary: Teacher's Manual*

Vocabulary Development

If we want students to develop sophisticated language, we need to speak to them in a sophisticated manner. In addition, all learners, especially those learning English, benefit from intentional vocabulary instruction linked to content-area learning. To plan for vocabulary development within the context of a unit, we first consider which content-specific terms are integral. Also, which transferrable academic language terms, such as *model, critique,* or *thesis,* are crucial? Then, we can plan for instruction while remembering these key principles for effective vocabulary instruction:

* Meaningful context: Help me care about these word(s).

* Student-friendly explanations: Let me describe this in my own words.

* Multiple contexts and frequent exposure: Invite me to play with new vocabulary in many ways and across a series of days.

* Numerous interactions: Present oral, kinesthetic, graphic, written, and aural exposure to the terms.

* Frequent exposures: Play with the same short set of words at least every day for a week.

Discourse

In addition to the development of vocabulary, skills for speaking and listening are also integral to academic language development. These are best scaffolded through direct instruction and then intentional classroom practice between pairs, in small groups, and with the whole class. Chapter 6 explores discourse in greater depth, as it is a facet of phenomenal teaching unto itself, yet here is a quick idea to get you started thinking about this: Too often, a child contributes a thought or an answer, and teachers are quick to nod, smile, and move on. Instead, we can use this idea as a launchpad for further conversation, starting with "What do you all think of what Henry just said?" We might also provide scaffolds for the ensuring conversation, such as:

- "I agree because . . ."
- "I disagree because . . ."
- "I am wondering . . ."

This conversation could take place as a turn-and-talk or as a group, but the big idea is to offer time for students to respond to their peers' thinking. Plan time for these sorts of conversations, and know that this is one of the most important ways you can support the development of literate, agentic citizens.

Into the Classroom

Primary Students Discuss Hidden Figures

John had not been ready to share earlier, but his teacher offered him time to think about what he wanted to say, then circled back and invited him to speak his mind about their text, the Young Readers' version of *Hidden Figures*. "I was thinking it would be very hard for her to get the job to be a computer because there is segregation, and she wanted to be a computer. I was thinking it would be very hard because she is a black woman, and there is segregation."

The teacher, Mary, prompts, "Anyone else want to add on or speak back to John about his thinking? Who might have something to say back to John, who just shared his thinking really bravely with the group?"

"I am thinking maybe they didn't know she was African American, that she was a white person, but when she gets there, they might be mean to her," Mario explains.

"I agree. They might not know she is black yet, but if they did know somehow, it would be a really well-paying job," Jillian adds.

"Mario and Jillian were saying they thought they might not know she was black, and but then if they found out they might be mean to her. I am agreeing with them because there was segregation, but if this happened now, they would be fine," adds Jacob.

Discipline-Specific Language Demands

To those experienced with a discipline, discipline-specific language and language functions can seem innate, yet to new arrivals, they seem to represent a secret code that is challenging to crack. All learners benefit when we are transparent about the unique language patterns—both oral and written—in our disciplines and take the time to uncover and explain how to understand, read, write, and speak in those ways. What are the unique language demands of your discipline? Which of the genres in Figure 2.20 might learners benefit from studying, understanding, and creating? What else?

Argument	Essay	Map	Rules	
Bibliography	Graph	Multimedia presentation	Proof	
Critique	Infographic	Music score	Proposal	
Debate	Infomercial	News article	Script	
Diagram	Instructions	Op-ed	Slide show	
Discussion	Lab report	Poem	Table	

Figure 2.20 Discipline-Specific Genres

Resources

Now that we know where we are headed, what will help us get there most efficiently? Oftentimes, learners benefit from delving into a shared study around a common text or problem set to practice skills and strategies together, then branching off to use those skills to explore other sources in greater depth. Spend some time before the launch of each unit gathering articles, books, images, and realia: What might trigger questions and curiosity? What might you bring in that can illustrate and authenticate the enduring understandings you seek to explore?

Your class may include readers at all levels, so consider resource gathering as an opportunity to enhance differentiation, knowing that you will meet more learners with diverse but related content in a variety of formats. (See Figure 2.21 for the PEBC Teaching Framework for Resources.)

	First Steps	Next Steps	Advancing	Peak Performance
Resources	Offer resources.	Leverage selected resources to differentiate instruction. Match resources, including technology, to learners' needs.	Provide an abundance of varied texts, imagery, media, realia, and manipulatives to support thinking and understanding. Integrate technology as a tool to increase rigor, depth, access, and opportunity.	Learners explore and make connections between information from multiple sources (some of which they self-select) in varied ways.

Figure 2.21 Plan: Resources

Where to Shop for Resources

Learners benefit from exploring content in a variety of texts and formats. When talking about Antarctic explorers, we can show slides and videos to set the scene, bring in ice cubes to test our own endurance, examine large-scale maps of the area, and read firsthand accounts of Ernest Shackleton and his colleagues. When learning about geometry, we might read *The Librarian Who Measured the Earth* and look for ways to use our tools to enact similar feats around our own school and community to bring that work to life.

Consider all the places you might find resources. You might consider gathering:

* text sets from the library

* articles from online sources

* realia from a local museum

* maps from the United States Geological Survey or other sources

* data sets from government agencies and other reliable sources

* infographics produced by nongovernmental organizations and other agencies

* guest speakers from a related profession

* video conferences with researchers or leaders in the field.

REFLECTION: RESOURCES

What resources might you bring in to help learners engage and connect with the content of your unit?

Technology

How can we capitalize on technology to enhance and enrich learning and connection? Some educators have been seduced by the belief that technology is always better than a traditional form of instruction, and yet research shows that students actually comprehend text better when reading on paper rather than on a screen, and many of us have witnessed the ways in which technology can waste valuable learning time or isolate individuals rather than enhance collaboration.

Education researcher Dr. Ruben Puentedura describes four levels of technology integration into instructional experiences, from low-impact to high-impact on learners' thinking: at the earliest or simplest stage, a digital version of student work replaces some other version (such as a paper worksheet). In the second stage, technology can be used to enhance traditional learning experiences. At the third stage, the technology makes significant changes to how learning happens, and in the fourth, the technology completely changes the experience.

In considering these stages, we can be thoughtful about the ways in which we incorporate technology into our plans, asking ourselves:

* When is the appropriate time in the learning sequence to incorporate technology?

* Why are we using technology at this time for this learning?

* How will we capitalize on the benefits of technology to deepen thinking and understanding?

* In what ways will we ensure access for all?

* What are the costs to using technology in this way, and how might we address them?

* What will learners do if the technology is not working on one or more learning days?

Related Resources for Further Study

Ron Berger, *An Ethic of Excellence*

Lisa Delpit, *"Multiplication Is for White People"*

Zaretta Hammond, *Culturally Responsive Teaching and the Brain*

Stevi Quate and John McDermott, *Clock Watchers*

Michael Schmoker, *Results*

Grant Wiggins and Jay McTighe, *Understanding by Design*

Dylan Wiliam, *Creating the Schools Our Children Need*

Jeff Zwiers, *The Communication Effect*

As critical consumers of the technology available to us in our schools and classrooms, let us seek the best-case scenarios for welcoming learners in the twenty-first century to engage with up-to-date experiences, as well as remember that it is OK to be low tech on purpose, at times, to meet students' needs to work with concrete materials and kinesthetic experiences. When technology can enhance the rigor and depth of our work, open new doors for learners' understanding, and activate their sense of agency, turn it on.

PLANNING TO PLAN

This chapter gives you a lot to think about in planning a unit, I know, and yet the more of these elements we intentionally consider, the more likely that our students will gain full benefit from the learning experiences we design. With clear purpose, clear understanding of our people, and distinct processes for learning in place, we can launch consciously into our year or unit, incorporating all the other aspects of phenomenal teaching presented in this text as they come. Figure 2.22 presents a unit plan, while Figure 2.23 shows the unit calendar.

In considering how to make the work of finding volumes and surface areas of geometric solids life-worthy and interesting for middle school learners, a teacher elected to introduce them to the problem of water transportation in developing countries and one solution, the Q Drum (https://www.qdrum.co.za). This rollable, fifty-liter plastic water container was developed by engineers for use in rural regions. In this unit, learners will apply their knowledge of relationships between dimensions of a cylinder to develop Q Drums with a volume of one hundred liters.

Purpose		
Clarity:	**Life-worthiness:**	**Content and process:**
Question: How can geometry help us solve problems?	Learners see shapes all around them, from package designs to buildings and vehicles. They can be agentic in understanding why specific designs are used for certain purposes as well as considering how mathematicians work within constraints to solve problems in the real world.	Content: Solve real-world and mathematical problems involving volume of cylinders, cones, and spheres.
Understand: We can efficiently use knowns to find unknowns when we know the patterns of their relationships.		Practices (CCSSMP):
		3. Construct viable arguments and critique the reasoning of others.
		4. Model with mathematics.
		6. Attend to precision.
		Process: Monitor for meaning and ask questions.

Figure 2.22 Sample Unit Overview: Eighth-Grade Geometry Study of Cones, Cylinders, and Spheres. CCSMP = Common Core State Standards for Mathematical Practice (2010).

People

Context:

Many students have background knowledge of life in other parts of the world where tap water is not available or not potable.

Responsiveness:

Most learners in this group know about two-dimensional shapes and how to find their areas, as well as how to find the volume of a cube.

Most have not yet worked with cylinders, cones, and spheres.

Inquiry:

Hook: We will discuss water transportation needs in the developing world and the ways in which those transform lives.

Learners will be welcome to play with design parameters to develop and justify the best Q Drum dimensions.

Process

Learning experiences:

- Doubling cube problem
- Measuring geometric solids
- Predicting relationships between volume, surface area, and dimensions
- Exploring formulae and why they hold true
- Practice problems on changing dimensions and finding volume

Final task: Design a Q Drum with a volume of one hundred liters. See that your design uses the minimum materials.

Language development:

Vocabulary: *area, cylinder, cone, dimension, height, pi, sphere, volume*

Discourse: Explain, justify, and critique solutions.

Genre: Create a design, as written mathematical explanation for dimensions, and construct a labeled scale model.

Resources:

- Realia: cylinders, cones, spheres
- Measuring tools
- Graph paper
- Q Drum video

Figure 2.22 *continued*

Here is an overview of the minilesson and task of each daily lesson planned within the unit described in Figure 2.22. More on daily lesson planning will be explored in Chapter 4, "Workshop."

Day 1	Day 2	Day 3	Day 4	Day 5
Minilesson: Determining importance **Task:** If you double a cube's side length, what happens to its volume? Surface area? What if it's tripled? Quadrupled? **Homework:** What if we double one dimension of a rectangular prism?	**Minilesson:** We can efficiently use knowns to find unknowns when we know the patterns of their relationships. **Task:** Give-get geometric relationships we know. Brainstorm geometric relationships we don't yet know. Discuss: How do mathematicians find these?	**Minilesson:** How can geometry help us solve problems? **Task:** Intro Q Drum. Consider challenge to design a Q Drum with a volume of one hundred liters. What would we need to know? **Homework:** Watch Q Drum video.	**Minilesson:** CCSSMP 6. Attend to precision. **Task:** Building background knowledge. Jigsaw solids exploration: cones, cylinders, spheres. Find relationships between dimensions, surface area, volume. Day 1: Expert groups **Homework:** Find geometric solids in the real world.	**Minilesson:** CCSSMP 6. Attend to precision. **Task:** Building background knowledge. Jigsaw solids exploration Day 2: Jigsaw groups

Day 6	Day 7	Day 8	Day 9	Day 10
Minilesson: Monitor for meaning **Task:** Problem-solving. Find the dimensions of a cone, cylinder, and sphere that all have the same volume. **Homework:** Explain class work finding.	**Minilesson:** Monitor for meaning **Task:** Problem-solving. What happens to the volume when you double the height of a cylinder or cone, or double the radius of a sphere? **Homework:** Explain class work finding.	**Minilesson:** Asking questions **Task:** Problem-solving. Doubling discussion: Why? **Homework:** Naked math: solve for given dimensions or volumes of cylinders, cones, and spheres.	**Minilesson:** CCSSMP 6. Attend to precision. **Task:** Problem-solving. Design a Q Drum with a given volume. **Homework:** Continue class work.	**Minilesson:** CCSSMP 3. Construct viable arguments and critique the reasoning of others. **Task:** Problem-solving. Share and critique Q Drum solutions.

Day 11	Day 12	Day 13	Day 14	Day 15
Minilesson: Asking questions **Task:** Finalize Q Drum design to use minimal materials for set volume. Write a mathematical explanation for its dimensions, and construct a labeled scale model. **Homework:** Complete class work.	**Minilesson:** CCSSMP 3. Construct viable arguments and critique the reasoning of others. **Task:** Museum share of Q Drum designs. **Homework:** So what synthesis on Q Drum project	**Minilesson:** Monitor for meaning **Task:** Review carousel solving volume problems. **Homework:** Review for assessment.	**Minilesson:** CCSSMP 6. Attend to precision. **Task:** Unit assessment.	**Task:** Reflection: How can geometry help us solve problems?

Figure 2.23 Sample Unit Calendar
CCSMP = Common Core State Standards for Mathematical Practice (2010)

Planning FAQs

- **"How am I supposed to have time for all this planning?"**

    High-quality planning does take time; there is no way around that. Enlist the collaboration of colleagues; divide and conquer. Save everything that worked so you can refine and reuse it next year. Recycle effective tasks and structures for use with other content (for example, if a fishbowl discussion worked well in your unit on the thirteen colonies, try another during your study of the Civil War).

- **"What about the curriculum?"**

    As described above, you are responsible for the standards and learning targets, yet might not realistically have time for every task and topic listed in the teacher's guide. Let that go. If you focus on supporting learners as thinkers capable of pursuing understanding independently, they will be ready to grapple with unfamiliar tasks in the future.

- **"What about the _____ students?"** (insert your concern group on the line)

    Learners rise to our expectations. A colleague was recently planning a lesson on spatial reasoning with an elementary-level math teacher. One student classified as "special education" was scheduled to return from her individualized help session partway through the math lesson, so the teacher was reluctant to invite her to engage with the tangram puzzle alongside classmates. After a coaching conversation, though, she agreed to invite that student to give the work a try. Guess who started last but finished first? The "special needs" student. Let's assume they _can_.

- **"But really, this particular group can't, so what do I do for them?"**

    Another teacher had decided to keep learners with low skills out of this mix for general math work time and instead to sequester them at the kidney table practicing math facts. They continued to fail on their skills assessment. A few weeks after she chose to release these students to grapple with the complex problem-solving work alongside peers, one of the "low-skills" learners got 100 percent on her skills assessment. Consider what caused this identity shift.

- **"Come on, I really have to differentiate for _____."**

    Yes. Differentiation by process (how learners approach the task), product (how learners document or present their learning), or content (what learners actually study) are all appropriate ways to modify work in the event that a learner truly needs a unique experience. But first, please let them have a go.

Your Turn

Using the template in Figure 2.24, think through your planning for an upcoming unit. In what ways might considering purpose, people, and process advance agency and understanding?

Purpose

Clarity: What is the purpose?	Life-worthiness: Why does this matter for learners?	Content and process: What and how are we learning?

People

Context: Who are the learners?	Responsiveness: What will these learners need?	Inquiry: How will learners' curiosity, voice, and choice be incorporated?

Process

Learning experiences: How will students develop and demonstrate understanding?	Language development: How will learners develop academic vocabulary and discourse skills?	Resources: What will best support learning?

Figure 2.24 Planning for Understanding and Agency Unit Design Template

REFLECTION

- How does your current understanding of planning for understanding and agency compare to your prior knowledge?

- What questions are still lingering?

- Which approaches to planning feel most natural to you?

- Which aspects might you want to refine? How?

- What changes do you feel inspired to make in your own instructional designs?

- What difference will those changes make for students?

- How will you know you have succeeded?

REFLECTION ON CHAPTER QUESTION: HOW CAN WE DESIGN LEARNING EXPERIENCES THAT CULTIVATE STUDENTS' UNDERSTANDING AND AGENCY?

Invitation: Summarize and reflect on the chapter by annotating the planning template in Figure 2.25 with your own notes and questions about each element.

Purpose		
Clarity	Life-worthiness	Content and process

People		
Context	Responsiveness	Inquiry

Process		
Learning experiences	Language development	Resources

Figure 2.25 Planning Template

3 COMMUNITY

CHAPTER QUESTION: IN WHAT WAYS MIGHT WE DEVELOP CLASSROOM COMMUNITIES THAT SUPPORT THE AGENCY AND UNDERSTANDING OF EVERY LEARNER?

ANTICIPATION QUESTIONS

• Why is community important to you? To your students?

• What is at the heart of your classroom community?

• In what ways do you intentionally build community?

• What challenges arise in the process of cultivating or sustaining community?

• What questions do you have about classroom community?

Teacher Voice: Community Magic

"It feels like magic. Community is that element that is least tangible, toughest to explain and quantify, and yet when you walk into a classroom that has it, you are mesmerized, can feel that energy in the room. People think it's magic, that it just happens. But magic isn't magic. As Don Murray said, a magician knows what she is doing. Community that feels magical is intentionally built."

—LORI CONRAD

Community Support in the Real World

If you've ever raised an infant, or even watched someone puzzle through the complexity of that challenge, you know how full responsibility for the life of a tiny human being with limited communication skills and lots of needs can be both phenomenal and overwhelming. So, there I was with a newborn in my arms, no relatives in town. Excitement coalesced with exhaustion, mingled with miraculous awe and sometimes sheer peril. I felt both elated and very much alone.

Fortunately, that was only a fleeting feeling—a savvy teacher, friend of a friend, with a newborn of her own, corralled a few of us new moms together to start a playgroup and meet weekly to do an activity with our children. The first several months, our gatherings consisted of plopping the babies together on a blanket in the middle of someone's living room and sipping tea while discussing what we wondered or had figured out about diapers, breastfeeding, sex, car seats, and just about everything else that had changed. As the kids got older and the blanket felt small, we started taking the babies on outings—to the museum, the park, the farm—anyplace to be together with other try-hard mamas and talk through our challenges, opportunities, solutions, and dilemmas. We worked through everything: anatomical changes, children's developmental milestones, preschool recommendations, work scheduling, the possibility of exercise, and more. Email the group about diaper prices, and you'd get back a spreadsheet about where to buy each brand, each size, for the best unit price. Call in a last-minute childcare pinch, and you had a safe, happy place for your little one to be, no questions asked, and no score-keeping about returning the favor. Isolation melted away in the bright warmth of community support; confusion gave way to confidence as we shared problems and insight. Not only are we moms still friends to this day, but so are our children, now in high school. And we still ask each other anything.

REFLECTION: COMMUNITY SUPPORT IN THE REAL WORLD

Tell the story of a time when you experienced a strong and supportive community. What conditions spawned, developed, and sustained your group? What were the results?

What: Community in the Classroom

Trust, shared purpose, interdependence, mutual support, and safety in taking risks are some of the features of an effective community. Your own community might be your neighborhood, your faith group, your colleagues, your extended family. For students, their learning community, the space in which and the people with whom they spend their learning time, is of primary importance. The powerful influence of both adults and peers in schools shapes learners' experience, self-perceptions, hopes, and dreams.

By putting students in a room together, we create a community. With intention and perseverance, we can create a productive culture on purpose. A productive community of thinkers is one where learners see peers as resources, rather than competitors. Participants help one another pick up dropped pencils, find missing books, troubleshoot wayward laptops, research ideas. Students feel confident to share their thinking, to risk making a mistake in front of the group, knowing that they will be supported and learn from the experience. Productive communities of thinkers buoy progress and offer participants opportunities to achieve more as part of the collective than they ever might individually (Vygotsky 1978). Community is a place where students linger, a place they want to be.

Education expert Ron Ritchhart (2015) describes the primacy of culture in any school reform effort:

> I believe that culture is the hidden tool for transforming our schools and offering our students the best learning possible. Traditionally, policymakers have focused on curriculum as the tool for transformation, naively assuming that teachers merely deliver curriculum to their students. Change the deliverable—Common Core, National Curriculum, International Baccalaureate Diploma—and you will have transformed education, they assume. In reality, curriculum is something that is *enacted* with students. It plays out within the dynamics of the school and classroom culture. Thus culture is foundational. It will determine how any curriculum comes to life.

Many forces interact to inform our classroom culture: the physical environment; the participants' attitudes, words, and actions; and the nature of the work we engage in together, and yet as lead learners, we have the opportunity to set the tone and to hold the bar high. We can intentionally create a classroom com munity that reflects our best hopes for all students and invites them to draw forth the unique potential in one another.

Why Community?

Important socioemotional development takes place in the context of community. "Supportive Relationships and Active Skill-Building Strenghten the Foundations of Resilience" found: "All prevention and intervention programs would benefit from focusing on combinations of the following factors: (1) facilitating supportive adult-child relationships; (2) building a sense of self-efficacy and perceived control; (3) providing opportunities to strengthen adaptive skills and self-regulatory capacities; and (4) mobilizing sources of faith, hope, and cultural traditions" Center on the Developing Child at Harvard University 2015). Furthermore, "Key Findings and Implications of the Science of Learning and Development," gathered by education and policy experts, described that children's development requires "the integration and interconnectivity—both anatomically and functionally—of affective, cognitive, social, and emotional processes. Though these processes—particularly

"When children are motivated, responsible, and focused, they are more able to persist in hard tasks and respond to good teaching. These capabilities are a booster rocket for everything we measure, including test scores. But the point is larger. No one involved in education can view the values and beliefs held by students as trivial or secondary. They are the very things that can grip the imagination and determine the direction of a life."

—The Aspen Institute (2018)

cognition and emotion—have historically been dichotomized, they are inextricably linked, co-organizing and fueling all human thought and behavior" (Turnaround for Children 2018). Community is the cauldron within which all socioemotional learning takes place. Community also has the power to make us safer, smarter, and more resilient.

COMMUNITY MAKES US SAFER

Students need safety to live, let alone to learn. Although rates of violent crimes in American schools, according to the National Center for Education Statistics, have remained steady for the past twenty years, bullying continues to plague more than 11 percent of all schools on a weekly basis, and in a 2015 study of Organization for Economic Cooperation and Development nations, 14 percent of U.S. fifteen-year-olds reported that "student learning is hindered to some extent or a lot by students intimidating or bullying other students." Eighteen percent of U.S. fifteen-year-olds report "student learning is hindered to some extent or a lot by students lacking respect for teachers" (Organization for Economic Cooperation and Development 2015). One in every six to ten schools, and disproportionately more in high-poverty neighborhood schools, is experiencing low levels of safety. Proactive community building can serve as an antidote to bullying or other unsafe behaviors in schools.

Furthermore, students' involvement with one or more stable, caring adult in their lives serves as a buffer against undesirable outcomes: learners with these productive, secure relationships are better able to "focus attention, solve problems, plan ahead, adjust to new circumstances, regulate behavior, and control impulses" (Center on the Developing Child at Harvard University 2015)—all behaviors that bode well for their own safety, and the safety of their school, as well as the lifelong outcomes of the children. Building positive relationships one-on-one, as well as productive communities at large, positively impacts school safety, as well as student outcomes across time.

SAFETY MAKES US SMARTER

We learn more when we feel safe. According to Stanford's Linda Darling-Hammond, "The science says to us that, in fact, the way the brain functions and grows, it needs safety, it needs warmth, it actually even needs hugs. We actually learn in a state of positive emotion much more effectively than we can learn in a state of negative emotion. That has huge implications for what we do in schools" (quoted in Riley and Terada 2019). We can support learners in feeling safe and therefore ready to learn by establishing productive and positive communities of learners. The outcomes of those efforts have been aptly documented: according to John Hattie's (2009) meta-analyses of educational research, students' self-efficacy (beliefs, attitudes, dispositions) creates a very strong positive impact on learning outcomes, as does students' seeking help from peers, followed closely by reciprocal teaching. We also know that the outcomes pay off across time: a 2016 World Bank report found that "8 in 10 employers say social emotional skills are the most important to success and yet are also the hardest to find" (Cunningham and Villasenor 2016). Teaching students the life skills of collaboration and community benefits them across their lifetimes.

Safety does not mean low expectations, an absence of rigor, or a cap on struggle; rather, it suggests developing a classroom climate where learners can step into unknown territory and tackle tough tasks knowing they are safe to make mistakes, experience confusion, and seek support. Building community in our classrooms yields positive returns in terms of overall school climate, learning outcomes for our students this year, and the futures our learners will design for themselves.

COMMUNITY TEACHES SOCIOEMOTIONAL SKILLS

The 2018 *From a Nation at Risk to a Nation at Hope* report published by the Aspen Institute National Commission on Social, Emotional, and Academic Development recommends that all schools change instruction to teach students social, emotional, and cognitive skills, that we embed these skills in academics and school-wide practices, and that learners be asked to exercise these skills while learning academic content and interacting with peers and adults each day at school. Giving learners a chance to try on these skills as they navigate and negotiate peer conversations and develop their own identities enhances their capacity for empathy, collaboration, and conflict resolution. The imperative to put the development of socioemotional skills at the forefront of our instruction suggests that we intentionally plan and allot time for teaching learners how to be engaged, productive community members, rather than assume these are skill sets they bring with them to school. (See Figure 3.1.)

> "Despite the widespread belief that individual grit, extraordinary self-reliance, or some in-born, heroic strength of character triumph over calamity, science now tells us that it is the reliable presence of at least one supportive relationship and multiple opportunities for developing effective coping skills that are essential building blocks for the capacity to do well in the face of significant adversity."
>
> —*Harvard University Center on the Developing Child (2015)*

Community *Is* . . .	Community *Is Not* . . .	Your Thinking . . .
Welcoming	Rigid	
Inclusive	Exclusive	
Student led	Teacher directed	
Engaging	Compliant	
Open-minded	Dogmatic	
Joyful routines	Scripted silence	

Figure 3.1 Clarification Corner

Teacher Voice: Why Community?

"Learning can't take place in a space void of relationship. Not just student to teacher but student to student. Learning is vulnerable, involves failing. We learn through the mistakes we make, how we question. We can't do that in a space where we don't feel safe, heard, valued," explains sixth-grade teacher Andrea Overton.

Her teaching partner, Rachel Gardner, adds, "We expect kids to be vulnerable and celebrate their vulnerability. We pull random kids to come up to the board and share their thinking, and then we celebrate, whether right or wrong. What's your mistake? What celebration would you like? Kids really own the celebrations. They are kid driven, student centered, and become part of their working culture."

Andrea continues, "We can't just start in the fall and build relationships, and then let it go for the rest of the year. We don't have an hour a day for deep connections, but we address it in five minutes with our attendance question: How are you today, 1–5? Why? Who is your hero? Who's your help and why? If you could only eat one thing for ninety-nine days, what food would you choose? What's something from your weekend that you hope happens again? What are you looking forward to? What are you curious about? A question like that, every day. It takes five minutes."

REFLECTION

- In what ways might learners benefit from strong classroom communities?

- What is the relationship between community and academic success?

- In what ways do you intentionally integrate socioemotional learning into your instruction?

- What is your vision for your own classroom community?

CONVERSATION INVITATION

What can you infer about Andrea and Rachel's beliefs in the Teacher Voice box above?

How: The Elements of Community

As teacher and staff developer Lori Conrad described in the epigraph of this chapter, community can appear to arrive by magic. Yet any teacher whose magical community we covet will confess that the self-efficacy and interdependence of their students was not conjured by a wand and a spell, but in fact fostered by a great deal of intentional design, conversation, modeling, and reflection. To that end, we've found six key components of a productive and thoughtful culture of thinkers:

- identity development
- environment
- relationships
- norms
- ownership
- collaboration.

PRODUCTIVE DISPOSITIONS

As described in Chapter 1, agency is self-determination, the ability to make decisions in response to our own hopes and interests, then to see the results of those choices in our lives. Productive dispositions breed agency as learners feel the power and promise of their own ideas and actions. As we develop a culture, we influence both individual and collective identities in service of the greater good, modeling, teaching, practicing, and reflecting upon identities such as, "We are people who look out for one another," or, "We are people who take responsibility." (See Figure 3.2 for students' ideas about their identities and Figure 3.3 for the PEBC Teaching Framework for Productive Dispositions.)

Cultivating productive identities begins with our stance toward learners, as expressed by our behavior and language: how we refer to students and respond to their ideas. Explicitly teaching socioemotional skills further fosters students' development of agency and identity.

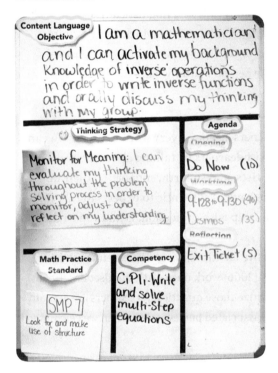

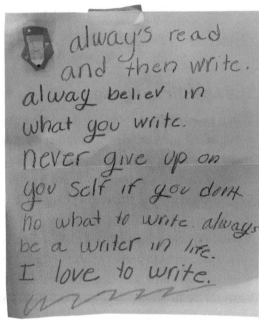

Figure 3.2 Students' Ideas About Their Identities

	First Steps	**Next Steps**	**Advancing**	**Peak Performance**
Productive Dispositions	Acknowledge each and every learner. Refer to learners as *readers, writers, mathematicians, scientists,* etc. Describe and model growth mindset.	Notice, name, and acknowledge the assets of culturally and linguistically diverse learners. Model and encourage empathy and perspective bending. Celebrate effort. Share own mistakes and self-corrections.	Include and celebrate learners of all backgrounds and abilities. Teach self-advocacy, goal setting, and self-regulation. Encourage perseverance; honor mistakes as learning experiences.	Learners demonstrate respect for and curiosity about people and cultures different from themselves and their own. Learners persevere, self-advocate, and encourage peers.

Figure 3.3 Community: Productive Dispositions

Teacher Voice: I Am a Mathematician

"I think calling my students mathematicians, and just switching from, okay friends, okay students, okay boys and girls, really does put that role in their hands. They become mathematicians. They think of themselves as mathematicians, which is really cool. And it was just one small change that we made, but as far as mindsets, it definitely helps. I think that for them to be able to visualize or use the words that have those positive connotations—I am a mathematician—it's just great."

—*Tara Stephens*

Inclusivity

Community is belonging. As described in Chapter 2, representing the diverse perspectives of all the world's citizens in our classrooms, studies, and instruction is key to raising global citizens. Beyond planning, we can model daily the respect we hold for learners of diverse backgrounds and abilities with our words and interactions. As described by the authors of "Turnaround for Children's Key Findings," "Cultural competence and responsiveness can address the impacts of institutionalized racism, discrimination, and inequality; promote the development of positive mindsets and behaviors; and build self-efficacy in all students, particularly those from culturally and linguistically diverse backgrounds" (Turnaround for Children 2018). Inclusivity requires appreciating and honoring differences and extending positive regard toward each learner, no matter what.

Use Agentic Language

When we strive to support the development of learners' agency, every word matters. We can demonstrate our confidence in and comaraderie with learners by talking about them as one might refer to experts in the field, as writers, scientists, and so forth, supporting their understanding that they, at some level, are engaging in behaviors authentic to experts in that field. Language cues invite students to explore in partnership with professionals and you as the lead learner.

In addition to using language that ascribes productive identities, we can be careful with language that aspires to praise. As author Carol Dweck's (2006) work on growth mindset described, when we label learners as "smart" or "quick," we prioritize those qualities, yet learners are actually better served in developing growth mindsets and the associated perseverance when we celebrate effort and determination.

Here is some growth mindset phrasing we might incorporate; what else might you add?

- "What a tremendous effort you made!"
- "Explain how you figured that out."
- "Tell how you considered your options before deciding."
- "What are you wondering now?"
- "You got stuck and then kept going; what was your strategy for getting unstuck?"
- "How are you going to go about that?"
- "What problems did you come across today?"
-

Teach Socioemotional Skills

Socioemotional skills are integral to every child's success. Some learners walk into our rooms with these skills, and others benefit from explicit instruction; mastery of cognitive, social, and emotional skills is integral to the development of productive identities. There are many collections of such skills. Check out the list developed by the Aspen Institute National Commission on Social, Emotional, and Academic Development in Figure 3.4: Which of these do your students bring to school? Which do they need to learn or practice? Mark up the list.

Cognitive	Social and Interpersonal	Emotional
• Focus and pay attention. • Set goals. • Plan and organize. • Persevere. • Problem solve.	• Navigate social situations. • Solve conflicts. • Demonstrate respect towards others. • Cooperate and work on a team. • Self-advocate and demonstrate agency.	• Recognize and manage emotions. • Understand emotions and perspectives of others. • Demonstrate empathy. • Cope with frustration and stress.

Figure 3.4 Socioemotional Skills (Aspen Institute 2018, 15)

Into the Classroom

Teaching Socioemotional Skills

Seated on the rug, Susan McIver invites first graders to ask themselves, "What do I need?" She then describes her own needs by way of modeling. "Me, I'm going to work on being flexible, because I know that if I get grumpy, that won't help me." Then, she looks up at the group and says, "What do you need? I have listed some ideas for you." She waves at the screen where the following words glow:

- empathy
- flexibility
- resilience
- persistence
- optimism

One at a time, she calls on students; each shares the qualities of character they will seek to embody this day while their teacher records. After a few students share, Susan walks them through an example. "If you happen to get grumpy, what can you do about it?"

The class chimes in with ideas. "Deep breaths."

"A drink of water."

"Walk around a little."

"Lucia, what do you need to make it a great day?"

Susan makes it all the way around the circle, discussing with learners the skills they will practice that morning, supporting learners' ideas to help them enact each one.

Figure 3.5 Classroom Chart Developed by Jamie Salterelli's Fourth Graders During Their Discussion on What to Do When They Feel Stuck

REFLECTION: STOP AND THINK

In what ways do you explicitly teach socioemotional skills? Which additional skills might students benefit from learning? How will you incorporate those?

ENVIRONMENT

Take a look around a classroom—your classroom, any classroom: What kinds of conversation patterns does the furniture suggest? How much of the work on the walls is teacher created? How easy would it be for you to find a pair of scissors, a ruler, or any other materials necessary for the work of this class? Environments speak to us, teach us, so let us be attentive to the sorts of environments we are creating for learners and the messages they convey. (See Figure 3.6 for the PEBC Teaching Framework for Environment.)

	First Steps	Next Steps	Advancing	Peak Performance
Environment	Display resources, strategies, norms, and content. Make learning materials available.	Arrange furniture to invite collaboration and accommodate learners' needs. Organize materials for ease of learner access. Post thinking on anchor charts.	Create an aesthetically pleasing, thoughtful, and thought-provoking environment. Display a variety of work representing diverse strategies and perspectives.	Learners independently use the environment—including materials, displayed work, and spaces for collaboration—as a resource for their learning.

Figure 3.6 Community: Environment

Furniture

My first year teaching, I arrived in a classroom with a grubby area rug and chairs lined up in rows, facing front. A few hours into my first day getting organized, my teaching partner, who had her desks in a circle, adorned her room with floor lamps and tapestries, and never turned on the overhead fluorescent lights, came in from across the hall to check on me. "You can move the chairs, you know," she said. Somehow that had not yet occurred to me. She helped me shift the tables into groups of four; pretty soon, I figured out how to orchestrate the groupings so that no one had their back to the front of the room, and sought a balance of their attention on me and their attention on their peers.

I know some of you reading this have desks bolted to the floor or light sockets in crummy places that need covering, but most of us can move the furniture around in our rooms. And as we consider those moves, we can think about the messages we want our arrangement to send to students.

What do these say? When might each be appropriate?

• **Desks in rows facing front:**

• Desks in table groups:

• Desks in a horseshoe with the board at the open end:

• Desks in a circle:

• No desks:

Walls

"Student learning is the core business of schools, and it needs to be made visible," explains Ron Ritchhart (2015) in *Creating Cultures of Thinking*. Our classrooms and hallways can be alive with the stories of thinking and learning that are taking place. Dedicating wall space to celebrating learners' ideas speaks volumes about our stance, more than could be conveyed through any commercially produced inspirational poster, however erudite.

Fifth-grade STEM (science, technology, engineering, and mathematics) teacher Tami Thompson asks learners each year what kind of scientists they aspire to be, photographs each student, and frames their photo with the name of their aspirational specialty, as in Dr. Leo Woodward, Botanist. Her walls scream productive identity development.

What do you want your walls to say? What might you put on them to get that message across? Here are some ideas. Add your own.

• Photos of students at work, captioned by learners themselves

• Annotated math solutions

• Unique artwork

• Writing in all stages of development

• Diverse samples of thinking about a shared question

• Learners' autobiographical displays

• Student-authored reflections

• Anchor charts of gathered student ideas

• Learners' own favorite inspirational quotes on posters they make themselves

•

•

RELATIONSHIPS

Parents sometimes chide children for copycat behavior: "Why did you wear flip-flops to school in the snow?"

"Well, Charlie wore flip-flops to school."

"Well, if Charlie jumped off a bridge, would *you*?"

We parents think we are making the point that Charlie is not always right, and yet the truth is that if Charlie jumped off a bridge, his friends might indeed be tempted as well. Relationships and the trust within them are powerful motivators of our behaviors. To build a productive learning community, we need to build relationships with students and families that demonstrate effort and care, as well as support them in building relationships with one another.

Relationships are based in trust; trust forms the foundation of our learning communities. "Trust among teachers, parents, and students produced schools that showed marked gains in student learning, whereas schools with weak trust relationships exhibited virtually no improvement," found education researchers Hoy, Tarter, and Woolfolk Hoy (2006). (See Figure 3.7 for the PEBC Teaching Framework for Relationships.)

	First Steps	Next Steps	Advancing	Peak Performance
Relationships	Learn and accurately pronounce learners' names. Appreciate differences between home cultures and school culture.	Devote time regularly to relationship building with and among students. Communicate with families about beliefs and purpose.	Know about learners' lives outside the classroom. Develop ongoing connections between home and school.	Learners belong to and care for the learning community. Families are engaged in supporting learners' success.

Figure 3.7 Community: Relationships

Know Students

I remember one of the first days of my graduate teacher preparation program: all one hundred or so of us piled into school buses and were taken on a tour of the surrounding communities' high-poverty neighborhoods. The intention had been to expose us—the young hopefuls—to the realities of our students' home lives, but there was one oversight: we did not get off the bus. Some years later, when I started a new teaching job, I learned that the K–8 school required home visits every fall by each student's homeroom teacher. "Even middle schoolers?" I wondered.

"Yes."

For three days, I snaked through unfamiliar neighborhoods and got lost in winding cul-de-sacs, but did eventually succeed in finding all of my students' homes; met their parents, some grandparents, and siblings; and learned about cancer diagnoses and a father in jail, immigration status issues, childhood traumas, adoption, lost jobs, and more. More than just the questions asked and answers given, I learned from the environment, the relationships, and the kindnesses I experienced. When school started a few days later, I felt much more aware not only of my learners' needs but also of the ways in which their families were counting on me—the teacher—to lift them as mathematicians and scholars from whatever circumstantial challenges they faced to hopeful high school careers. I did not take that responsibility lightly. Although home visits may not be practical in your setting or circumstance, every effort to know learners and their families is, in my experience, rewarded with effort and trust.

How do you build relationships with your students and their families? In Figure 3.8, reflect on what you have learned about relationship building.

What have you tried?	How did that work?	What did you learn?
Home visits		
Individual conferences		
Family events at school		

Figure 3.8 What have you tried?

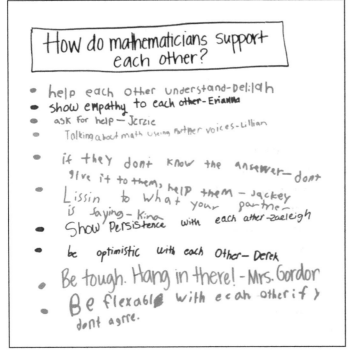

Figure 3.9 A Chart of Ideas from Keri Gordon's Class Discussion on How Students Can Support One Another as a Learning Community

Classroom Connections

Relationships take time, and time is hard to come by in schools. Still, our investments pay off. Creating regular routines that welcome learners' whole selves to class builds the connection between home and school, as well as creates opportunities for students to find common ground with their peers. Numerous guides and resources are available explaining structures for morning meetings, greetings, and group-building activities. These need not take hours out of our week but can prove a worthy investment.

Here are just a few surefire classroom connections routines. What rituals and routines do you incorporate regularly to build rapport with and among learners? What else might you add?

Community-Building Routines

◆ Doorway greeting: welcome learners at the door with a handshake.

◆ Morning meeting: gather in a circle, and each share out about a common question.

- Partner connections: have students pair up with a partner for a brief check-in.

- Written ranking: on paper, have students score their day so far (1–5) and explain why.

- Individual highlights: devote time to one student each day sharing something of themselves.

- Quote of the day: read and respond to an inspirational quote as a group.

- Students take turns leading morning meetings or other rituals.

Into the Classroom

Jamie Salterelli's Fourth-Grade Morning Meeting

All students are gathered in a tight circle on the rug at the side of the room. One boy perched on a chair leads the group. In turn he welcomes each classmate by name and invites them to share one sentence about how they are doing. In May, students know the routine, and the meeting flashes by.

"Good morning, Sylvie," the student leader says to the girl on his right.

"Good morning, Gaspar," she replies, then adds, "my baby cousin is coming to visit this weekend."

Peers smile and nod, and Gaspar moves things forward. "Good morning, Devon."

"Good morning, Gaspar. I caught all the fly balls at my baseball practice."

"Good morning, Max."

"Good morning, Gaspar." Max stops, takes a squirt of the hand sanitizer that is being passed around the circle, rubs it into his palms, hands on the pump bottle, and shares, "I feel like at 7:00, it's still light out, and I love that because I enjoy playing outside."

Peers use inside cheer sign language to show their agreement with Max's delight. Gaspar moves things forward. "Good morning, Lindsey."

"Good morning, Gaspar. My chameleon has been digging, and they said only girls do that so my chameleon is a girl."

In a few minutes, the circle is complete, and Ms. Salterelli invites Gaspar to choose tomorrow's meeting leader before transitioning into today's work on nonfiction writing.

NORMS

In *Life in a Crowded Place*, Ralph Peterson (1992) says, "Making a learning community—coming together, keeping together, and learning together—is not easy. It is far easier to dominate and require obedience. But if the prospect of encouraging the social nature of learning lets our students experience genuine learning and helps them to uncover ideas that make a sound in their hearts, isn't that a compelling argument for trying?" Establishing shared agreements about how we will live and talk and be together creates a foundation for safety that must be maintained all year long. Our agreements about behavior can be rooted in our shared values and represent a reflection of our ideals for ourselves, one another, and the group as a whole. (See Figure 3.10 for the PEBC Teaching Framework for Norms.)

	First Steps	Next Steps	Advancing	Peak Performance
Norms (also see Chapter 4, Workshop)	Refer to shared values, such as honesty, integrity, and responsibility. Establish behavior expectations.	Model and discuss shared values. Notice and name behaviors congruent with expectations. Invite learners to make decisions.	Weave intentional conversations about shared values into academic work. Cocreate and invite reflection on class agreements. Welcome learners' leadership in upholding agreements.	Learners exhibit integrity, agency, and kindness. Learners hold peers accountable for scholarly behavior.

Figure 3.10 Community: Norms

What are your shared values?

Does your school or district have shared values that you all agree to teach? If not yet, here's a list of some common virtues to consider:

courage faith
helpfulness respect
patience nonviolence
honesty gratitude
zeal responsibility
compassion
eco-friendliness agency valor
integrity confidence
peace joy kindness strength
discipline empathy
creativity service harmony

Which might you bring to life on purpose throughout the life of your classroom? Are there any you'd add? (Three to five are quite enough.)

Shared Values

Many school faculty take time to work together on a list of shared values they aspire to impart: compassion, courage, discipline, integrity, responsibility. Perhaps your school already has such a set of ideals, or maybe you need to establish your own short list, either independently or in collaboration with your students. Regardless of which values you choose to highlight, they need to come to life in the classroom, beyond just being posted on a wall. Here are some ways to bring shared values to life:

* Focus on one value at a time.
* Define the value.
* Identify exemplars of that value in your community.
* Read stories that present the value.
* Discuss ethical dilemmas where that value is in play.
* Create skits to teach the value.
* Read and respond to quotes addressing the value.
* Create artwork teaching the value.
* Invite learners to live that value during a specific project or time period.

Which of the ideas above might you try? What else?

Behavior Expectations

In addition to being built on shared values, communities sustain themselves based on shared agreements. Some teachers tell learners "the rules" directly, and others cocreate them as a group. Whatever your approach, keep the list short and inclusive. Here are a few we like:

- You are responsible for your own learning and for supporting the learning of others.
- Take care of yourself, each other, and our learning environment.
- Be where you are supposed to be; do what you are supposed to do.

Once the agreements are established, upholding them can become the responsibility of the group, yet you are still the leader of that group. How you respond to a transgression speaks volumes about your beliefs and your role in the classroom. When a student crosses an agreed-upon boundary, will you warn? Scold? Punish? Remove? Invite reflection? Propose amends? Wait?

REFLECTION WRITING: TALK BACK

What are your expectations for learners' behavior? How do you uphold them? In what ways do they foster community development?

OWNERSHIP

Whoever is doing the reading, writing, and talking is doing the learning. That cannot be said enough times. Students deserve ownership of their learning and thinking, as well as of the intellectual climate in the room. (See Figure 3.11 for the PEBC Teaching Framework for Ownership.)

	First Steps	Next Steps	Advancing	Peak Performance
Ownership	Listen. Welcome learners' ideas.	Recognize learners' thinking and understanding through paraphrasing and probing. Demonstrate the expectation that all are teachers and learners by using plural pronouns *we* and *our*.	Acknowledge, attribute, and record learners' ideas and refer to them throughout studies. Create explicit links between what learners say, do, and understand and instructional next steps.	Learners own their role in the intellectual life of the group, referring to and celebrating peers' thinking. Learners' questions and ideas influence teaching and learning.

Figure 3.11 Community: Ownership

Ownership in this context means connectedness to the intellectual life of the classroom. There are two straight-forward steps you can take to cultivate learner ownership: pronouns and attribution.

When launching our studies, we can be careful with our pronouns: rather than sending students off to learn something, as in "You are going to learn . . . ," join them in their endeavor, as in "We are about to explore . . ." The whole conversation can be about *us*, what *we* discovered, figured out, thought. This style of language, as noted by Peter Johnston (2004) in *Choice Words*, goes a long way toward inviting youth and adults to collaborate in one authentic, agentic learning community.

Furthermore, we can be on the constant lookout for learners' thinking and bright ideas. When learners talk, we can remain curious and ask for more rather than being satisfied with initial impressions. As they share, we can notice, name, record, and remember on sticky notes, on chart paper, in conferring logs. When a student comes up with a great new method for multiplication—even if it is commonly known as the partial product approach—we can call it by their name: "Graham's method." When a learner poses a question, we can catalogue it with their name and circle back: "So, Matty was wondering Monday whether these three *Refugee* stories would converge. What are we thinking now?" Hold the group while students share and grapple, but let the conversation, the intellectual joy, belong to the group.

Where and how and when will you hold—or invite peers to hold—learners' thinking for the group?

COLLABORATION

The skills of collaboration prepare us for membership in communities of all sizes and intentions. Getting along with others is difficult, and collaborating with peers on meaningful academic tasks even harder. And yet, there is no greater purpose to our learning community. To foster collaboration, we must first invite students into shared work, and, knowing conflict will arise, intentionally construct learning experiences where students can navigate through interpersonal challenges and succeed in gaining both content knowledge and social skills. (See Figure 3.12 for the PEBC Teaching Framework for Collaboration.)

Grouping Learners

One of the first questions teachers ask at the suggestion of collaborative work is how to group learners. I match my grouping methods to my beliefs: my belief as a teacher and as a parent and a human is that everyone needs to learn to get along with everyone. For that reason, I randomly

	First Steps	Next Steps	Advancing	Peak Performance
Collaboration (see also Chapter 4, Workshop)	Provide opportunities for learners to work together. Model conflict resolution.	Use multiple grouping strategies, including choice. Support learners' social problem-solving.	Invite regular reflection on learners' efficacy with interdependence. Strategically balance individual and collaborative work.	Learners make wise choices about when to work independently and interdependently. Learners collaborate inclusively, flexibly, and effectively.

Figure 3.12 Community: Collaboration

group learners and switch the groups often. There are many ways to do this for collaborations brief and lengthy, but here are a few of my favorites; what might you add?

- Matching visible appearance: shirt partners, shoe partners, height partners, hair length partners
- Inviting dialogue to navigate invisible qualities: same toothpaste, same favorite band, same favorite cereal; different favorite sport; different birthplace; different kind of pet at home
- Requesting learners to line up by a quality, and then make groups: shoe size, birthday (month and day), number of siblings, last digit of your phone number, and more!

One caution: although some instructional approaches assert the virtue of creating "heterogenous groups" by sorting and labeling groups, then assigning students to one another based on their perceived strengths and weaknesses, this approach can encourage fixed mindsets and unproductive identities, as in "I am the 'low' member of the group, so I may as well act like it." Yet, some intentional groupings do benefit students, such as pairing an English learner with a bilingual peer who will support with translation as needed.

Although it may be tempting to police every group and micromanage every step of a project, once we get students into collaborative learning, we need to let them run, puzzle, and problem solve, while sustaining high expectations for productivity and clear outcomes. Of learner collaboration, sixth-grade teacher Ryan Bentley explains, "It's easier to trust than control. It takes so much pressure off me."

Teaching Collaboration

Lab host Tracey Shaw teaches her high school students to be interdependent when it comes to group problem-solving. "Think of the teacher as the captain," she explains. "On a boat, you don't run to the captain every time there is a problem—you go to the crew to figure it out." Throughout the year, Tracey revisits this concept and teaches learners the skills for

Resources for Further Study

Harvey "Smokey" Daniels, *The Curious Classroom*

Peter Johnston, *Choice Words*

Peter Johnston, *Opening Minds*

Alfie Kohn, *Beyond Discipline*

Debbie Miller, *What's the Best That Could Happen?*

Ron Ritchhart, *Creating Cultures of Thinking*

group independence: they brainstorm problem-solving approaches, reflect on how and when they collaborated successfully, discuss dilemmas of collaboration, and give feedback to peers. In this way, she scaffolds learners' ability to seek support from one another when challenges arise.

Here are some discussion questions that can bring the focus on collaboration to life:

- What challenges did your group encounter today?

- How did you solve your problems?

- What did you learn from that experience?

- What will you need to focus on tomorrow to be more efficient as a group?

TALK BACK

How do you want learners to feel when they are with you?

Community FAQs

- **"How do I help the low group to believe in themselves?"**

    First, stop calling them that. Tracking sets kids in ruts before they know what hit them. To the extent possible, hold high expectations for all learners. Act as though you have full faith in their potential. Give them demanding work. Expect excellence. Reward effort. Celebrate perseverance and talk with whomever you can about heterogeneously grouping students.

- **"What if my room is so crowded that I can't move the furniture, and there is no place for students to get up and switch partners?"**

    I am sorry to hear of your overcrowded situation, and yet trust in your ability to improvise. Find ways to mix up the groups: Might students talk to the people in front of, then next to, then behind them? Or, find ways to get away from the furniture, either by removing it or by taking learners to a larger space. If you have concerns about their ability to behave appropriately in a new setting, level with them. "It's crowded in here. I want you to have space to move and talk so have arranged for us to use the library. I trust you will behave in ways that make this work so we can do it again."

- **"How can I get learners to buy into being a community when they are just used to teachers bossing them around?"**

    Talk about your hopes for them. Talk about your motives in establishing a learning community. Ask learners what they want, what they hope, what they need. Seek common ground. Be patient. If trust is low, it will take time to build.

- "But my students can't collaborate . . ."

   Collaboration, like shoe tying and bike riding, is a learned skill. Students can develop this skill with appropriate motivation, modeling, practice, and reflection. It is a tough one, no doubt, but what better way to prepare learners for life?

Your Turn

By attending to productive dispositions, the learning environment, relationships, norms, ownership, and collaboration, we can develop learning communities that support all students' agency and understanding. Consider the power of these approaches to help you envision the sort of learning community you'd like to create in your classroom. (See Figure 3.13.)

	Productive Dispositions	Environment	Relationships	Norms	Ownership	Collaboration
What I Already Know and Do						
New Ideas I Might Try						

Figure 3.13 Building Your Community

REFLECTION

- What new understanding do you have about the importance or the means of developing classroom community?

- What questions are still lingering?

• What changes do you feel inspired to make toward community development?

• What difference will those changes make for students?

• How will you know you have succeeded?

REFLECTION ON CHAPTER QUESTION: HOW CAN WE DEVELOP CLASSROOM COMMUNITIES THAT SUPPORT THE AGENCY AND UNDERSTANDING OF EACH AND EVERY LEARNER?

Invitation: Write a dialogue between a few of your students that depicts your vision for your own classroom community.

4 WORKSHOP

CHAPTER QUESTION: IN WHAT WAYS MIGHT WE FACILITATE LEARNING EXPERIENCES THAT SUPPORT STUDENTS GRAPPLING WITH CHALLENGING TASKS IN SERVICE OF CONCEPTUAL UNDERSTANDING?

ANTICIPATION QUESTIONS

• What does a great day look and sound like in your classroom?

• How do you organize learning time?

• What do you see as students' role during learning?

• How would you describe your role as teacher?

Teacher Voice: Transitioning to Workshop

"When I switched to workshop model instruction, my students' math achievement leapt up by 50 percent in a matter of months. I am not kidding. The principal was in my room asking, 'What is it you are doing in here?' And I told her, 'I read this book, and now it's all about the kids doing the thinking.' Even I was amazed."

—ELAINE LEE

• What do you already know about workshop model instruction?

• What questions do you have about implementing workshop?

Struggle in the Real World

Have you ever replaced a garbage disposal? I hadn't until a couple of months ago: ours completely died, and I was left with a sink full of slurry. I wouldn't be able to meet a plumber at the house for at least two weeks. I had a couple of options: shut down the kitchen sink, or replace the disposal myself. After watching a few handyman videos online, I braced for a trip to Home Depot. Materials in hand, I dove under the kitchen sink to extract the dead disposal. It came out according to the YouTube directions, without a hitch, but for the smell. When I sought to attach the new one, though, I was foiled—I could not figure out how to get it to clamp onto the base of the drain. I watched the video again, studied the lip of the drain, and the top of the disposal, and recruited my children to help. The three of us had to set the weighty machine in just the right position, then concurrently push the disposal straight up toward the lip of the drain while also twisting it. It took many attempts. There was some cursing involved. Finally, on trial five, it bit, and has been happily chomping under our sink ever since.

Nothing in the online tutorial or the multilingual pamphlet that came in the factory-packaged disposal box compared with the sweaty wrestling involved. Now I know how to replace a garbage disposal, because I had to grapple.

REFLECTION: STRUGGLE IN THE REAL WORLD

Tell the story of a time when you had to grapple to solve a problem or understand a concept. What happened? What supported your progress? What did you learn?

What: Workshop

A workshop—whether twenty or two hundred minutes in length—is a flexible structure that follows a predictable pattern. One format is to open with a hook of some sort, an invitation for learners to engage in thinking and surface preconceptions. The hook can be followed by the minilesson, a time for the teacher to apprentice students to the work they are about to do.

This might include introducing a strategy, thinking aloud, modeling a parallel task, or teaching a critical piece of content integral to the work ahead. The work time—the bulk of any given workshop—is devoted to students engaging independently or in small groups with a rich task that challenges their thinking and deepens their understanding within a conceptual framework. (This might be solving math problems, reading books independently or with partners, working on writing projects, or digging into a science investigation, for example.) The final segment of workshop is a critical opportunity for reflection to solidify and lock in learning.

Figure 4.1 shows what a generic workshop structure might look like. Typically, one-fifth of a class period is devoted to the minilesson, three-fifths to the work time, and the final fifth to sharing and reflection, though times can certainly vary. Although this classic structure features a particular sequence and use of time, segments can be longer or shorter, or rearranged based on the larger purpose: for example, one might feature a longer minilesson at the launch of a project and a brief reflection at the end of work time on day one, then start the second day by continuing the reflection at the beginning of the lesson, and save the minilesson for midway through work

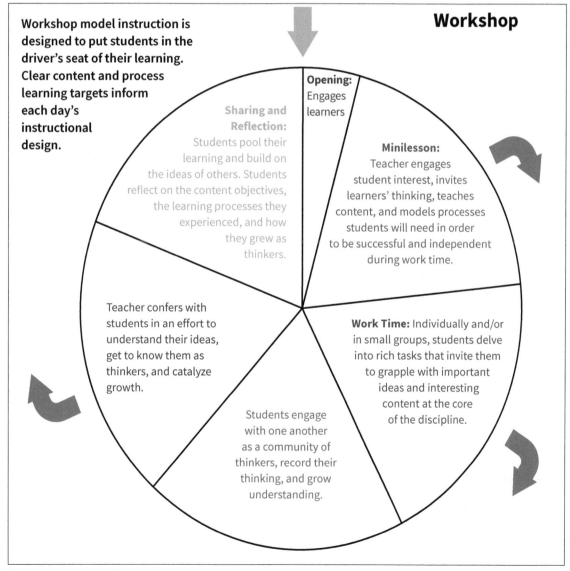

Workshop

Workshop model instruction is designed to put students in the driver's seat of their learning. Clear content and process learning targets inform each day's instructional design.

Opening: Engages learners

Minilesson: Teacher engages student interest, invites learners' thinking, teaches content, and models processes students will need in order to be successful and independent during work time.

Work Time: Individually and/or in small groups, students delve into rich tasks that invite them to grapple with important ideas and interesting content at the core of the discipline.

Students engage with one another as a community of thinkers, record their thinking, and grow understanding.

Teacher confers with students in an effort to understand their ideas, get to know them as thinkers, and catalyze growth.

Sharing and Reflection: Students pool their learning and build on the ideas of others. Students reflect on the content objectives, the learning processes they experienced, and how they grew as thinkers.

Figure 4.1 A Sample Workshop Structure

time. In adapting, teachers remain true to this big idea: students are capable apprentices on a journey toward understanding important ideas—as well as themselves.

In describing the big idea behind workshop, PEBC staff developer Dana Sorensen explained, "It's about releasing students to explore, rather than guiding them to replicate." Whoever is doing the work is doing the learning, so students should be doing the majority of the reading, writing, talking, problem-solving, and thinking in a classroom. Behind workshop is the belief that students are competent and capable, can be trusted, and want to engage in purposeful and meaningful work. The teacher's role, then, is to model, facilitate, coach, confer, and celebrate while learners do the work of learning. Well-crafted workshops give students the resources and support needed to persevere, but do not take away the struggle by simplifying tasks or offering critical information before it can be appreciated. (See Figure 4.2.)

MAKE CONNECTIONS

How does this description of workshop connect with your background knowledge?

Workshop *Is* . . .	Workshop *Is Not* . . .	Your Thinking . . .
Learners engaged in the pursuit of understanding important ideas around a shared theme or strategy through a rich task	Stations where students complete disconnected tasks at an appointed time by a system of rotations	
Aligned with clear understanding targets, yet flexible to address students' needs, perhaps speeding tasks along if learners are demonstrating mastery, or slowing the process down if learners are needing more support	A strictly paced scope and sequence that can be predicted before a unit begins	
Trusting students' thinking and allowing time for them to struggle and experience the complex journey to understanding	Chaos	
An opportunity for teachers to work side by side with learners, hear their ideas, and support their growth through intentional conferring conversations	Cold calling, shaming, blaming, or rescuing	
A stance that honors children, every day	A once-a-week "break" from real school	

Figure 4.2 Clarification Corner

PHENOMENAL TEACHING

Why Workshop?

Grappling helps us learn. Manu Kapur's research in Singapore on the value of productive failure informs us that grappling "affords better conceptual understanding, creative thinking, and helps students to transfer learning to novel situations" (Schwartz 2016). Furthermore, research by Ermeling, Hiebert, and Gallimore (2015) emphasizes the virtues of students making meaning while facing challenging tasks: through "an opportunity to struggle through a difficult problem with a clear learning goal in mind, combined with just enough stretch and strategic assistance, students can develop lasting connections about important ideas, increased capacity for productive struggle, and durable skills for solving novel problems in life." As Boston and colleagues (2017) explain, "Productive struggle comprises the work that students do to make sense of a situation and determine a course of action when a solution strategy is not stated, implied, or immediately obvious. From an equity perspective, this implies that each and every student must have the opportunity to struggle with challenging [content] and to receive support that encourages their persistence without removing the challenge."

How People Learn, the National Research Council's 2000 metasynthesis, boils a century of educational research into three important teacher actions that support all learners' comprehension: activate prior knowledge, provide conceptual frameworks, and invite metacognition. The structure of workshop naturally lends itself to doing all of these every day: a workshop typically opens with an invitation for students to draw upon their schema as they engage in the new topic; student work time offers opportunities for learners to think deeply about the concept at hand, making connections between these new ideas and their background knowledge; and reflection time is intentionally set aside for students to look back at their day's work and be metacognitive: What did I learn about the content? What did I learn about myself as a learner? Why is this important? What does this mean about me and my place in the world?

REFLECTION

- How comfortable are you allowing students to struggle? What seems exciting about this? What concerns does it raise?

- In what ways do you intentionally invite learners to engage their preconceptions?

- How do you support students in developing conceptual frameworks as they enter new territory in their studies?

Teacher Voice: Why Workshop?

"All I remember about being a student in eighth-grade geography is that my teacher made us pick up the floor every day before we left. You could not leave one scrap of paper there. I don't remember anything we read or talked about, though I imagine we studied the whole world that year. I remember what we did, pick up the floor. I want my students to know and remember important ideas in social studies, and within workshop they have chances to discuss their thinking and really make sense of the content in memorable ways. . . . It's about the strength of your argument, the power of your evidence. Thinking. That's what is important in my classroom."

—*RheaLynn Anderson, middle school social studies teacher*

CONVERSATION INVITATION

What do you infer about RheaLynn's beliefs in this Teacher Voice box?

Into the Classroom

First-Grade Math Workshop

First graders in Carrie Halbasch's class are gathered together on the rug at the front of the room. "How do mathematicians make sense and solve?" She invites them to share their ideas and records their thinking on a chart.

"Read."

"Reread and make a picture."

"Underline important parts."

"Think: What is known? What is unknown?"

"Use manipulatives, like the Unifix cubes, to make a model."

After this warm-up conversation about their own strategies for making meaning, Carrie poses a math challenge: 8 + 5 + 7 = ___. "Hmm. How can I solve without counting?" The class reads the problem again together, then Carrie says, "Turn and talk with a partner. We are not solving yet, we are just looking for clues. What do you see that is going to help you solve?" Students go knee to knee and start talking about their ideas, hands gesturing animatedly as they chat. Carrie leans in and listens.

After a few minutes of partner conversation, Carrie reconvenes the group as a collective and invites students to share their thinking.

"What I know is that eight is a part, five is a part, and a plus in the middle means that we need to add."

"We said that eight, five, and seven are the parts."

"We drew a picture." Carrie invites Lucy to share her image with the group. She comes to the board and sketches:

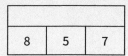

After students hear a few more of their peers' observations and ideas, Carrie sends them to their tables for some independent work on this problem. "Happy solving!" Learners open math journals, glue in the half sheet with the printed problem, and start to record their thinking. They whisper to one another. Some grab bins of manipulatives to work this out kinesthetically. Others sketch boxes or sticks or other representations as they think through their solutions. A handful, after gluing their papers into their notebooks, return to the rug to request their teacher's support getting started. Carrie talks through the problem with this small self-selected group, glancing up at the other mathematicians often. After about ten minutes of work time, Carrie calls for all the students' attention and identifies some of the strategies she is observing. "I see Felipe is using cubes and a balance scale, and Shawnia is drawing rows of dots." A few students grab new resources and persevere. And just to ensure no one is left at loose ends, Carrie layers in another challenge, holding another half sheet of colored paper in the air. "And this is the 'push me,' when that (pointing to 8 + 5 + 7) is done: 18 − 7 ___ 9 + 7. Make it true. Less than, greater than, or equal? Happy solving."

Throughout ten more minutes of diligent work time, Carrie moves from table to table, leaning in to confer with individuals and small groups: "Tell me about your thinking." "Show me how you got that." "And what are you thinking now?" Soon, with recess looming, Carrie calls all these young mathematicians back to the rug to share. Felipe carries his balance scale to the front of the group and explains his thinking. "I put eight black cubes on one side of the scale, and seven blue on the other side. Then, I broke the five apart to have 8 + 2 and 7 + 3, and that is ten on each side. They are even. It balances."

"Who sees it?" Carrie asks, and many hands shoot into the air. "What do you see?"

"I see two tens, and it's equal. And that's a double."

"And what did you get?" Carrie prompts Felipe.

"Twenty. 10 + 10 = 20." Carrie compliments Felipe's representation of his thinking, pointing out to the group how he used "make it a ten" twice, finding the hidden patterns to make those tens, and used his background knowledge of doubles. Then Jazlyn shows how she had the same idea, but wrote it out numerically.

"So, what helped us solve without counting, in the most efficient way?" she addresses the group, and invites students once again to turn and talk with a partner. They conclude their workshop by going back to the opening question, "How do mathematicians make sense and solve?" The students offer new ideas to add to their chart based on the work today:

- Look for patterns.
- Use background knowledge.

Recess, well earned.

How: The Elements of Workshop

We have identified eight transferable elements of workshop at every grade level and across the content areas:

- independence
- rituals and routines
- opening
- minilessons
- work time
- awareness and response
- conferring
- sharing and reflection.

Let's take these one at a time, knowing that each is integral to the design of a productive workshop, and yet emphasis on refining one will surely influence the implementation of all other subcomponents.

INDEPENDENCE

Workshop requires confidence that students can be the thinkers and workers in our classrooms and faith that they can succeed without our holding their hands. The most important litmus test of any workshop learning experience is: Are students thinking deeply about content in a manner authentic to the discipline? (See Figure 4.3 for the PEBC Teaching Framework for Independence.)

	First Steps	Next Steps	Advancing	Peak Performance
Independence	Create daily opportunities for learners' independence and collaboration.	Match resources, supports, and time to work with complexity of task(s) and individual needs.	Engage learners in authentic work of the discipline for the majority of learning time.	Learners lead meaning making throughout learning time.

Figure 4.3 Workshop: Independence

A first step in fostering student independence is to shift our planning perspective: rather than focusing on what we as the teacher will be doing during the learning time, instead we need to consider what students will be doing and how we will ensure that they can do so independently.

Teaching Independence

No one was born knowing how to tie their shoes, flush a toilet, drive a car, or pay taxes—and yet nearly all of us learned. We learned because we had to.

Once we identify the skills for independence our students need for a given task—say, how to infer the meaning of a haiku or how to use a protractor to measure an angle—we can devote time to teaching them explicitly, then lean back and let students grapple to master them. We do not need to hover. (See Figure 4.4 for some help with planning independence.) A primary-grades literacy teacher recently lamented how her students rotated through guided reading groups and were very productive during the six minutes they met her at the kidney table but then languished for the remainder of the reading time. She recognized that she had not been modeling or expecting them to be independently productive, and so they weren't. She realized that she needed to teach them how to read on their own, without direct guidance.

Building Stamina and Focus

Maintaining stamina is a key aspect of independence. Students may not have prior experience sustaining their own focus throughout an extended work time, yet we can build toward that goal with

- Open conversations about the value of stamina: try Thomas Edison, Abebe Bikila, Yo-Yo Ma, Marie Curie, and William Kamkwamba as role models.
- Discussion of the ways in which learners—as well as folks in all walks of life—sustain their own stamina: try microgoal setting, self-monitoring, self-talk.
- Preselection of tools or strategies to sustain stamina: try "Choose one thing you could do today to help yourself keep focused."
- Reflection on the efficacy of selected tools: try "What built your stamina today? What detracted from your stamina? What will you do next time?"

How else might you invite learners to develop awareness of and confidence with stamina and focus?

What are the prerequisites for learners' independence in your classroom? How will you intentionally teach them? Here are some categories to consider:

	Productive Dispositions	Access to Materials	Understanding of the Task	Strategies for Getting Unstuck
What Do They Need to Know?				
How Will You Teach This?				

Figure 4.4 Planning for Independence

RITUALS AND ROUTINES

The workshop structure is predictable, even as it evolves daily based on the work of yesterday, the needs of today, and the goals for tomorrow. Students are served best when they know the routine and develop automatic responses to the rhythm of the room. Teachers establish daily rituals—how we start class, how our activities progress, how we close, the signals we use for transitions—which become predictable patterns students can expect, smoothing the need for explanation and expediting transitions. (See Figure 4.5 for the PEBC Teaching Framework for Rituals and Routines.)

	First Steps	Next Steps	Advancing	Peak Performance
Rituals and Routines	Experiment with routine and structure.	Enact a daily routine to guide workshop. Prioritize learner work time.	Learners understand and independently follow rituals to efficiently transition through workshop. Workshop elements sequenced effectively, flexibly.	Learners own and operate the workshop in the absence of their teacher.

Figure 4.5 Workshop: Rituals and Routines

PHENOMENAL TEACHING

Punctuate Your Workshop with Rituals

Routine and ritual bring order into an often chaotic world, supporting students in efficiently engaging in meaningful thinking. As you grow into the workshop model, consider creating regular routines that can support students in learning the life of your classroom. You might consider establishing rituals that reinforce the cultural norms and learning expectations, all of which strengthen the community of learners (see Chapter 3). Figure 4.6 lists some opportunities to establish rituals; add your own ideas.

REFLECTION

What are your class rituals and routines now? In what ways might you adjust or expand them later?

Student Voice: Workshop Is . . .

"I like this class because I know what is coming. It's not like it's the same thing every day, but it is kind of predictable. We know what to expect. We have the lesson and then the work time and then the reflection. And the time goes by really fast because she always has something interesting for us to do."

—*Javier Guttierez*

Workshop Resources for Further Study

Samantha Bennett, *That Workshop Book* (K–8 humanities)

Wendy Ward Hoffer, *Minds on Mathematics* (K–12 math)

Wendy Ward Hoffer, *Science as Thinking* (6–12 science)

Debbie Miller, *What's the Best That Could Happen?* (elementary)

Wendy Saul, *Science Workshop* (K–6 science)

Cris Tovani and Elizabeth Birr Moje, *No More Teaching as Telling* (6–12 humanities)

Moment for Ritual	Ponder	Possibilities	Plan (Your Turn)
Greeting	How will you welcome students? How will you invite learners to welcome one another?	• Morning circle • Paired greeting • Silent sitting	
Launch	How will you get learners started on some thinking in the opening minutes of class?	Invite them to respond to content-related • Cartoons • Photos • Questions	
Conversation (See Chapter 6 for more on discourse.)	What regular habits for focused and efficient student-to-student conversation can you practice and instill?	• Turn and talk • Trios • Tea party (rapidly changing partners)	
Movement	When will it be appropriate to ask learners to move about the classroom? What signals will you use to prompt these transitions? What will you need to practice?	• Brain breaks • Kinesthetic memory joggers • Furniture-moving routines	
Grouping Strategies	How will you organize learners to collaborate?	• Choice partners • Partner based on visible traits (shirts, shoes, etc.) • Assigned partners	
Gathering	How will you signal and invite learners to gather?	• Chimes • Music • Clapping routines • Call and response	
Cleanup	How can you make cleanup time efficient and effective?	• Jobs • Labeled storage • Timing	
Closing	How will you end class with what matters most?	• Celebrations • Words to the wise • Farewells	

Figure 4.6 Moments for Ritual

OPENING

One routine that deserves particular attention is the opening, a self-directed moment of connection as learners enter the space. They can acknowledge you, the environment, their peers, and the content at hand in a calm, predictable manner that supports their settling into productive work. The opening says to learners, "You are a thinker, and your thinking is welcome and expected here."

Learners benefit when they see the thread between their previous learning and the new experience they are about to enjoy. For these reasons, the opening is a key moment to connect with students: What do we already know—or think we know—about this topic? This is also a moment to invite students to start some thinking and ask some questions, even if their questions are not ones we immediately answer.

Our opening needs to be more riveting than what just happened at recess, got said in the hall, or came across the screens of their phones. It could be a writing or drawing task, an invitation to conversation, an opportunity to vote, a responsibility to move in reply to a question. The big goal is to get the engines of learners' minds warmed up and the vehicle of their thinking pointed in the right direction to maximize upcoming learning time. (See Figure 4.7 for the PEBC Teaching Framework for the Opening.)

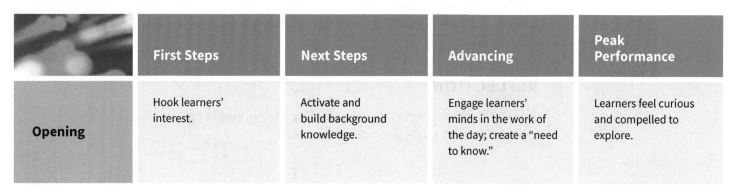

	First Steps	Next Steps	Advancing	Peak Performance
Opening	Hook learners' interest.	Activate and build background knowledge.	Engage learners' minds in the work of the day; create a "need to know."	Learners feel curious and compelled to explore.

Figure 4.7 Workshop: Opening

Plan Your Hook!

There are many ways to hook learners: with images to pique interest, cartoons to convey a stance, connections to personal experiences, current events, or evocative questions. When I am planning a lesson about a potentially unfamiliar topic, I often gather a series of related images to show as slides while learners notice and wonder with a shoulder partner. This is one format for a quick and engaging opening.

High school science teacher Erika Schenk has her own effective routine for her opening: whenever learners enter her room, they know to get out their Do Now sheet and respond to the question on the screen. One recent day, she asked juniors and seniors, "Psychopaths are people who lack emotion and empathy and can be manipulative, violent, and impulsive. Several studies suggest that psychopathy may be an evolutionary strategy. This suggests that the qualities that bring about psychopathy are also qualities that encourage more frequent reproduction, making psychopathy an advantageous strategy. What do you wonder?" Who wouldn't like to spend a few minutes pondering that evocative question?

Topic	Possible Juicy Opening Question	Other Juicy Question Ideas
Poetry	Who is a better poet, Emerson or Dr. Seuss?	
Fractions	Would you rather have one-half or two-thirds of a pizza? Why?	
Density	What if ice sank instead of floating?	
Space	Should humans explore space?	

Figure 4.8 Juicy Opening Questions

Let's think about how Erika got to her good opening question: students were studying genetics and evolution, and she thought about their interests in things like reproduction and mental health. What's your big idea for the day? What's the topic? Where does it live in the real world? How can you make it juicy? Figure 4.8 has a few sample opening questions from fourth grade to get you started.

REFLECTION

Think of an upcoming lesson. Considering the options in Figure 4.8 and your own experience, how might you open with gusto?

MINILESSON (CRAFTING)

The purpose of the minilesson—or crafting, as it is sometimes called—is to set the stage for student independence during work time. Minilessons involve setting purpose for the learning time. In addition, we may prepare learners for their work by thinking aloud about a task similar to what they will encounter, modeling processes parallel to their upcoming work, offering direct instruction on critical points of content, or introducing or revisiting a useful thinking strategy. For example, before releasing learners to analyze a collection of population graphs, we might think aloud about a specific graph to narrate how we make meaning of it. Or, before inviting learners to write their own personal narratives, we might think aloud as we begin penning a story of our own.

At times, the minilesson is devoted to reviewing recent work, revisiting strategies practiced, or analyzing sample products. The litmus test for a good minilesson is: Did it set learners up to engage deeply in the meaningful work of thinking during their work time? (See Figure 4.9 for the PEBC Teaching Framework for Minilesson.)

	First Steps	Next Steps	Advancing	Peak Performance
Minilesson (Crafting)	Communicate purpose for learning. Provide directions.	Efficiently demonstrate processes integral to learners' independence. Model precise academic language that facilitates learners' discourse.	Teachers or learners think aloud, model, or demonstrate one or more specific thinking strategies in service of metacognition. Flexibly time minilesson in response to learners' needs.	Learners actively listen and set purpose for learning. Learners know why and how to persevere during work time.

Figure 4.9 Workshop: Minilesson

Into the Classroom

Sounds Like: Think Aloud

A fifth-grade teacher launches her literacy workshop with a minilesson on the thinking strategy *determining importance*. (See Chapter 5 for more on thinking strategies.) She opens by reviewing learners' prior experiences with the strategy and how it helped them as nonfiction readers.

"The next great place for us to move is to consider, 'How do we determine importance as readers all the time, in every kind of text?' It involves a super important word: *purpose*. What does purpose mean?" Students discuss, referring to the movie *A Dog's Purpose* and a fellow student's dedication to gymnastics.

"What we are going to do today is think about the author's purpose in the text we are reading." She slides a copy of a news article on immigration under the document camera. "In my mind, I am zooming in to ask, 'Why on earth did this author write the piece I am reading?' Finding the purpose is like being a detective. We look for evidence. You need to be able to explain how you know what you know."

She reads aloud a couple of paragraphs from the article, pausing to circle and underline clues she believes are important, terms such as *cost, taxpayers, expenses, dollars*. After finishing a section, she pauses and says, "So, I am thinking this author is concerned about money. So far, all she has mentioned is finances, nothing about families or opportunities or human rights. I am thinking her purpose is to persuade me that immigration is expensive to our country. But I need to keep reading. I bet she has some other ideas in here as well.

"So, what did you see me do as a reader, trying to understand the author's purpose?"

Students respond: underlined important words, reread some parts, used background knowledge, kept an open mind, looked for patterns.

Satisfied that these learners understand enough to get started, she turns to the group and invites students to select one of several articles on immigration and to devote their work time to reading in pursuit of understanding that author's purpose.

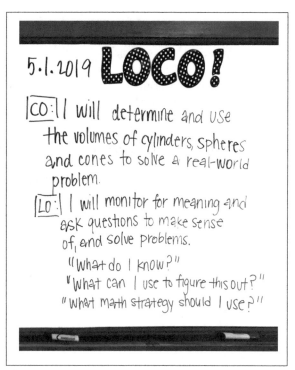

Figure 4.10 Middle school math teacher Jessica Piwko orients learners to the lesson by providing the daily LOCO: a language objective (LO) and a content objective (CO).

REFLECTION

What do you notice about the minilesson on the previous page? What do you wonder? What new ideas do you have about developing your own minilessons?

WORK TIME

To be the lead actors in their own learning, students need independent work time to pursue worthy tasks. (See Figure 4.11 for the PEBC Teaching Framework for Work Time.)

	First Steps	Next Steps	Advancing	Peak Performance
Work Time (Composing) **(also see Chapter 3, Community)**	Structure time so that the majority is devoted to learners' independent and collaborative work. Redirect as needed.	Invite learners to read, write, solve, talk, create, and/or think, then document their understanding. Integrate independent, paired, and group work as appropriate.	Offer choice among various levels of challenge aligned with the learning goals and resources. Create opportunities for learners to work and share with a variety of peers.	Learners use work time efficiently for purposeful and meaningful learning authentic to the discipline.

Figure 4.11 Workshop: Work Time

The Grapple

As described in Chapter 2, the nature of the work time work is pivotal to the work time's success. (See that chapter for ideas to help you design tasks that engage everyone in purposeful and meaningful work.) As I refine a workshop plan, I review the task by asking myself (or a colleague) some clarifying questions. As I answer each question, I attend to the why: Why is this the best choice for my purpose here?

- How will learners grapple? What thinking does the task invite?
  » Learners might ask questions, visualize and represent, determine importance, infer, synthesize, argue, critique, problem solve, predict, or design.
- When and how will learners experience choice?
  » Learners could choose partners, their work location, perhaps the task itself, where to begin, resources to use, the recording format.
- In what ways will they be invited to record their thinking?
  » Learners might record in notebooks, take photos and annotate, create and complete a data table or other graphic organizer, vlog.
- What resources will be available?
  » Learners could use peers, reference materials, visuals, charts, manipulatives and/or tools, adult-led groups, graphic organizers, sentence stems, word walls.

- What extensions will be available for those ready for more?

  » Learners could engage with further research, challenge questions, new resources to study, peer coaching, designing their own questions or prompts, synthesizing perspectives, developing a presentation.

  - What scaffolds will you have for students who encounter challenges?

  » You might provide buddies, realia and audiovisual aids, alternate texts, additional instructions, chances for movement, alternate formats for products, or other ideas.

REFLECTION

Think about an upcoming lesson or unit. Consider the previous questions. What opportunities for grappling will you provide? Why are they the right options for your students?

Talk During Work Time

Learners need a balance of collaborative talk and independent work to grow understanding. Many teachers invite students to begin a task alone for a few minutes before creating space for them to discuss. Other teachers, such as Carrie (whose class you read about previously), will welcome students to talk about their first thinking before beginning the task independently. During or after work is completed, students benefit from opportunities to relate their experience to peers. Our workshops need a balance of think time and talk time. Here are two go-to structures for work time conversations. (We'll discuss much more about discourse in Chapter 6.)

- Conversation sandwich: At the beginning of a work time, invite students to pair up and talk for a few minutes about their plans or initial thinking. During work time, students may work independently or with a different partner. Toward the close of the work time, or even during a pause (if you like multilayered sandwiches), invite students to reconnect with their first partner to share progress or insight about the work.

- Expanding universe: After some initial alone time to begin to understand a text or grapple with a task, put students into pairs or trios to apply that understanding or complete the problem-solving. Once the small groups are ready with ideas or work to share, clump them, so two pairs make a quad or two trios make a group of six, to compare their thinking, find similarities and differences, or critique peers' reasoning.

AWARENESS AND RESPONSE

While students are immersed in the work of work time, we can enjoy these opportunities to listen and learn about their thinking, as well as to respond in ways that facilitate independence and scaffold success.

Visitors to Jessica Piwko's eighth-grade classroom describe her as being "everywhere." During work time, she zips from table to table, listening and observing, yet not lingering. "Praise, prompt, and leave," she explains. "I look at what they are up to, ask a question, and move on. That's my strategy. If I stay there too long, they look to me and expect answers. Instead, I leave them with a question and walk away." Yet she walks away with data about what students in each group understand, what they need, and how she will propel thinking forward.

What do you do with the information you learn this way? Samantha Bennett (2007), author of *That Workshop Book*, popularized the phrase "catch and release" to describe the ways in which teachers briefly gather the students' attention during work time for some just-in-time instruction, to add a new layer of challenge to a task, or to redirect learners' attention toward productive strategies. The catch might involve further tips on the task, direct instruction of content, noticing and naming of learner behaviors, revelations, sharing of examples, celebrations of progress, or other topics relevant to the whole group. A catch is typically signaled by a gentle interruption, a request for learners' undivided attention, and usually allows students to remain in the place they are working, with their hands off their materials, while listening. The beauty of the catch is that it is quick and powerful: in fewer than five minutes of worthwhile interruption to learners' independence, a teacher can catapult students forward in their understanding and efficiency. (See Figure 4.12 for the PEBC Teaching Framework for Awareness and Response.)

	First Steps	Next Steps	Advancing	Peak Performance
Awareness and Response (also see Chapter 7, Assessment)	Watch and listen to learners. Check in with individuals and small groups to reengage them in the task as needed.	Provide clear expectations and appropriate supports to ensure that learners use time wisely. Notice and name strategic thinking to propel learning and engagement. Provide general feedback to learners at the end of the workshop.	Respond to patterns and trends in learners' thinking by extending challenges, and adjusting available scaffolds, including invitational groups, as needed. Catch and release learners for timely, intentional instruction that deepens understanding or enhances efficiency.	Learners are able to provide feedback about their progress and needs. Learners make efficient and wise choices about their task, use of resources, pursuit of scaffolds, and selection of collaboration partners.

Figure 4.12 Workshop: Awareness and Response

Into the Classroom

Sounds Like: Catch

Middle school science teacher Chris Martin calls for his class' attention. Students let go of the rock samples on their desks and turn their eyes to the front of the room. "I just want to show you guys what Noah is doing." Chris slides a student's science notebook under the document camera. "He has made a table for himself as a way to organize the data he is gathering. What do you notice about his table?"

"The columns are labeled."

"There is plenty of space to write."

"He is not done yet."

"Right," Chris affirms, "he is not done yet, but he has really set himself up for success by creating a structure to hold his thinking. If you haven't yet organized your notes in some fashion, you might consider adopting Noah's strategy. We have about fifteen more minutes to look at these samples. Go for it."

Conferring Resources for Further Study

Patrick Allen, *Conferring: The Keystone of Readers' Workshop*

Carl Anderson, *How's It Going? A Practical Guide to Conferring with Student Writers*

Catherine Fosnot, *Conferring with Young Mathematicians at Work*

Jen Munson, *In the Moment*

Jennifer Serravallo and Gravity Goldberg, *Conferring with Readers*

Possible Catch Topics

- Notice and name effective approaches students are using, as in "Wow, when I look around the room, I see . . ."

- Provide brief instruction on an important point that will support the whole group's thinking, as in "I am noticing a lot of you are choosing to . . ."

- Offer feedback on learners' participation, as in "I see seven groups all digging in to . . ."

- Highlight a student's contribution, as in "I noticed Devi doing something really interesting . . ."

- Introduce a new resource, as in "Also, we have . . ."

- Present the next layer of challenge, as in "If you are ready to move on, next . . ."

REFLECTION

What else might you insert as a catch to support learners' ongoing independence?

CONFERRING

While students are knee-deep in their own thinking and solving during work time, our role is to engage side by side with them as curious colleagues and coaches. Conferring—the act of getting eye to eye with a learner and listening in as they think aloud—can strengthen our appreciation for a student's learning process, alert us to misconceptions or needs, and create opportunities for targeted just-in-time instruction. It is not necessary to confer with every child every day, or even every week, so don't let that notion prevent you from beginning.

Staff developer Heather Kuzma invites us to make our conferring questions about learners and their thinking. "When crafting our questions, we can avoid statements like 'Tell me what you are thinking.' That makes it about us. Really, what we want to know is what is happening for learners. It's not about us. We want students to own this." (See Figure 4.13 for the PEBC Teaching Framework for Conferring.)

Some Conferring Questions

Annotate this list: Underline the ones you like. Cross out what you'd never use. Add your own.

- What are you doing?
- How's it going?
- What's a problem you liked solving?
- How does this work?
- Wow! How did you do that?
- What's up?
- How might you show what you understand in a picture?
- Explain what parts you do understand.
- What questions do you have?
- Can you remember any similar problems and how you solved those?
- What would help look like?
- What was important to remember about what you did here?
- How did this conversation help you?
- What did you learn?
-
-

	First Steps	Next Steps	Advancing	Peak Performance
Conferring	Circulate during work time. Monitor and record learners' growth.	Listen in on individual or collaborative work to formatively assess. Ask learners questions about their progress. Individualize instruction as needed.	Notice and name attributes of high-quality thinking and engagement. Research learners' thinking and understanding by asking questions that promote insight and metacognition. Cocreate goals and next steps.	Learners confer with peers. Learners own progress toward their goals.

Figure 4.13 Workshop: Conferring

Into the Classroom

Sounds Like: Conferring

A third-grade teacher crouches down beside a young reader. "What are you reading?" Azalea shows her teacher the cover of a Baby-Sitters Club book and tells a bit about where she is in the story. As she listens, her teacher jots some conferring notes in her notebook. (She has a section for each student.) "Azalea, it amazes me the amount of detail you can recall as you are summarizing. So, what are you thinking?"

"I am inferring that she feels really sad and afraid."

"You are also monitoring for meaning and also predicting as a reader. What about this idea of determining importance? How do you do that as a reader?"

"I stop and think about what I am going to remember."

"And what will you remember about this chapter?"

"That she is very brave."

"And so are you."

I think that throughout my math career, I had always been taught to just learn when to plug something into an equation. But, your class was much more challenging than that because you actually made us learn the WHY behind the math and why it works, which was the most helpful aspect of it all.

Finally, metacognition. As an IB student, I think I have been trained to be somewhat mechanical with my learning. But, there was nothing like that in your class. Every single problem that we did, we used the process of metacognition. I think that you helped me bridge the process of applying what I know really effectively. There was no review that was the same as the test/repeat questions - I really had to know my math. You gave us challenging questions at the beginning of the year but walked us through how to solve it/ proving that we already knew how to do it. We just needed to apply our knowledge. Towards the end of the year, I think I became much stronger at solving those questions and applying my knowledge.

Figure 4.14 Student Reflection on the Power of Metacognition in Math

METACOGNITION AND REFLECTION

Research on metacognition clearly underlines the importance of pausing at regular intervals to check in with ourselves: What do I understand? What does this mean? How does this fit with what I already know? Creating formal opportunities for learners to engage with these types of questions not only solidifies comprehension but also enhances efficiency, prompting students to move with purpose through a learning experience in pursuit of a clear target. Individually, with a partner, or as a whole group; recorded on a sticky note, on loose paper, or in a journal or demonstrated visually—student reflection is a critical component of effective workshops, not to be skipped even under the tyranny of time. (See Figure 4.14 for a student work sample and Figure 4.15 for the PEBC Teaching Framework for Sharing and Reflection.)

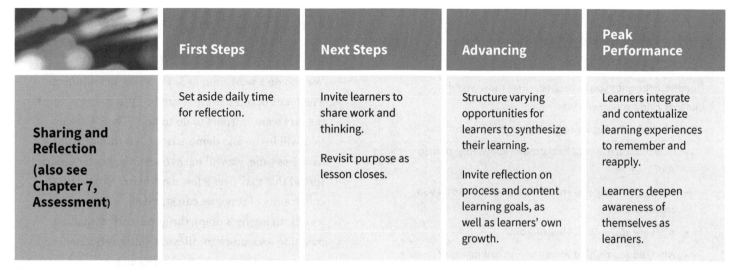

	First Steps	Next Steps	Advancing	Peak Performance
Sharing and Reflection (also see Chapter 7, Assessment)	Set aside daily time for reflection.	Invite learners to share work and thinking. Revisit purpose as lesson closes.	Structure varying opportunities for learners to synthesize their learning. Invite reflection on process and content learning goals, as well as learners' own growth.	Learners integrate and contextualize learning experiences to remember and reapply. Learners deepen awareness of themselves as learners.

Figure 4.15 Workshop: Sharing and Reflection

Nonlinguistic Reflection Options

Underline the ones you have used; circle those you'd like to try. Add your own ideas.

- Fist of five: "Show me on a fist of five (five fingers being the most and zero fingers being the least) how confident you feel about this concept."

- Thumbs: "Thumbs up, sideways, or down to show how well you understand."

- Four corners: Assign topics or feelings to each corner of the room and invite students to move to the one they most understand or identify with, then the one they least do. Additionally, they could find a partner there and discuss their choices.

- Temperature: "If this wall is freezing and this wall is boiling, stand in the place that represents how hot your understanding of ___ is."

- Magnets: Write each child's name on a magnet; they stick them to the whiteboard in the column that best describes how they feel at the end of the lesson: "Got it." "Thinking hard." "Not yet."

- Strike a pose: "Without a sound, hold your body in a position that represents how you feel about your learning today."

-

-

Reflection Questions (to Write About, Discuss, or Ponder)

Underline the ones you have used; circle those you'd like to try. Add your own ideas.

- What was the big idea of today's lesson?
- How did you use your background knowledge to help you?
- What's one thing you are sure about and one that you are unsure of?
- What are you proud of figuring out?
- What did you do, and what are you thinking now?
- What are you still wondering about?
- Describe why you believe your thinking is correct.
- Describe two other ways you could have approached this task.
- Describe what you have accomplished and what you plan to do next.
- What patterns have you noticed?
- What's one thing you learned from a classmate today?
- What was your biggest "aha" moment today?
- What's the most important thing you want to remember?
- If we had more time, what would you wish to investigate further?
- How could today's lesson have been even better?
- What will you say when your friends ask you what you did in class today?
- If we were starting class with a pop quiz tomorrow, what would the questions be?
- What do you think we are going to do next?
- I used to think _____. Now, I think _____.
- In one word, share how you feel about your learning today.
-
-
-

Workshop FAQs

- **"What if I only have learners for ___ minutes?"**

  We can do a workshop in 5, 15, 50, or 105 minutes. The focus of our planning can be "What sort of thinking do I want learners to do today?" Then, "What task will invite and demonstrate that thinking?" If we have less time, we will have to select a shorter task or spread that task over a few days' work. No matter the constraints of time, we can still dedicate the majority of it to learners doing the good work of making meaning—so, quick minilesson, quick reflection, and strong routines to maximize efficiency.

- **"But I thought workshop meant stations?"**

  No. Workshop is not stations. Stations are typically a series of learning experiences about sometimes related topics designed to keep learners busy while the teacher guides a group toward a learning goal. Workshop, in contrast, involves all students pursuing meaning of a common understanding target while working independently and in small groups, with flexible levels of teacher support. Workshops launch with a shared purpose and intentional instruction designed to scaffold learners' independence. Workshops also include sharing and reflection about progress toward collective goals.

- **"What if my curriculum does not lend itself to workshop?"**

  You can't do a workshop about a worksheet. Dig into your curriculum in search of rich tasks; this might involve skipping over some of the more rote materials. If the depth is not there, modify what you have or develop your own.

- **"But students aren't ready for this level of independence."**

  They might not be, yet. Learners need us to prepare them and expect them to be independent. Start small. Build slowly. Narrate your vision, as Jamie Salterelli does each year with a chart such as hers in Figure 4.16. Highlight progress. You will get there. Any effort toward learners' independence is a better step than sustaining dependence out of fear or mistrust.

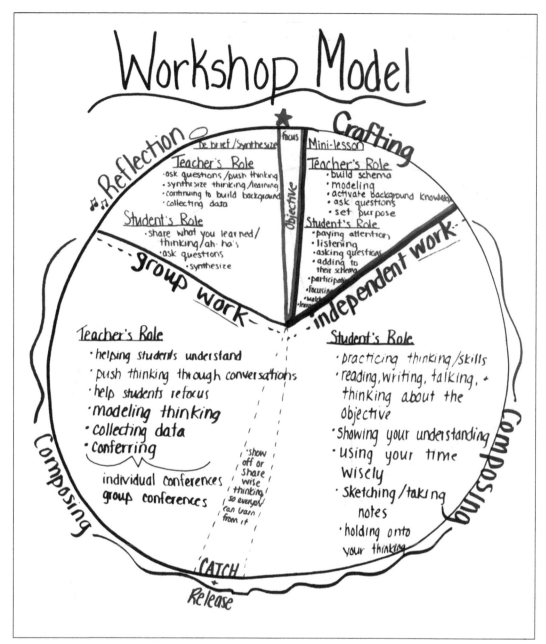

Figure 4.16 Jamie Salterelli explains workshop to her students with an anchor chart.

Your Turn

When we plan a workshop, we start by considering the work—what it is that learners will do to grow or demonstrate understanding. From there, we back up to consider how we will hook learners' interest, then design the minilesson by asking ourselves what learners need to succeed independently. Our reflection typically refers back to our learning targets and invites deeper consideration. Figure 4.17 is a planning tool with questions to cue your thinking about each segment of a workshop. Test it out as you consider an upcoming workshop model lesson. Figure 4.18, the empty workshop wheel, is a space to record your answers to the questions in the first wheel.

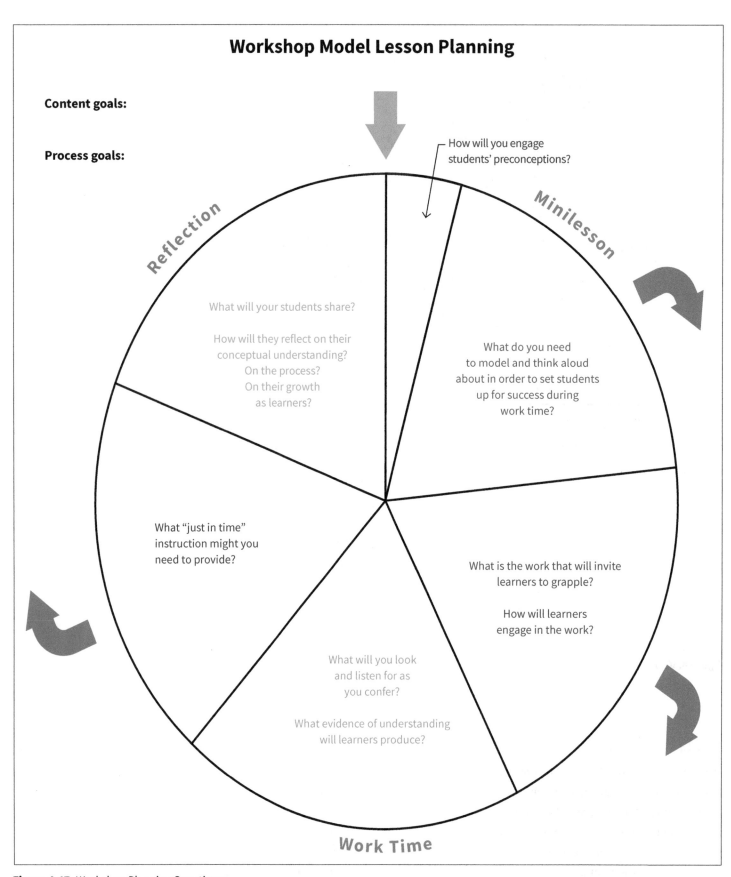

Workshop Model Lesson Planning

Content goals:

Process goals:

How will you engage students' preconceptions?

Minilesson

Reflection

What will your students share?

How will they reflect on their conceptual understanding?
On the process?
On their growth
as learners?

What do you need
to model and think aloud
about in order to set students
up for success during
work time?

What "just in time" instruction might you need to provide?

What is the work that will invite learners to grapple?

How will learners engage in the work?

What will you look and listen for as you confer?

What evidence of understanding will learners produce?

Work Time

Figure 4.17 Workshop Planning Questions

Workshop Model Lesson Planning

Content goals:

Process goals:

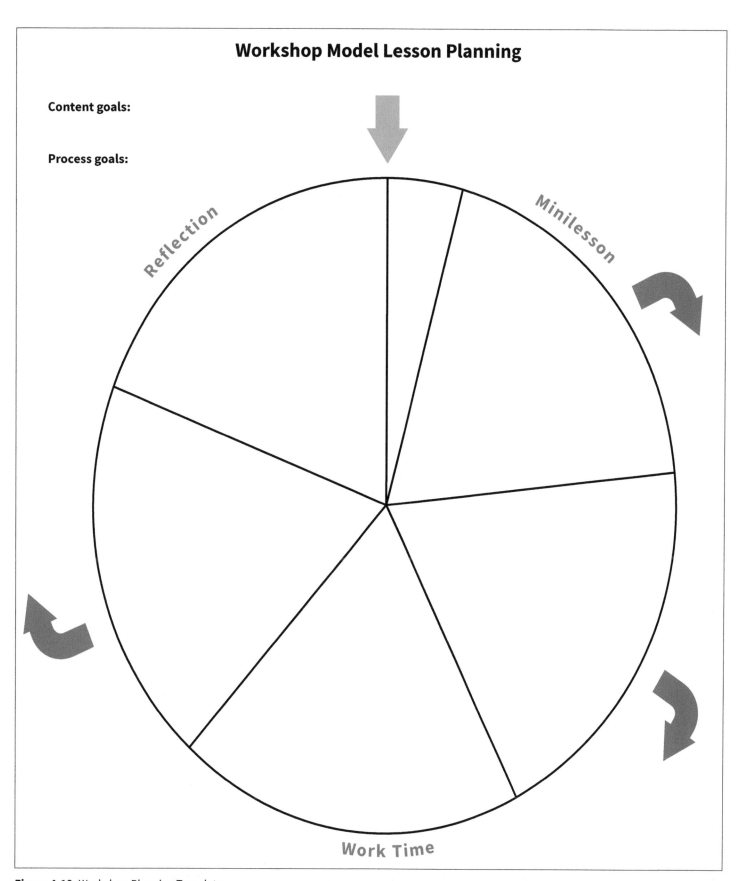

Figure 4.18 Workshop Planning Template

content: Author's message

Process: Inferring

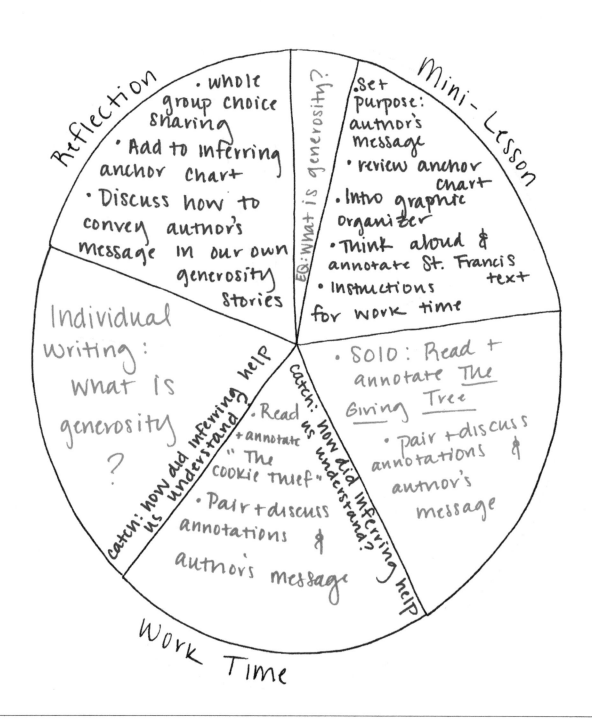

The circular diagram contains the following sections:

Mini-Lesson
- Set purpose: author's message
- review anchor chart
- Intro graphic organizer
- Think aloud & annotate St. Francis text
- Instructions for work time

(center divider: EQ: What is generosity?)

Reflection
- whole group choice sharing
- Add to inferring anchor chart
- Discuss how to convey author's message in our own generosity stories

Individual writing: what is generosity?

Work Time
- SOLO: Read + annotate The Giving Tree
- Pair + discuss annotations & author's message
(Catch: how did inferring help us understand?)
- Read + annotate "The cookie thief"
- Pair + discuss annotations & author's message
(Catch: how did inferring help us understand?)

Figure 4.19 What Observers Noticed During a Workshop Model Language Arts Lesson with Layered Texts Targeting the Question, "What is Generosity?"

REFLECTION

- How does your current understanding of workshop compare to your prior knowledge?

- What questions are still lingering?

- Which aspects of the workshop feel most natural to you?

- Which segments might you want to refine in your work? How?

- What changes do you feel inspired to make in your own instruction?

- What difference will those changes make for students?

- How will you know you have succeeded?

REFLECTION ON CHAPTER QUESTION: HOW CAN WE FACILITATE LEARNING EXPERIENCES THAT SUPPORT STUDENTS GRAPPLING WITH CHALLENGING TASKS IN SERVICE OF CONCEPTUAL UNDERSTANDING?

Invitation: Create a one-frame cartoon that synthesizes your learning from this chapter in answer to this question.

THINKING
5 STRATEGIES

ANTICIPATION QUESTIONS

- What resources and scaffolds do you currently provide that support learners in making meaning of complex content?

- Share what you already know about thinking strategies.

- What questions do you hope to answer as you explore this chapter?

Teacher Voice: Thinking Strategies

"Thinking strategy instruction gives learners the power to fend off confusion and persevere. It takes them from helpless hand-raisers to agentic meaning-makers."

—MOKER KLAUS-QUINLAN

Making Meaning in the Real World

In local elections, decisions on candidates are typically straightforward for me once I read the news and hear their positions. Ballot measures, on the other hand, often leave me stumped. Check out Ballot Measure 110 from Colorado's 2018 election:

> Shall state taxes be increased $766,700,000 annually for a twenty-year period, and state debt shall be increased $6,000,000,000 with a maximum repayment cost of $9,400,000,000, to pay for state and local transportation projects, and, in connection therewith, changing the Colorado revised statutes to: 1) increase the state sales and use tax rate by 0.62% beginning January 1, 2019; requiring 45% of the new revenue to fund state transportation safety, maintenance, and congestion related projects, 40% to fund municipal and county transportation projects, and 15% to fund multimodal transportation projects, including bike, pedestrian, and transit infrastructure; 2) authorize the issuance of additional transportation revenue anticipation notes to fund priority state transportation maintenance and construction projects, including multimodal capital projects; and 3) provide that all revenue resulting from the tax rate increase and proceeds from issuance of revenue anticipation notes are voter-approved revenue changes exempt from any state or local revenue, spending, or other limitations in law.

"To think incisively and to think for one's self is very difficult. . . . Education must enable one to sift and weigh evidence, to discern the true from the false, the real from the unreal and the facts from the fiction."

—*Dr. Martin Luther King (1947)*

That one got me. I did not understand. I stopped and reread it. I reread it again. I did a little math on my phone. I wondered what this would really mean to voters today and to our children in the future. I thought about the money involved and picked through the sections one at a time. I read a few websites describing the measure and talked it over with some politically savvy friends. It took me a while to get to a place where I could explain Measure 110 to my children, answer their questions, and discuss as a family whether this was a good idea and whether it deserved our vote. Understanding was a lot of work.

REFLECTION: MAKING MEANING IN THE REAL WORLD

Tell the story of a time when you worked hard to make meaning. What did you need to understand? Why did you need to make sense of it? What supported your success? What did you learn about yourself as a thinker?

What: Thinking Strategies

Look at Figure 5.1. Strive to make sense of it, as though you were going to have a quiz on its meaning.

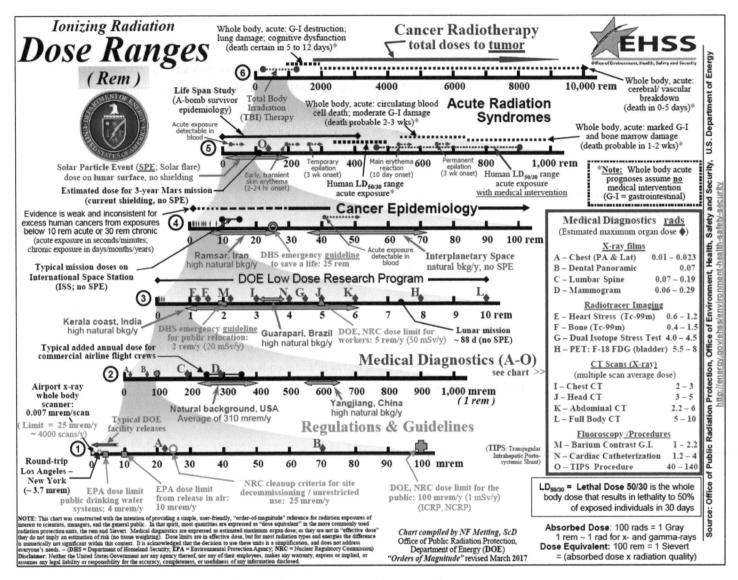

Figure 5.1 How can you make sense of this diagram? (U.S. Department of Energy 2017)

What did you find yourself doing in your effort to understand? What helped?

You probably used a lot of different strategies to make sense of that chart, perhaps relating to familiar terms like *x-rays* or *cancer*, or noticing and wondering about the color codes and the orders of magnitude graphics. Or, maybe you got annoyed and gave up—which is OK, too, under the circumstances. But the big idea of thinking strategy instruction is giving learners something to do instead of give up.

In 1983, P. David Pearson and M. C. Gallagher first published their research on how proficient readers make sense of complex texts. When thinkers are stumped by a puzzle, researchers found, most readers will try one or more of the following to make meaning:

- Draw on background knowledge.
- Ask questions.
- Infer.
- Develop sensory images (initially referred to as visualizing).
- Determine importance.
- Synthesize.
- Monitor for meaning.

When one of those approaches doesn't work, we are likely to try another, persevering to understand.

Once this research went public, studies continued to explore the effectiveness of explicit strategy instruction for fostering learners' independence as meaning makers. In 1992, Pearson and colleagues wrote,

> We really do expect all readers of all ages to engage in all of these strategies at some level of sophistication. We really are arguing that there are no first grade skills, third grade skills, sixth grade skills, and so on. Readers of all ages should engage in these strategies: with age and experience, they get better and are able to apply them to a wider range of texts, tasks, and situations. But these strategies are as important for the novice as they are for the expert. Granted, first graders may not ask sophisticated questions, but they can ask something, and what they ask is likely to be important to them. . . . What we have, then, is more of an emerging expertise model of strategy acquisition instead of a scope and sequence of skills.

This research in hand, smart teachers got to work providing thinking strategy instruction for learners at all levels to enrich their ability to make meaning of complex texts. Ellin Oliver Keene, Steph Harvey, Chryse Hutchins, Anne Goodvis, Debbie Miller, Cris Tovani, Susan Zimmermann, and so many other empowered teachers led the way, starting first in elementary classrooms, but soon expanding to reach learners of all ages and across content areas. And these strategies aren't just for fiction, or even just for narrative text, they found; we can use thinking strategies to make sense of everything: graphs, maps, pictures, word problems, cartoons, facial expressions, clouds in the sky.

Thinking strategies as tools can be thoughtfully paired with content instruction to enhance learners' understanding of the topic in front of them while also equipping students with tools to carry forward into other studies and stages of their schooling. While exploring volcanoes, for example, we learn to ask questions as scientists, a transferrable skill we can take with us as we study earthquakes or electromagnetism or elections or economics. We do not study strategies for their sake alone, but rather as a means to the important end of expanding learners' comprehension and independence.

Thinking Strategy	Definition and Real-World Example	Classroom Examples	Classroom Anchor Chart
Draw on Background Knowledge (Schema)	• Seek and build connections between what is known and unknown. • Include connections between text and self, text and the world, or this text and another text. *Example:* Even though the airline said my flight was delayed, I knew from experience that it could leave any time after the originally scheduled departure, so I stayed at the gate.	• Activate relevant, prior knowledge before, during, and after reading. • Build knowledge by deliberately assimilating new learning with their related prior knowledge. • Clarify new learning by deleting inaccurate schema. • Notice what a story or problem reminds us of.	
Ask Questions	• Be curious, wonder about a great many things. • Questions might be answered in text, through research, or via discussion, or may not be answerable. *Example:* When I saw a wet spot under my car, I wondered: Do I have an oil leak? A radiator leak? An engine problem? Is it safe to drive? How much will this cost me to fix?	• Generate questions before, during, and after reading about the text's content, structure, and language. • Ask questions for different purposes, including clarifying, making predictions, and wondering about the choices the author made. • Realize that one question may lead to others. • Question texts, peers, reasoning, solutions . . .	

Figure 5.2 Thinking Strategies in Summary

continues

Thinking Strategy	Definition and Real-World Example	Classroom Examples	Classroom Anchor Chart
Infer	• Merge background knowledge and new learning to reach conclusions, make predictions, or galvanize big ideas. • "Read between the lines." *Example:* Observing my mother's face as she opened her present, I knew I had better find the receipt.	• Draw conclusions about their reading by connecting the text with their schema. • Make, confirm, and/or revise reasonable predictions. • Know when and how to infer answers to unanswered questions. • Extrapolate from data sets or find meaning not explicitly stated.	
Develop Sensory Images	• Visualize and represent learning in a new format. • Present understanding in a variety of formats, including models, manipulatives, and drawing. *Example:* When I read the recipe for a lattice pie crust, I pictured how I would weave the strips of dough together.	• Create images connected to the senses to enhance and personalize understandings. • Revise their images to incorporate new information and new ideas revealed in the text. • Develop models to represent understanding.	
Determine Importance	• Based on purpose, sift and sort to select key information. • Know why that information is important and how it can support your understanding. *Example:* A political candidate's flyer listed his stance on an array of issues, and I focused on those I care about most in making my decision about whether to support him.	• Identify key ideas, themes, and elements as they read. • Distinguish between important and unimportant information using our own purpose(s). • Use text structures and text features to help decide what is essential and what is extraneous. • Use purpose as problem solvers to identify important information.	

Figure 5.2 *continued*

Thinking Strategy	Definition and Real-World Example	Classroom Examples	Classroom Anchor Chart
Synthesize	• Notice and apply patterns. • Observe how understanding evolves over time. *Example:* I watched the waves for a while before jumping into the ocean, observing how they broke and where. When I got in to swim, I used those observations to help me decide which waves to try to catch and which ones to swim under.	• Continually monitor overall meaning, important concepts, and themes while reading. • Recognize ways in which text elements or data sets fit together to create larger meaning. • Find and use patterns to make predictions.	
Monitor for Meaning	• Be aware of your own thinking and when your comprehension breaks down. • Pause and use fix-up strategies when stuck or confused. *Example:* Reading a letter from the phone company about my bill, I felt confused, so I reread it and then asked a friend to read it to see if we understood it the same way.	• Pause to reflect on growing understandings. • Recognize when we understand the text and when we don't. • Identify when and why the meaning is unclear, and use fix-up strategies to address confusion. • Catch ourselves being "stuck" and make a plan for getting "unstuck."	

Figure 5.2 *continued*

THINKING STRATEGIES AND YOU

Reread and annotate the list of thinking strategies in Figure 5.2. Star the ones you already use with automaticity. Add to their definitions and examples. Put question marks next to the strategies that are less comfortable for you. What are you wondering? Record your questions about these strategies. Now, consider which strategies come most naturally to your students; emphasize those with an exclamation point. And what would you like to teach them next? Why?

Why Thinking Strategies?

As teachers, our purpose is to support all learners' success at independently grappling with challenging content and making sense so that some day in the future, when they are all alone facing a state test or a medical challenge or a lawsuit or a tax problem or any of the million other life challenges that might present themselves, our kids know how to understand and take action. Knowing how to make meaning, rather than shy away from difficulties or act out, gives learners the strength and power to be leaders in their own lives.

A key support for learners is possessing a cognitive tool kit into which they can dive for help when comprehension breaks down. The thinking strategies are the essential components in this tool kit, and so their study, deep and wide, affirms learners' access to these cognitive resources as readers and thinkers every day. Liben and Pearson (2018) note: "When the text stops making sense, the readers must take stock, reconsider options, and look for ways to achieve the coherence they seek. The processes they invoke when things don't make sense are what we call cognitive or comprehension strategies. These strategies are a set of deliberate mental procedures (corrective or 'fix-up' routines) that students invoke when they sense that comprehension has broken down."

Cognitive strategy instruction serves all learners. Researcher Jill Fitzgerald (1995) demonstrated that both native and nonnative English speakers benefit from balanced reading instruction and that there is "virtually no evidence that ESL [English as a second language] learners need notably divergent forms of instruction to guide or develop their cognitive reading process." The Pathways Project, an eight-year study developed by researchers at the California Writing Project, offered rich cognitive strategy instruction to 2,000 English language learners each year in thirteen California secondary schools. With intensive support applying thinking strategies, as well as work refining their writing skills in light of exemplars, 93 percent of seniors who participated in this study passed the state high school exit exam, as compared with an average pass rate of 39 percent among all English language learners.

This process of noticing confusion and doing something about it is not unique to one age or stage of education: as students progress in their learning and lives, the challenges of comprehension grow steeper. Hence, strategies are worth teaching at every stage and in each content area. In this light, author Stevi Quate affirmed our need for strategy instruction at all levels: "Comprehension is going to be part of pre-K until death" (personal communication, 2016).

"Knowledge is now a commodity, and what our children need to learn is where to find it, how to evaluate it, how to select what is germane, and how to apply it to the problem *they* are trying to solve."

—*Gisèle Huff (2019)*

With agency as our goal, we must focus our efforts toward supporting learners' understanding—not only of the content before them, but, more importantly, of how they can independently persevere in making sense of new information in novel contexts. Planned, intentional thinking strategy instruction is a critical means to that end.

REFLECTION ON RESEARCH

- In what ways are you already incorporating thinking strategy instruction into your class(es)?

- What is compelling about the research on thinking strategy instruction?

- What concerns do you have about focusing on thinking strategies for all learners and across the curriculum?

CONVERSATION INVITATION

- What can you infer about Deb's instruction from the description of her beliefs in the Teacher Voice box?

- What are you wondering now about thinking strategy instruction?

Teacher Voice: Why Take Time Teaching Thinking Strategies?

"Determining importance, making connections, and recognizing and articulating when, where, and why one becomes stuck or unstuck all require critical thinking skills. We are learning to construct, name, recognize, and use mental models to help us start managing the very messy process of learning and integrating new information. To cope with new information, students develop different thinking routines. It is fascinating to listen to students explain their thinking. Through differing processes they arrive at a common solution. Articulating and sharing their thinking is powerful. It allows them to identify and fix possible thinking flaws as well as affirm thinking strengths. Finding and grouping common thinking patterns allows those processes to be named. By naming a thinking routine, students can then use it as 'an engine/catalyst,' which with practice speeds and strengthens connections between new and established knowledge. For both student and instructor, this process is also very messy, and exciting! *We* are learning together."

—*Deb Maruyama*

Mrs. Blake's Fifth Grade

Mrs. Blake's students have been fifth graders for seven days. This time of year is all about growing independence and learning the rituals and routines of readers' workshop. But Mrs. Blake's fifth graders are also knee-deep into an inquiry of how monitoring for meaning and envisioning help them understand a text more deeply. They have begun to define what it means to understand, they have practiced envisioning during read-aloud and with really challenging nonfiction texts, and they have had opportunities to confer with Mrs. Blake about their thinking. Let's listen in on the reflection component of today's workshop.

After students record the titles of their books and how much they read, they gather on the rug. Mrs. Blake begins, "In readers' workshop, we are really working on figuring out what it means to understand. During our minilesson today, we talked about the differences between a simple retell and an extreme retell, and we created this chart of strategies. Turn and tell your partner which of these strategies you used today and how it helped you understand."

Students huddle together and jump into their conversations. Mrs. Blake listens in for insights and trends.

"The book I am reading is also called *The Sun Becomes a Star*, and I made a connection to the text."

"Well, I thought about the struggles the character is facing."

Mrs. Blake asks, "Who wants to share a strategy they used and how it helped them understand?" She had noticed that students were simply sharing their strategies, but not elaborating.

One student shares, "I'm reading *The Land of Stories* right now, and these kids are trying to get to another world. I really had to think about the main idea."

Mrs. Blake probes, "How did that help you understand?"

"Well, when I thought about the main idea, I could focus on what was going on. This book gets confusing as the characters try to get back home. So, the main idea helped me monitor and make predictions."

Mrs. Blake thanks the student for sharing and recognizes another volunteer who says, "In my book, I am thinking about all of the struggles the characters face."

Mrs. Blake asks again: "How is that helping you understand?"

"Well, I can picture the problems, and then I make predictions."

Mrs. Blake takes a moment to recap and paraphrase. "So, readers, today we noticed that when we use strategies, we can monitor for meaning and have a deeper understanding of our books."

And then students cozy up for read-aloud. Laughter permeates the room as Mrs. Blake reenacts the bee sting from yesterday's reading. "Can you just see it? Here we are envisioning again."

In what ways does the thinking strategy deepen learners' understanding and agency in this vignette?

Thinking Strategies *Are* . . .	Thinking Strategies *Are Not* . . .	Your Thinking . . .
Research based	Made up from scratch	
Flexible tools to mix and match	Rigid and isolated	
Processes applied in support of content understanding	A content of their own	
Scaffolds for learners' independence	Extra work	

Figure 5.3 Clarification Corner

How: The Elements of Thinking Strategy Instruction

Thinking strategies scaffold learners' independence. With this purpose in mind, we can provide thinking strategy instruction that enhances self-awareness, metacognition, and understanding. When teaching thinking strategies at any grade levels, here are some essential elements that support learners' success. In this chapter, we will explore each, one at a time:

- metacognition
- intention
- tasks
- gradual release of responsibility
- speaking and listening
- documentation
- reflection.

METACOGNITION

Simply put, metacognition is self-awareness: awareness of our thinking, feelings, and attitudes, as well as of how we do what we do. To be metacognitive, we need to slow down, observe our own selves, name our processes, and notice what helps us to remember, transfer, and reapply our knowledge. In the context

> "Some books pose problems in comprehension—we might feel thrust into a situation that is confusing. Unless readers know how to pause and think through these difficulties (and learn that difficulties are natural for many kinds of reading), they will feel inadequate and stupid."
>
> **—Thomas Newkirk (2011)**

of thinking strategy instruction, metacognition invites learners to become aware of what is taking place in their own minds, as well as to learn new processes they can intentionally employ to build, repair, or enhance understanding. This thinking takes time; as one recent guest to a lab classroom described, "You know, they talk about slow food. This is slow teaching. And it works." (See Figure 5.4 for the PEBC Teaching Framework for Metacognition.)

	First Steps	Next Steps	Advancing	Peak Performance
Metacognition	Honor all thinking. Notice and name strategies used to make meaning.	Create time for thinking, dwelling with ideas; highlight understanding as the purpose of thinking. Describe own experiences of thinking that led to understanding. Notice and name learners' progress using the language of thinking strategies.	Narrate the evolution of individuals' and the group's thinking and learning. Engage learners in conversations about how and why thinking strategies support their understanding. Celebrate insight, as well as growth and revision.	Learners notice and name how thinking strategies support their journey toward understanding. Learners use thinking strategies to persevere in the face of challenge or confusion.

Figure 5.4 Thinking Strategies: Metacognition

Start with You

To best prepare to teach these thinking strategies, we need to first understand our own use of them. We might have a lot of unconscious competence as readers and thinkers, yet when we pause to notice what we did to fix up our own confusion, we can share that approach with learners, an authentic example of our own thinking and problem-solving.

Literacy expert Michelle Morris Jones describes, "Teachers need opportunities to unpack the thinking strategies themselves and their own understanding processes. We approach text in lots of different ways. We each have our go-to strategies, and some strategies that don't work as well for us. We need to be able to describe our own experience, 'I am the type of reader who . . .' From this awareness of self, we can build towards awareness of others and facilitate their understanding" (personal communication 2019). My colleague Kirsten Myers-Blake visualizes each individual's progress toward metacognition as a staircase (see Figure 5.5); we need each step to support the next.

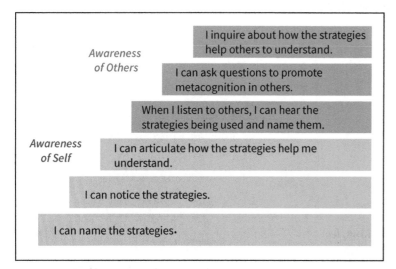

Figure 5.5 Kirsten Myers-Blake's staircase image describes the steps we each take as we grow to impactfully employ the thinking strategies.

REFLECTION

- Where are you on this staircase? Why?

- How do you support metacognition now? In what ways might you take it to the next level later?

Space for Thinking

We scaffold learners' awareness of thinking by inviting frequent reflection and conversation about how they are using strategies, how the strategies are helping, and why. These discussions might take place one-on-one, with small groups as learners delve together into a task, or with the whole group as part of the minilesson or sharing time of a workshop.

Here are a few phrases that might be used to elicit learners' ideas in any of these settings:

- "Say more."
- "Wow! How did you do that?"
- "Help us understand why."
- "What is making sense to you?"
- "Hmm . . ."
- (Add your own.)
-
-

When we ask learners to describe their thinking—to tell the story of how they made sense or developed ideas or arrived at solutions—we are inviting them to be metacognitive. (See Figure 5.6 for anchor charts on metacognition.)

Which words might you use to demonstrate your interest in learners' thinking?

Figure 5.6 Jamie Salterelli uses anchor charts on metacognition with her fourth graders.

INTENTION

Within each unit and lesson, we need to set clear goals and establish strong pathways to support learners' acquisition of thinking strategies and other skills for independence. This means planning each day thinking not only about what students will learn, but also about how. Our strategy instruction needs to be responsive rather than mechanical, consistent rather than spotty, and connected rather than removed from content studies. As described previously, the strategies do interconnect, yet even introducing and scaffolding learners' understanding around one can uplift their understanding of others. As one teacher described, "It's like cleaning a vacuum cleaner—start with just one section, then the whole vacuum works better." (See Figure 5.7 for the PEBC Teaching Framework for Intention.)

	First Steps	Next Steps	Advancing	Peak Performance
Intention	Expect learners to use one or more thinking strategy(ies). Communicate the need for and value of thinking.	Set goals for learners' acquisition of thinking strategies. Match thinking strategies to learning experiences.	Leverage understanding with thinking strategies. Weave thinking strategy instruction consistently over time into content learning experiences.	Learners honor thinking, as demonstrated by careful listening, articulate speech, and clear written communication.

Figure 5.7 Thinking Strategies: Intention

Getting Started

Here are some first steps toward being intentional with thinking strategy instruction:

- Spend time as a learner yourself, noticing your own thinking.

- Define and describe one or more strategies to your students, sharing your own experiences; invite learners to consider how they may also unconsciously use the same strategy to make meaning.

- Develop one or more thinking strategy anchor charts in the room for ready reference; each might include an explanation of the strategy, quotes describing learners' experiences with the strategy, or reflections on how the strategy helps learners to understand.

- Identify thinking strategy learning targets for each unit that authentically connect to the work learners will do: if you are reading poetry, perhaps students will benefit from a focus on inferring; if you are studying algebraic patterns, perhaps a focus on determining importance. Choose what makes sense.

- Make time for thinking and listening to thinking every day; make space for recording thinking.

- Work toward a gradual release of responsibility in learners' implementation of that strategy.

TALK BACK

In what ways do these thinking strategies feel authentic to your content instruction? How might you be more intentional about using them to scaffold learners' independence?

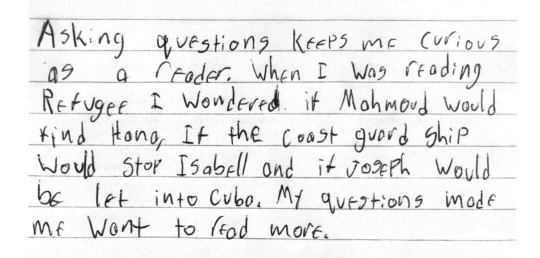

Figure 5.8 Student's Reflection on the Value of Questioning While Reading *Refugee*

TASKS

For thinking strategies to flourish and take root in our classrooms, we need to provide learners with evocative and interesting content to ponder, and we need to interweave that content learning with invitations for thinking. (For more details on tasks, see Chapter 2, "Plan.")

Secondary humanities teacher Alisa Wills-Keely brought the classic play *The Taming of the Shrew* to life by inviting learners to look at contemporary social issues and take a stance on forgiveness or revenge: Which will set us free? Students saw a film about a suitor in Iran who poured acid on a woman who rejected his proposal and read an article about violence

against women in Afghanistan. Learners determined importance, inferred and synthesized their thinking about each of these events, engaged in a pop-up debate about the nature of revenge and forgiveness, and then wrote their own position papers taking a stance for which of those will set us free, using evidence from their own lives as well as from the texts they studied to support their arguments. In this way, Alisa moved learners beyond simply reading an old play and invited them to connect that text with current issues to gather evidence to evaluate and justify their own moral compasses. What could be more worthy of students' thought and time? (See Figure 5.9 for the PEBC Teaching Framework for Tasks.)

	First Steps	Next Steps	Advancing	Peak Performance
Tasks (also see Chapter 2, Plan)	Welcome learners to share their own ideas about content.	Provide rich tasks and diverse texts that spark learners to respond.	Intentionally layer ideas and learning experiences that invite learners to deepen and refine conceptual understanding.	Learners make meaning over time and take action to apply their understanding.

Figure 5.9 Thinking Strategies: Tasks

Elevating Tasks

Figure 5.10 offers some ideas for refining a task to create richer invitations for thinking.

Idea	Planning Question to Ponder	Sample Unit	Possible Task
Go big: Instead of reading a textbook or studying a concept for the sake of that text or concept alone, connect it to a bigger story. Check out the Next Generation Science Standards' Crosscutting Concepts or the National Curriculum Standards for Social Studies Ten Themes for ideas.	Zoom out: What's the big idea?	Studying the civil rights period of American history, we might focus on the broader social issue of equity, or consider current dilemmas that challenge the United States Declaration of Independence's assertion that "all men are created equal."	Write a letter to the authors of the Declaration of Independence about the ways in which their words do or do not ring true in the United States today.
Go outside: Instead of restricting our study of content standards to school settings, consider the real-world application of the knowledge students are pursuing, akin to problem-based learning.	Zoom out: How does this content connect beyond the classroom?	While studying water in a science unit, we might explore water sources, resources, use, conservation, and pollution in our own community.	*(Your turn)*
Go for controversy: Often, we can connect the content at hand with a current paradox, dilemma, or moral question or an as yet unsolved problem, using that as the crux issue of our unit, as Alisa did.	Zoom in: Where is the controversy or challenge where this concept comes to life?	*(Your turn)*	*(Your turn)*
(What else?)			

Figure 5.10 Ideas for Elevating Tasks

TALK BACK

- Can you remember being riveted as a learner, madly wanting to understand something? What was it? Why did you care?

- What are you teaching? Why is it interesting, important, connected, or controversial? How will you make it evocative for your thinkers?

GRADUAL RELEASE OF RESPONSIBILITY

Learners effectively adopt thinking strategies when we, the teachers, release responsibility for implementing them to the students. We could name this approach a "gradual increase of responsibility," because, from a learner's perspective, that is what is happening: more and more, they are asked to own the tools for building their own understanding. In their article "A Cognitive Strategies Approach to Reading and Writing Instruction for English Language Learners in Secondary School," education researchers Carol Booth Olson and Robert Land describe the case for gradual release: "In their analysis of over 20 years of research on comprehension instruction, Block and Pressley (2002) note widespread agreement among scholars that students should be taught cognitive and metacognitive processes and that, regardless of the program used, instruction should include modeling, scaffolding, guided practice, and independent use of strategies so that students develop the ability to select and implement appropriate strategies independently and to monitor and regulate their use" (2007). (See Figure 5.11 for the PEBC Teaching Framework for Gradual Release of Responsibility.)

	First Steps	Next Steps	Advancing	Peak Performance
Gradual Release of Responsibility	Post the thinking strategies in the room. Refer to the thinking strategies. Describe strategies and their use.	Describe thinking strategies as transferable tools for meaning making. Model thinking strategies during minilessons and while conferring.	Create and scaffold intentional and varied opportunities for learners to authentically apply thinking strategies as tools for comprehension. Appreciate learners' innate knowledge of thinking strategies as tools for living.	Learners use thinking strategies authentically, flexibly, and independently in a variety of genres and across disciplines in service of understanding.

Figure 5.11 Thinking Strategies: Gradual Release of Responsibility

Plan a Strategy Study

Many teachers embed a strategy study within a content unit. Figure 5.12 suggests some steps to planning a strategy study, with ideas for introducing the strategy early in the unit, focusing on strategy development in the middle of the unit, and continuing to hand off the responsibility for learners' leadership late in the unit. A similar approach could be adopted across a semester or year.

	Planning	Early	Middle	Late
Goal	• Match the strategy to the content.	• Introduce with stories and description. • Think aloud about content using the strategy. • Create an anchor chart.	• Model the strategy. • Confer with learners about the strategy.	• Invite learners to think aloud. • Invite all to reflect on how this strategy serves their understanding.
Questions to Ponder	• How do I approach this content? • What strategy might be most authentic to professionals in this field of study?	• When have I used this strategy in my life? • What accessible task might I use to introduce this strategy? • How might I visually represent this strategy for learners?	• How can I describe my use of this strategy and how it helps me understand this content? • What questions will I ask learners about their use of this strategy?	• How will I know when learners are ready to demonstrate their own use of this strategy? • What invitations will I create for learners to consider how this strategy helps them to understand?
Example	*Wonder*, a teacher decides, matches well with inferring because with that text learners can practice empathy.	• Introduce the strategy by talking about how we infer by the look on someone's face. • Read a passage from the text and talk about what I infer. • Show a picture that can be interpreted in multiple ways.	• Continue to model with images and picture books, as well as *Wonder* think-alouds. • Ask, "What are you thinking? How do you imagine Auggie is feeling? Why? What is the author's message?"	• When students can talk about thoughts, guesses. and predictions that match evidence from the text, they will be ready to model for peers. • How did inferring engage you as a thinker? In what ways did this strategy support your understanding?
Your Turn				

Figure 5.12 Planning a Strategy Study

Thinking Aloud

Thinking aloud is a gift to our students. It invites them to glimpse how proficient thinkers make sense. This is something we can do often, not just once with any given strategy. We might think aloud about a strategy in the real world, how it serves us in our content area, how it comes to life in a particular genre of text, or how it helps us to solve a problem.

Planning a Think-Aloud

- Select text that lends itself to the strategy we seek to model.
- Preview the text to identify think-aloud points.
- If helpful, preannotate the text with key ideas worth mentioning.

Conducting a Think-Aloud

- Be precise about when you're thinking aloud versus reading aloud, or just sharing, as in "The author started with, 'Once upon a time,' which reminds me of fairy tales that I have read and makes me think this will be a work of fiction."

- Explain how being metacognitive helps you comprehend, as in "My schema is helping me to make a prediction."

- Be clear that students will be expected to be metacognitive in the same way about their own work, as in "You got to hear what happens in my head while I read; now you will have an opportunity to listen to your own thinking and make your own connections as a reader."

Into the Classroom

Sounds Like: Thinking Aloud About Determining Importance

Caitlin Moore shows a word problem on the screen, then invites her students to join her. "Your job is to listen, to keep your thinking in your brain." She reads the problem once, slowly, then thinks aloud, "One thing I know is to reread. This time as I read, I am going to try determining importance, so I am going to get my highlighter." She reads again, more slowly this time, and highlights the numbers in the problem. "As a mathematician, I have learned that numbers are usually helpful," she narrates. "Now, I am going to ask myself, 'What am I trying to find out?'" She scans for the question. "Aha! I am trying to find out how much it will cost her for this year. I am going back to my toolbox. I am realizing I need to understand this idea of a year. I need to dip into my schema, and I know a year is 365 days . . . when I go back to determining importance, I realize I saw prices given by the month, so I see that I will have to convert. Turn and talk to a friend. What are some strategies I just talked myself through? How will you determine importance as a mathematician?"

As Caitlin sends learners out to work on their own parallel problem, she reminds them, "If the hammer doesn't work, use a screwdriver. If you are stuck, check your toolbox. What have you not used?"

REFLECTION

What do you notice about Caitlin's think-aloud? What transferable elements might you include in think-alouds of your own?

SPEAKING AND LISTENING

By developing a common language of thinking, we support learners in replicating and refining the complex process of coming to understand. Language acquisition expert Jeff Zwiers (2014) describes the importance of conversation for learners today: "The better students get at negotiating and explaining content ideas, the better they learn them. The better students get at communication, the better prepared they are for communicating in college, careers, and life."

We'll look more closely at productive classroom discourse in Chapter 6. For now, let us note that the thinking strategies provide scaffolds to support students in developing not only the internal dialogue of their own metacognition but also the academic language required to engage and express their ideas in a community of learners. We need to invite learners to speak often and much about their thinking, as well as to respond to the ideas of their peers. (See Figure 5.13 for the PEBC Teaching Framework for Speaking and Listening.)

Teacher Voice: Why Use Strategy Language?

"In the beginning, I was really shy about the language, and thought, 'This is like teaching young kids to say humongous dinosaur words and thinking that that makes them smart.' But soon I saw how these strategies become tools for learners to increase their thinking. Our conversations through strategies have widened, deepened, and enriched the learning tremendously."

—*Ana Mettler, primary teacher*

	First Steps	Next Steps	Advancing	Peak Performance
Speaking and Listening (also see Chapter 6, Discourse)	Invite conversations about thinking.	Provide explicit vocabulary instruction to amplify learners' use of thinking strategies and academic language.	As needed, provide sentence stems, protocols, and conversation structures to facilitate meaningful discourse about thinking.	Learners socially construct knowledge through purposeful and meaningful conversations.

Figure 5.13 Thinking Strategies: Speaking and Listening

How Does Thinking Sound?

Once we begin to fill learners' ears with our own thinking strategy language, they will naturally begin to incorporate similar speech patterns in their peer-to-peer conversation. Figure 5.14 includes some Invitations—questions you might ask—and Statements—stems you might invite learners to use—to articulate their thinking through the lens of a particular strategy. Take some time to digest this list: highlight the sentences and phrases that seem most natural to you, and add your own as well!

Thinking Strategy	Invitations	Statements
Draw on Background Knowledge (Schema)	"What does this remind you of?" "What might you connect this to?" "How does this link help you understand more deeply?" "Where would you file this information?" "How is this like . . . ?"	"This is just like . . ." "This reminds me of . . ." "A connection I made to this is . . ." "This matches the ideas/information in my brain's file folder . . ." "I know that . . ."
Ask Questions	"What are you wondering?" "What questions do you have?" "In what ways will those questions help you understand this?" "What are you curious about?"	"My question is . . ." "I'm wondering . . ." "How . . . what . . . why . . . when . . . who . . .?" "I wondered . . . and I found out . . ."
Infer	"What are you thinking?" "What do you think this author is really trying to say or ask?" "What conclusions can you draw?" "How does this thinking beyond the text help you make deeper meaning of your reading?"	"I'm thinking that . . ." "I predict . . ." "Even though the text doesn't say so, I think . . ." "I bet . . . I knew it . . ." "I am guessing that . . ."
Develop Sensory Images	"When you read that, what did you see/hear/smell/feel/taste?" "What words led you to that image?" "How does that image help you understand this?"	"In my mind, I can see/hear/smell/feel/taste . . ." "My image is . . ." "The movie in my head . . ." "The picture is on/off . . ." "Making a movie in my mind of my reading, I saw . . ."

Figure 5.14 Invitations and Statements for Classroom Discourse

Thinking Strategy	Invitations	Statements
Determine Importance	"So, what's essential here?" "Is that important to understand?" "What are the main ideas or messages?" "How does the author show us what they think is important?" "What does the author want us to do or learn?"	"I think this is really important . . ." "This is essential . . . This is extra . . ." "When I sort this out, these things seem to stick . . ." "I'll remember . . ." "I learned . . ." "The big ideas are . . ."
Synthesize	"Now what are you thinking?" "What's changed about your ideas or thinking?" "Tell about the quilt of your thinking." "How are you connecting all of these texts and experiences?"	"At first I thought . . . but now I'm thinking . . ." "Now I understand that . . ." "My thoughts have really changed . . ." "Like putting a puzzle together, the pieces of my thinking are . . ."
Monitor for Meaning	"What makes sense?" "What's confusing?" "Where are you 'clue-full'? 'Clueless'?" "What will you do now to restore meaning?" "So, what did you do to repair meaning?" "Now what are you going to do?" "Knowing that it doesn't make sense is only part of the work. "Now you have to fix it up to make better sense."	"I'm confused here" or "I'm clear here . . ." "I don't get it / I get it . . ." "This doesn't make sense." "I understand . . ." "I think I'll reread to make better sense . . ." "I'm going to slow down here . . ." "Wait a minute, I'm not making sense here . . . I'll try . . ."

Figure 5.14 *continued*

Into the Classroom

Sounds Like: Conferring About History and Thinking Strategies

"I used to think the Cold War was an actual thing that happened, like a war with fighting and battles, but now I understand it was just this time where everyone was building weapons," describes a high school student in World History class.

"So, you are changing your thinking?" his teacher asks.

"Yeah, my background knowledge was wrong, and I had to recycle it and build some new schema."

"What helped you do that?"

"The film and then reading the newspaper articles, also talking with my group."

"So, you are synthesizing based on a number of texts."

"Yeah."

"And what do you understand now?"

"What the Cold War really was. And, also, that the names of things in history—like the Boston Tea Party—can sometimes be misleading. You have to know what actually happened."

"You are building schema about this event but also learning about how history can be misunderstood. Beautiful synthesis."

DOCUMENTATION

In addition to talking, we benefit from holding our thinking, recording it in some form so we can remember, revisit, and reuse it as our understanding grows. Learners can record thinking in a wide variety of ways: in or on the text, on the board or a shared chart created with the class, on index cards, on sticky notes, on half sheets of paper, on graphic organizers, in notebooks, on class blogs. The format itself is not important per se, but rather the expectation: I know you are here having wonderful ideas, and I invite you to record them so we can share and discuss and build from yours and one another's. We support this expectation with explicit modeling. (See Figure 5.15 for the PEBC Teaching Framework for Documentation.)

	First Steps	Next Steps	Advancing	Peak Performance
Documentation	Provide structures for learners to document thinking. Post individual and group thinking in the classroom.	Model and invite learners to record thinking in multiple formats. Match method of holding thinking to the text or task.	Demonstrate how to reference and reapply "held" thinking. Create ongoing need and use for learners to access their recorded thinking.	Learners independently select appropriate structures to hold their thinking, and then use those intentionally.

Figure 5.15 Thinking Strategies: Documentation

Annotation

Effective annotation—with symbols, words, images, colors—is a scaffold to practicing thinking strategies. While asking questions, I might record my questions in margins; while determining importance, I might underline and circle key ideas; while inferring, I might jot my predictions at the end of every page. There is no wrong way to annotate—it is all about responding to the text while reading.

Remember those old overhead transparencies? Back in the day, I saw one teacher overlay a blank one on top of a text, write on the transparency, then take the text away to show what she had recorded. The idea was that the annotations themselves tell a story of the reader's comprehension. (See Figure 5.16 for a fifth-grade student's annotations on the Declaration of Independence.)

Graphic Organizers

Many teachers scaffold early work around thinking strategies with graphic organizers. These are distinct from worksheets—where there is one known right answer—and instead serve as frames to invite an array of thoughts and ideas. Many authors on thinking strategies (see Resources for Further Study box on page 126) have published lesson ideas and specific recording structures for you to peruse. Choose one that works for you, for your students, for the task and text. And yet recognize that the ultimate goal of thinking strategy instruction is to remove the scaffolds of graphic organizers and encourage learners to develop their own methods of recording and revisiting.

Matching Task and Text

How you decide which method of documentation to use depends ultimately on your purpose. Some questions you might ask yourself in making that decision:

- What systems and routines do learners already have or know for documentation? What else might they benefit from trying?

- How much do I expect them to record?

- How will this thinking be shared with peers? (Visually? Orally?)

- When will we revisit this thinking?

- How will this documentation be preserved?

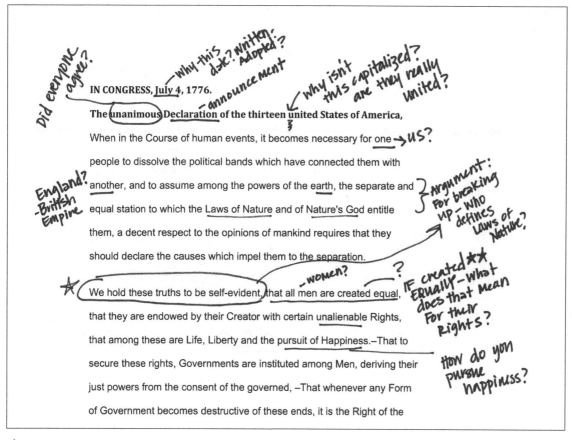

Figure 5.16 Annotations on the Declaration of Independence

Resources for Further Study

Lori Conrad, Missy Matthews, Patrick Allen, and Cheryl Zimmerman, *Put Thinking to the Test*

Stephanie Harvey and Anne Goudvis, *Strategies That Work*

Wendy Ward Hoffer, *Developing Literate Mathematicians*

Arthur Hyde, *Comprehending Math*

Arthur Hyde, *Comprehending Problem Solving*

Ellin Oliver Keene, *To Understand*

Ellin Oliver Keene and Susan Zimmermann, *Mosaic of Thought*

Ellin Oliver Keene et al., *Comprehension Going Forward*

Sue Kempton, *The Literate Kindergarten*

Debbie Miller, *Reading with Meaning*

Cris Tovani, *Do I Really Have to Teach Reading?*

Cris Tovani, *I Read It, but I Don't Get It*

Modeling Documentation

Learners need to document thinking before, during, and after engaging with a text or a group conversation. Holding thinking thoughtfully and thoroughly is a learned skill. As with any task, students benefit from seeing and discussing examples, elevating their own vision for how the work might look. Invite students to analyze work samples—either your own, their peers', or artifacts from another class—to discuss and arrive at shared descriptors of quality. With effort, learners can develop stamina for thoroughly recording their ideas.

REFLECTION

Researchers Lerch, Bilics, and Colley (2006) demonstrated that through reflection, learners develop higher-order thinking skills, an ability to analyze their own learning, and the self-awareness to become effective learners. In the case of thinking strategies, learners benefit from stopping and asking themselves, "How did this strategy help me to understand? How has my thinking changed? What do I know and wonder now?" This invitation to pause, step back, and think about the *what* and the *so what* helps students to lock in their learning.

Although metacognition asks us to think about what we are thinking, reflection invites us to ponder *how* that thinking is helping us to make meaning. Thinking strategies are not just about thinking for thinking's sake, but rather about focused, productive thinking that results in understanding. To this end, learners benefit from regular opportunities to reflect. (See Figure 5.17 for the PEBC Teaching Framework for Reflection.)

	First Steps	Next Steps	Advancing	Peak Performance
Reflection (also see Chapter 4, Workshop)	Model reflection about strategy use.	Structure reflection about how thinking strategies help learners understand.	Establish routines of self-monitoring that support learners' ongoing awareness of thinking strategies as tools for understanding.	Learners naturally consider, "How is this thinking helping me to understand?" and, "What strategies work best for me to independently create meaning?"

Figure 5.17 Thinking Strategies: Reflection

Purposeful Reflection

My PEBC colleagues Moker Klaus-Quinlan and Emily Quinty have identified key purposes for reflection: thinking about our thinking, and thinking about ourselves as learners. Figure 5.18 summarizes some of their clarity about purposes and strategies for reflection. Add your own.

Purpose	Outcome for Students	Prompts	Structures
Thinking About Our Thinking	• Be strategic as a reader, writer, thinker. • Be able to set purpose for yourself. • Build stamina. • Be able to "fix it" when meaning breaks down.	• What do you understand now? • What did you notice yourself doing as you read/solved? • How did you use ____ strategy to help you understand? • How did you revise your thinking? • How did you fix up misunderstandings?	• Annotating text • Completing graphic organizers • Responding in notebooks or on sticky notes • Exit tickets • Conversation • Whole-group sharing
Thinking About Ourselves as Learners	• Know yourself as a learner. • Be able to self-advocate. • Feel confident. • Be independent. • Courageously take risks. • Stay motivated and engaged.	• What works for you? • What are you learning about yourself as a learner? • How do you learn best? • How did you stretch yourself today? • How did you contribute to the understanding of your peers? • How could you improve your own stamina and engagement?	

Figure 5.18 Purposes for Reflection

Sounds Like: Reflection

As reading work time ends, Val Beckler calls her class to gather together at the front of the room. "Today's work was complicated to me. I was asking you to do something simple, find the author's purpose, but it led us down this whole road: How did the author do this? And then, how did that help you understand? Robert and I had an interesting conversation at the beginning, and we went to our understanding poster, which will grow all year long. We asked ourselves, 'What are the signs and signals for the way that we know we are understanding?' Do you remember some of the ways that we can mark it? I've got it, I understand, and I know that I understand because . . ."

A student chimes in, "When I understand, I can teach it, explain about it." Students use hand signals to acknowledge agreement.

"Another way?" Val invites.

"If you have a question about it, you can answer it."

"We don't have that on our chart yet. Can you write that on a sticky, and we'll put it up there?" Val requests. Then, "How else?"

"I know I understand when I don't have any more questions."

"You also know you understand if you feel it," Val explains. "Raise your hand if you felt what you read today in your book." Many hands shoot into the air.

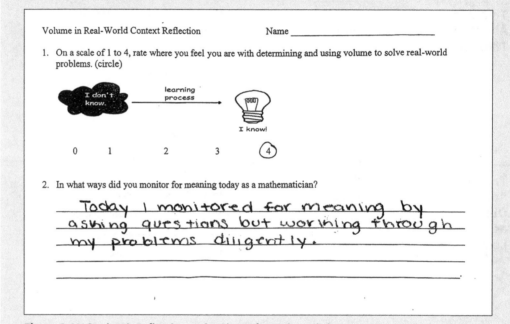

Figure 5.19 Student's Reflection at the Close of a Math Workshop

TALK BACK

When is reflection worth the time?

Thinking Strategies FAQs

- **"Which thinking strategy should I start with?"**

  Start with what makes sense to you. If you are naturally drawn to a strategy yourself, experiment with it in your own reading and studies until you can effectively narrate how it works to help you understand. Then, look for a topic in your students' learning where it can come to life, and introduce the strategy by describing your own experience.

- **"Do I teach them separately?"**

  The thinking strategies are interdependent and inseparable; you cannot quite infer without your background knowledge or synthesize without determining importance. Still, learners benefit from understanding them as distinct but overlapping, so you might try explaining them individually—like naming the rainbow's colors—then, invite learners to mix and match with the strategies they know to paint the full canvas of their understanding.

- **"How do I match the thinking strategy to the thinking of my content area?"**

  Look for authenticity. Ask yourself, is this what you really do to make sense of this content? Is this what professionals in the field actually do? If the answer is yes, then go for it. Geographers visualize and represent by making maps. Mathematicians determine importance as they read word problems. Athletes infer to decide their best position on the field. Readers draw on their background knowledge to understand stories. Go with what is true.

- **"Do I have to teach all seven of these thinking strategies?"**

  No! Any thinking strategy you teach learners is a gift. Select the one or ones that match most authentically with your content and best support learners' understanding, and see where that leads you. Middle school teacher Jessica Piwko, after striving for years to introduce a new thinking strategy with each unit, decided recently to just focus on monitoring for meaning, all year. What could eighth graders need more?

- **"Won't this take a lot of time away from our work?"**

  Thinking and understanding *is* the work of learners in school. Thinking strategy instruction supports students in doing so efficiently. Yet, we must go slow to go fast. In the early stages of understanding thinking strategies, students need examples and structures like graphic organizers and time to reflect to build metacognition. The goal is for them to internalize these tools, to apply the strategies automatically and independently as needed, yet building toward that goal requires time and intention.

Your Turn

As you step into exploring these strategies with students, start by noticing how they come to life for you as a thinker. Remember those moments. Tell learners stories of what you do to understand. In this way, we begin to make the invisible visible for students, effectively apprenticing them in the craft of making meaning.

THINKING STRATEGIES REFLECTION

• How does your current understanding of thinking strategies compare with your prior knowledge?

• What questions are still lingering?

• Which thinking strategies would you like to bring to life more in your work?

• What new ideas do you have for thinking strategy instruction?

• What will be different for students because of your learning from this chapter?

• How will success look?

REFLECTION ON CHAPTER QUESTION: IN WHAT WAYS MIGHT WE PROVIDE TOOLS THAT INCREASE LEARNERS' AGENCY AND UNDERSTANDING?

Invitation: Write a script of a future conversation you envision having with a student about their use of thinking strategies and how these tools helped them to understand.

6 DISCOURSE

ANTICIPATION QUESTIONS

• What are the benefits of student discourse?

• How do we prepare learners for productive conversations?

• What conditions foster meaningful discourse?

Leader Voice: Discourse Is Key

"The new focus on discourse, to me, was the biggest difference. Students learned that it's OK to talk, first of all, and secondly, that it actually assists with learning and thinking. The discourse was so important because kids got to be experts, explain to their partners, 'Here's what I did, what it looks like. Tell me about your work.' They were talking that whole time.

In planning, teachers ask, 'So, when I want kids to do this, what questions can I ask?' rather than leading with a low-level question that doesn't get to understanding."

—HANS BARBER

Talking to Learn in the Real World

It was time to get a new car. I don't know a lot about cars, nor am I too interested in them generally, so I knew I needed help deciding what to buy. My goal was a new, economical vehicle to take me to work and around town, nothing fancy, but reliable and with great fuel efficiency. I started to ask around, just telling people I knew or met what I needed to find.

Most everyone, I found, had an opinion. "You don't want a new car; they lose their value as soon as you drive them off the lot."

"You definitely want an electric vehicle. They are far easier on the environment."

"Straight electric cars don't have enough range. You want a plug-in hybrid."

To each opinion, I asked questions, probed for explanations, argued back at times.

I visited a few dealerships, and they had their opinions as well. Finally, I sat down with my dad, who knows a lot about cars and wants what is best for me. I told him what I needed, and

what I had learned and asked his advice. He had been doing some research of his own ever since I had started shopping and had some ideas, but he started with some clarifying questions: "So, you want something fuel efficient? And you only need five seats, not seven at this point? And you are thinking new?"

He had been listening intently, so my answers were all yes. We went out together to test-drive two cars he recommended, and on the way home, we had a chat, discussing which we liked, and why.

Through all of these conversations, I learned from others, grew my thinking, gained understanding, tested my ideas, and came to a decision. Collaborative conversations helped me to get smarter.

REFLECTION: TALKING TO LEARN IN THE REAL WORLD

Tell the story of a time when you learned through conversation. What happened? What supported your understanding?

What: Discourse

Discourse is engaged, academic conversation in pursuit of meaning. It is not necessarily debate, though it might be. It is not a contest, and it is not a waste of time. Discourse is devoting learning time to sharing ideas, growing thinking, and evolving understanding. Discourse builds agency because learners get to hear and reflect on the power of their own ideas and to deepen their understanding in light of the thinking of others. What richer fodder for democracy?

And yet traditional school norms have shuttered learners' mouths. Still today, we find classrooms where teacher voices dominate the airwaves, or the conversation reflects the initiate, response, evaluation (IRE) format, in which the teacher poses a question, allows a student to respond, and then evaluates that response. Maps of conversations like this will show the teacher at the hub of the wheel, each student at the end of a spoke, reliant on the stance and permission of the teacher to mediate the conversation. Yet, to promote effective discourse, we must get out of the center of that wheel, and take the wise stance of math teacher Steven Reinhart (2000) to "Never Say Anything a Kid Can Say." Author Marty Nystrand (1997) invites us to use talk to *create*, rather than assess, understanding, an approach that raises student achievement and encourages higher-level thinking.

Classroom discourse is our opportunity to teach, model, and practice the skills of engaged, academic conversation. Speaking and listening need to be taught across the content areas. For example, according to the Common Core, our high school learners are expected to:

- Initiate and participate effectively in a range of collaborative discussions (one-on-one, in groups, and teacher-led) with diverse partners on grades 9–10 topics, texts, and issues, building on others' ideas and expressing their own clearly and persuasively. (CCSS.ELA-LITERACY.SL.9-10.1)

- Present information, findings, and supporting evidence clearly, concisely, and logically such that listeners can follow the line of reasoning and the organization, development, substance, and style are appropriate to purpose, audience, and task. (CCSS.ELA-LITERACY.SL.9-10.4)

- Adapt speech to a variety of contexts and tasks, demonstrating command of formal English when indicated or appropriate. (CCSS.ELA-LITERACY.SL.9-10.6)

In preparation for these, fourth graders are invited to:

- Engage effectively in a range of collaborative discussions (one-on-one, in groups, and teacher-led) with diverse partners on grade 4 topics and texts, building on others' ideas and expressing their own clearly. (CCSS.ELA-LITERACY.SL.4.1)

- Report on a topic or text, tell a story, or recount an experience in an organized manner, using appropriate facts and relevant, descriptive details to support main ideas or themes; speak clearly at an understandable pace. (CCSS.ELA-LITERACY.SL.4.4)

- Differentiate between contexts that call for formal English (e.g., presenting ideas) and situations where informal discourse is appropriate (e.g., small-group discussion); use formal English when appropriate to task and situation. (CCSS.ELA-LITERACY.SL.4.6)

Teacher Voice: Why Discourse?

"The purpose of including reading, writing, and talking in every single workshop is so that they then can have that opportunity to converse, they can practice getting their thinking out, constructing their thoughts critically, questioning their perspectives, and then reading to get smarter, and then writing to either support an argument and a stance, or to find meaning in what it is that they are thinking and go beyond what they may have started thinking at the beginning of class."

—*Alisa Wills-Keely, high school teacher*

Speaking and listening skills are integral to learning at every level, in all content areas, and so time devoted to developing learners' capacity for high-quality discourse will certainly support their lifelong success.

Why Discourse?

A recent study of the eighth- and ninth-grade English classes found that students averaged fifty seconds a day of dialogue (Nystrand 2012). Fast-forward to college, and professors now walk in to find young adults hunched in silence over their own devices, unaware of their peers just inches from their elbows.

Yet, research points to the high value of discourse in promoting language development, academic understanding, and lifelong success. We must prioritize instruction for and experience with academic conversations within our daily instruction. Hattie (2009) found classroom discussion led to significant gains in student achievement. Authors Douglas Fisher, Nancy Frey, and Carol Rothenberg (2008), in their book *Content-Area Conversations*, explain the importance of classroom talk: "Put simply, talk, or oracy, is the foundation of literacy. This should not come as a surprise to anyone. We have all observed that young children listen and speak well before they can read or write. Children learn to manipulate their environment with spoken words well before they learn to do so with written words. It seems that this pattern is developmental in nature and that our brains are wired for language. Young children learn that language is power and that they can use words to express their needs, wants, and desires." They go on to describe how much of classroom talk is of the call-and-response variety, with teachers checking for understanding rather than asking learners to delve deeply into a discussion of the sort we are seeking.

A recent Stanford study found that students of lower socioeconomic status enter kindergarten two years behind their affluent peers in some measures of language development. Researcher Anne Fernald explained, "For lots of reasons, there is generally less supportive talk to children in families living in poverty, which could partially explain the differences we found in children's early processing skill and vocabulary learning" (quoted in Carey 2013).

Evidence from the National Assessment of Educational Progress demonstrates the powerful impact of regular discussion; simply put, the more frequently learners discussed their reading material, the higher their test scores (U.S. Department of Education, Institute of Education Sciences 2013). (See Figure 6.1 and Figure 6.2.)

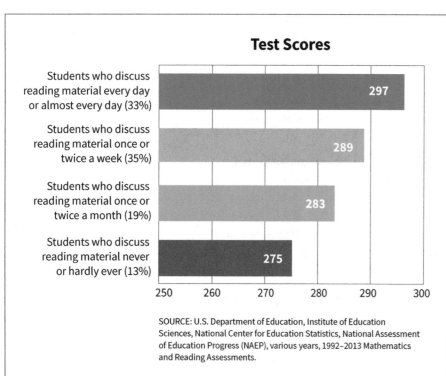

SOURCE: U.S. Department of Education, Institute of Education Sciences, National Center for Education Statistics, National Assessment of Education Progress (NAEP), various years, 1992–2013 Mathematics and Reading Assessments.

Figure 6.1 The Effect of Discussing Reading

PHENOMENAL TEACHING

Discourse Is . . .	Discourse Is Not . . .	Your Thinking . . .
Logical discussion	Emotional debate	
Open-ended	Pursuit of a singular correct answer	
Student driven	Teacher directed	
Engaging	A spectator sport	
Collaborative	Scripted	

Figure 6.2 Clarification Corner

REFLECTION ON RESEARCH

• What is the value of discourse?

• What is the relationship between discourse, agency, and understanding?

• What does or might discourse look like in your classroom?

"Why bother with student-driven discussions? Here's my first answer: Talking matters for learning. Although it's possible to think without talking—and to talk without much thinking— each can strengthen the other. Talking also provides windows into what students are learning. I want schools to be places of rich learning, and therefore I want them to be places of rich talk. Here's my second answer: Deep down in my 'why I'm an educator' bones, I believe that dialogue matters for democracy and for making the world a better place. Thinking, speaking, and listening are practices of freedom. Schools should help students learn to exercise that freedom, for their own good and for the collective good. And here's my third answer: It's fun. Some of my happiest, most rewarding moments as an educator have been hearing what comes out of learners' mouths when I get out of the way. Learning, freedom, and fun seem like a potent combination. So why are teachers still doing most of the talking in the classroom? And even when students are talking, why are they so often doing more talking than learning?"

—*Elizabeth A. City (2014)*

First-Grade Discourse

Susan McIver gathers her first graders on the rug at the close of readers' workshop. "Today, we were doing a lot of reading, thinking, and working to understand the books in front of us. Malia, will you share what you did today as a reader and a thinker?"

Malia reads her page of writing aloud. "Butterflies are nice. Butterflies start like caterpillars. A butterfly lays eggs under a leaf. Most of the time butterflies come in spring or summer. Butterflies use antennae to find their way."

Learners around the circle raise their hands.

Susan calls on Patricia, who says, "At home, for my birthday, I got a butterfly thing, and my mom ordered caterpillars, and we think that at night they eat because they get this wide, and we bet they will turn into butterflies."

Susan then calls on Charlie, who adds, "I like looking for bugs, but one day my cat brought in a moth caterpillar that will turn into a moth. That got roasted in the sun by accident. I have another one. I have that one alive. I checked under the rocks where they normally hide, and I had a wood spider as a pet, and I also had a centipede, but I had to release both of them."

"Thank you Malia, Patricia, and Charlie. We have a lot of experience with insects! Malia, you got us all thinking when you shared from your reading about butterflies. Thank you!"

What do you notice about this discussion? About Susan's role in the conversation? What do you wonder?

How: The Elements of Discourse

When we see learners immersed in a conversation about a learning target, listening to and responding to peers' ideas, and seeking intently to make meaning for themselves, we can be certain we are witnessing the wonder of discourse. As with most magical moments in teaching, discourse at this level does not happen by accident. Effective classroom talk is the result of intential preparation, thoughtful scaffolding, and targeted facilitation. Here are six elements we find to be alive and well in all discourse:

- learning
- structure
- expectations
- access
- language development
- facilitation.

LEARNING

I met a special education teacher who shared a story about a boy with autism who had not spoken a word all year. Then one day she gave the group a uniquely challenging math problem. This boy figured it out before all his peers; everyone saw his solution and believed that it was correct, but no one quite understood how he had gotten there. They begged him to explain, and sure enough he did. In great detail. For about ten minutes. This teacher was amazed. This experience taught her how giving learners something challenging and interesting to explore can evoke language production from even the most reluctant.

If we invite learners to discuss low-level questions, seek definitions, and verify known answers, there will be little to say, and soon their focus will drift. Instead, to invite rigorous dialogue in our classrooms, we must offer students something juicy to talk about, a struggle for insight and meaning. Our discourse requires a focus, a purpose, a quest for understanding that will motivate and engage participants to grapple in earnest with the conversation. We can support their grappling through the questions we ask. (See Figure 6.3 for the PEBC Teaching Framework for Learning.)

	First Steps	Next Steps	Advancing	Peak Performance
Learning (also see Chapter 2, Plan)	Focus discussions around making meaning of standards-based content.	Present important concepts, challenges, or paradoxes that invite rigorous thinking and conversation.	Use discussion to build enduring understanding of complex ideas. Structure opportunities for learners to provide and discuss claims, evidence, and reasoning.	Learners capitalize on the perspectives of their peers to explore depth and complexity and make meaning as experts in the discipline.

Figure 6.3 Discourse: Learning

Struggle

We can ask ourselves, "What invitation will unsettle and challenge learners in such a way that their conversation will be rich and meaningful?" Sometimes these opportunities present themselves naturally: when eighth-grade teacher Jessica Piwko found her whole group mired in confusion about how to apply the Pythagorean theorem in a real-world context, she invited them to engage in an impromptu turn-and-talk: "Talk to your partner about how you find the hypotenuse of a right triangle." The air was electric as learners' confusion was at last allayed. That's a quick example of just-in-time discourse, which can flow from an authentic opportunity.

At other times, we need to plan ahead for a rich, deep discussion. In any content-area study, the true grapple is the fertile ground for discourse. When seeking to scaffold rich conversation, find the crux, the moral dilemma, the paradox, the puzzle. Figure 6.4 shows a few ideas; add yours.

Topic	Discourse-Worthy Challenge
Environmental challenges	What progress is worth what price?
Genetics	Are we all created equal?
World War I	How does the past predict the future?
Shakespeare	What is worth dying for?
Galileo	What is the role of geniuses?
Space exploration	What is the value of discovery?

Figure 6.4 Discourse-Worthy Challenges

Look back to Chapter 2 on planning for more ideas about generative topics worthy of discussion.

Deep Questions

The nature of the question(s) posed will have a bearing on the richness of the conversation. Although literacy experts caution us against the oft-promoted sequence of working from surface-level to deeper-thinking questions lest we languish too long in the shallows, we can provide learners with a range of prompts to foster fruitful dialogue. Consider the possibilities of employing the thinking strategies (Chapter 5) as tools to pose evocative questions, such as those in Figure 6.5. Annotate this list—highlight those that might feel authentic to your content and purpose; add your own thinking.

Thinking Strategy–Informed Questions

Monitoring for Meaning

- What makes sense?
- What's confusing?
- What are we being asked to do?
- Is our answer reasonable?

Background Knowledge

- What does this remind us of?
- How do our connections help us understand more deeply?
- Is this an example of a larger phenomenon that we have seen before?

Inferring

- Based on . . . what do we think will happen next?
- Based on . . . what do we think is going on?
- Based on our data, what might we conclude?

Determining Importance

- What is the main idea/purpose/theme of this text?
- What is this problem asking us to solve? How do we know?
- What patterns do we notice across the "text"?
- What's worth remembering? Why?

Creating Sensory Images

- In our minds, what do we see, feel, smell, taste?
- What's the movie in your mind?
- What might we draw/map out to represent this information to help build understanding?
- In what ways might we model or represent this situation?

Asking Questions

- What are we wondering?
- What do we need to know in order to solve?
- What is the most efficient way to solve?
- In what ways will our questions help us understand this?

Synthesizing

- What do we understand now?
- How has our thinking changed?
- What new ideas emerged based on key themes/ideas/data from the text set?
- What patterns do we see?

Figure 6.5 Questions to Foster Discourse Based on Thinking Strategies

STRUCTURE

Discourse, large or small, short or long, takes time and space. We serve learners best when we intentionally plan by providing protocols or structures that will ensure focus, progress, and accountability. (See Figure 6.6 for the PEBC Teaching Framework for Structure.)

	First Steps	Next Steps	Advancing	Peak Performance
Structure	Plan time for discussion.	Create time for learners to independently generate ideas and questions before or during discussion. Use a variety of discussion formats regularly.	Invite partners and small groups to construct meaning before engaging in whole-class discussions. Purposefully select protocols, thinking routines, and linguistic frames to guide group conversation and promote participation by all.	Learners take ownership of the structure and content of engaged, academic conversations in service of understanding.

Figure 6.6 Discourse: Structure

Teacher Voice: Thinking Strategies and Discourse

"I think that the thinking strategies have been giving students a way to express their amazing thinking. We have known all along that kids are brilliant philosophers at heart, but it is not always easy for kids to articulate their deep thinking. Often in the past, we have been stuck with short answers and then moving on to the next 'What are you thinking?' The thinking strategies, the discourse they have ignited, allow students to have the vocabulary to express how they connect text and life experiences and insights. How they connect—by way of inference, schema, or in other ways—creates a network of thought. As well, it helps individual students who would be saying, 'This makes me think of that. I am inferring, or I am synthesizing...'"

—*Ana Mettler, primary teacher*

Purpose

We need to be clear with learners about the purpose of our discourse: What are we trying to accomplish? The possibilities are plentiful. We can engage in discourse to:

- build oral language fluency
- prioritize values
- craft a proposal
- develop relationships
- solve a problem
- find the most efficient method
- hone an argument
- respond to a news story
- take a moral stance
- prove a theory
- develop a position
- debunk a statement
- critique a solution
- understand a question
- create a vision . . .

Preparation

In preparing for discourse, even brief conversations, students benefit from time to gather their thoughts, as well as from formats to hold their thinking. Research on think time suggests that when participants are afforded ample time to ponder, their responses will be more thoughtful and in-depth. Consider the following means to help learners prepare for conversations:

- Provide silent think time: "Take thirty seconds to think about whether you agree or disagree with Beth's prediction and why."

- Offer a choice of questions to consider: "You can choose to explain your thinking on the first poem or your response to the second one. Those who want to discuss the first will meet on this side of the room, and those interested in the second will gather and find partners on the other side."

- Model phrases about a parallel topic: "For example, if I were going to argue that we should have recess before lunch, I might say, 'Everyone wants to play first and eat later . . .'"

- Provide written sentence stems: "Based on . . . I infer . . ."

- Invite students to nonlinguistically represent ideas through a sketch, diagram, or model.

- Use a sequence of preparatory steps, such as

  » think, write, talk

  » draw, talk, write, talk

  » read, talk, write, talk

  » read, draw, talk

Sentence Stems for Discourse

What to say when we *disagree*:

- "Then again, we shouldn't forget . . ."
- "I see things differently based on . . ."
- "That is a valid point, but I think . . ."
- "I understand what you're saying. Have you thought about . . . ?"

What to say when we want to *affirm* others' ideas:

- "My idea is related to _____'s idea . . ."
- "I really liked _____'s idea about . . ."
- "What _____ said resonates with me . . ."
- "You made a great point about . . ."
- "I hadn't thought about that . . ."
- "My idea builds on _____'s idea . . ."
- "I'd like to piggyback off that idea . . ."

What to say when we express *cause and effect*:

- "I think . . . was caused by . . . because . . ."
- "The main cause was probably . . . because . . ."
- "I think . . . led to . . . which led to . . ."
- "The effects of . . . were . . . which is evidenced by . . ."

What to say when we want *clarification*:

- "Can you elaborate on that?"
- "In other words, are you saying . . . ?"
- "I have a question about . . ."
- "I'm not quite clear about . . ."
- "Can you explain . . . ?"
- "Do you mean that . . . ?"
- "Can you clarify _____ for me?"

What to say when we *connect* learning to other subjects:

- "This reminds me of (subject) when we were doing . . ."
- "We also learned about . . . in (subject). Remember when we . . . ?"
- "There was a strategy we used in (subject) when we were . . . That might help us think about . . ."
- "This reading strategy works for both (subject) and (subject) because . . ."
- "This is similar to what we do in (subject) when we . . . because . . ."

TALK BACK

What is your experience scaffolding discourse? What else might you try?

Into the Classroom

Making Meaning Through Discourse

Fifth-grade teacher Tami Thompson starts her science workshop about photosynthesis by inviting learners to gather their background knowledge about the sun and its role in the food chain. Before opening the conversation to the group, she poses a few questions and offers students time to record their thinking. After this silent work time on the rug, she calls students together.

"Let's do some sharing," Tami begins. "Ashley, why is the sun important?"

"It gives us light and heat."

"If you hear something from another scientist that you agree with but have not recorded, make sure you jot it down on the bottom of your paper," Tami prompts.

"And we need plants," Ashley continues.

"What has that got to do with the sun?" Tami asks.

"The sun fuels the plants."

"Then the plants will grow and give us oxygen," Vikram chimes in.

Ashley clarifies, "If the sun didn't give the plants energy, there wouldn't be anything to eat."

"The sun gives the plant light, and it also needs water and photosynthesis and gets the carbon dioxide and the oxygen it needs to breathe," Thomas shares.

"What do you understand about what Thomas is saying, Brie?"

"The sun is helping the plants. We wouldn't have oxygen without the sun."

Tami just looks at Brie, waiting. Nelson decides to help out. "Adding on to what Brie said, the sun drives the whole process. Plants take in the oxygen, the water, and the sunlight and make the food. Food for themselves and food for us."

Tami waits some more. Students look around expectantly. After a moment, she instructs, "Turn and tell your shoulder partner what you understand now about the sun's role in the food chain." Students quickly spin and chat animatedly for a couple of minutes, then come back to the whole group at Tami's signal. "So, what do we know?" she asks the group.

"We need the sun to eat."

"It starts this whole food chain, that we benefit from."

"Plants turn sunlight into food."

"We can't live without plants, and they can't live without us."

"Plants can't live without the sun. No one can."

Tami pauses there. "Let's go back to our notes. What else might you add, after hearing your colleagues' thinking?"

Protocols

Igniting great conversation is an art. Some learners are ready to dive in and discuss in rich, meaningful ways, but most benefit from structures and protocols designed to surface ideas, equalize voices, and create fertile ground for thinking. When selecting a discourse protocol, we consider:

- Groupings—what size will work best, from pairs to whole class?

- Timing—will this discussion happen in a few minutes or span the length of a week or more?

- Content—what structures will most successfully support the grapple for understanding?

There are many protocols available that span the range of complexity, purpose, and topics. Figures 6.7 and 6.8 show a few favorites to get you started. Make notes about which appeal to you. As you begin experimenting with a new format, remember that even with a routine, learners need modeling, scaffolding, and repetition to develop discourse skills.

Structure	Purpose	Ideal Application	Sounds Like
Turn and Talk	Articulating understanding	Brief conversations synthesizing learning	"Pair up and tell your shoulder partner what you understand now about similes and metaphors."
Trios	Brainstorming, discussion	Short discussion where multiple perspectives shed light on complexity	"What if the earth's magnetic poles were reversed? Form a trio with two people not at your table."
Kinesthetic Voting	Justifying thinking	Finding common ground, deepening understanding	"Of capitalism, communism, and monarchy, which is the best form of government? If you think it's capitalism, go to the front of the room; communism to the side door; monarchy to the middle. Once there, find a partner and discuss. You must choose one form of government and move to that part of the room."

Figure 6.7 Quick Discourse Moves

Sources for Discussion Protocols

EL Education: Classroom Protocols: https://curriculum.eleducation.org/sites /default/files/curriculumtools_classroom protocols_053017.pdf

National School Reform Faculty: https://nsrfharmony.org/protocols/

School Reform Initiative: https://www.schoolreforminitiative.org

Teaching and Learning Lab at Harvard Graduate School of Education: https://www.gse.harvard .edu/sites/default/files/Protocols_Handout.pdf

Visible Thinking Routines: http://www .visiblethinkingpz.org/VisibleThinking_html_files /03_ThinkingRoutines/03c_CoreRoutines.html

That was just enough to get you started. For more ideas on discourse structures, check out the Sources for Discussion Protocols box.

TALK BACK

Which protocols have you experienced as a learner? As a teacher? Which do you feel inspired to refine or try?

Structure	Purpose	Set Up	Process
Partner Gallery Walk: view and respond to the work of peers	Analysis, comparison	Post photos, text, or student work on a shared task on the walls throughout the room.	Invite classmates to travel quietly with a partner, as though visiting an art gallery, quietly discussing the exhibits, possibly leaving notes behind.
Wagon Wheels: learners speak in quick sequence to a series of partners	Generating thinking	Gather in concentric circles, the inside circle facing out, the outside facing in, so that each student has a partner.	Pose a question for pairs to discuss. After a minute or so of talk with this partner, spin one of the wheels ("Outside circle, move two partners to the left"), and either invite them to continue the conversation or to explore a new question.
Carousel Discussion: small groups gather around an artifact to discuss	Interpreting	Prepare for each table a different "text" requiring response: a problem to solve, a piece of student work to examine, a reading, an infographic.	Give groups time to read, discuss, then respond in writing to the text (either on a poster, sticky notes, or a smaller piece of paper). Then rotate and invite learners to respond to the artifact and comments at the next table, and so forth.
Fishbowl: half the group listens as peers discuss	Analysis, critique	Arrange half of the group (the "fish") into a circle for discussion; invite the other half to gather on the periphery (the "bowl"). Pose a generative topic for discussion.	Outside circle students need a purpose for listening. They might attend to the content, the discussion process, the group dynamics—and be invited later to give feedback before changing roles and moving to the inner circle. Questions might include "What did you notice about the conversation?" "What did the speakers share?" "What did they do well?" "What could they have done better?" and "What will you try when you have your next discussion?"

Figure 6.8 Deep Discourse Structures

EXPECTATIONS

Close reading of the Common Core Standards for Speaking and Listening describe skills for high school discussions that all students can practice in age-appropriate ways:

- Come to discussions prepared.
- Work with peers to set agreements for collegial discussions.
- Propel conversations by posing and responding to questions.
- Reply thoughtfully to diverse perspectives, summarize points of agreement and disagreement, and, when warranted, qualify or justify their own views and understanding.

We cultivate effective discourse when we invest the time to teach necessary skills and develop productive agreements about the nature of our conversations, regardless of the structures we are employing. We need to explain, post, and model these skills and agreements, and students need to practice and reflect on them. (See Figure 6.9 for the PEBC Teaching Framework for Expectations.)

	First Steps	Next Steps	Advancing	Peak Performance
Expectations	Invite discussion. Expect learners to deepen understanding through conversation.	Cocreate and post agreements that describe participation in discourse. Uphold agreements. Asks learners to reflect during or after discussion on both content and process.	Model effective speaking, active listening, pausing, probing, and paraphrasing. Model and practice accountable talk.	Learners invest in the success of each discussion and hold peers accountable for upholding norms of productive discourse.

Figure 6.9 Discourse: Expectations

Discussion Skills

To engage effectively in classroom discourse, students need to develop and practice a known set of skills that will serve them throughout their relational lives. We need to provide clarity on how each looks and sounds, then to offer models, scaffolds, ongoing practice, and reflection. You might take them one at a time with your students, providing a minilesson on each over the course of a few weeks, circling back to provide additional modeling as needed. See how the discourse flourishes as a result.

Figure 6.10 lists some starting places for teaching discussion skills. What might you add?

Into the Classroom

Sounds Like: High School Discourse

High school social studies teacher Ryan McKillop leverages the power of thinking strategies to get learners talking. This day, their target is to utilize questioning and background knowledge to infer the impact of agriculture on current-day people and countries.

She starts by modeling her own thinking about a graph, drawing inferences about overcrowding in cities based on her background knowledge and the data given. Soon, she hands students graphs of their own and invites them to ask their own questions, draw their own inferences.

As table groups get started, Ryan invites, "You have six minutes to create as many questions as you can to push your thinking." Students lean in, shuffle through the range of data sets in the middles of their tables, spill out, and record questions: Is this worldwide? Will the percentage of child labor increase or decrease in the future? Is the problem getting worse or better? How can 21 billion chickens lay only 7 billion eggs? How often are the 7 billion eggs laid? Which agricultural industry is most valuable? Has demand for vegetables decreased? How has new technology affected agriculture? Who are the major importers and exporters?

After some time to pose questions as a group, share those out to the class, and highlight key queries, Ryan directs the groups to their task for the balance of work time:

Discussion Skill	Looks Like	Sounds Like
Thoughtfully prepare.	Read and think about materials.	
Maintain eye contact and physical rapport.	Look at the speaker. Turn body toward speaker.	Keep hands, mouth, and body quiet when another is speaking.
Practice respectful, patient listening.	Nod and keep your body calm.	"Hmm." "Mm-hmm."
Question to deepen understanding.	Raise a hand or provide another signal that you have a question.	"I wonder . . ." "Why do you think . . ."
Paraphrase to clarify ideas.		"So, the main idea is . . ." "You are confident that . . ."
Pause to allow for think time.	Keep mouth closed, eyes open, thinking.	Quiet.
Support statements with evidence.		"For example . . ." "I agree because . . ."

Figure 6.10 Discussion Skills

create a mind map of how agriculture impacts economy, culture, politics, and the environment. "Now is the time to infer."

Let's listen in as students get to work. "It says here that 50 percent of chickens are in Asia."

"Maybe Asia is where they catch the most fish. Southeast Asia is on the Pacific. Cattle probably come mostly from the U.S. or Latin or South America . . ."

"Agriculture is all around the world," a student clarifies.

"What was that place we talked about yesterday that transformed all small farms into one giant farm?"

"Deforestation."

"That is happening in developing countries, but what about the U.S.?"

The conversations continue table to table as learners explore thinking about issues of income disparity, child labor, environmental impacts, and animal rights.

After a hearty segment of work time, Ryan calls for students' attention and checks in about their experiences with this process. "What's the difference between collaboration and group work?"

"Collaboration is like bouncing ideas off each other and taking in feedback; group work is like everyone is contributing."

Ryan affirms, "I'm seeing some great collaboration, like over here, talking about the cost of water. When Lucy stated that the cost of water would increase, what did everyone do?"

"We made connections."

"Yes, instead of just letting her write that, they started making more connections while she was writing. Keep up that great work."

Students dive back in.

Accountable Talk

Lauren Resnick, Sarah Michaels, and M. C. O'Connor (2010) described effective discourse as accountable in three ways: to the community, to the content, and to rigorous thinking. Our conversations are accountable to the learning community when we listen attentively, build on or probe for deeper understanding of peers' ideas, and disagree respectfully. We demonstrate accountability to content when we cite facts, evidence, and examples and refer to texts and prompt peers to do the same. Accountability to rigorous thinking involves explaining reasoning, justifying claims with evidence, and respectfully challenging or strengthening the arguments of others. (See Figure 6.11.)

The Learning Community	Knowledge	Rigorous Thinking
• "Can you please repeat that?" • "Can you help me understand?" • "So, are you saying . . . ?" • "I would like to add on to ___'s thinking . . ." • "I respectfully disagree because . . ." • "Take your time."	• "I looked up ___ and learned ___." • "On page ___, the author says . . ." • "Can you show me where you found that?" • "What evidence do you have?"	• "Based on my evidence (cite), I believe . . ." • "So one example might be . . ." • "Why do you think so?" • "Where is your evidence?" • "Could that be interpreted in a different way?"

Figure 6.11 Phrases That Demonstrate Accountability to the Community, to the Content, and to Rigorous Thinking

Forging Agreements

• What are the attributes of an effective conversation?

• What do you need in order to feel heard?

• How can we show with our bodies that we are ready for conversation or discussion?

• How can our comments draw forth the thinking of peers?

Discuss these questions with your students. Their answers can form the foundation for shared agreements about classroom discourse. Although there are many lists of discussion norms available online and in books, developing these agreements collaboratively will ensure student ownership of establishing and upholding the norms.

TALK BACK

What agreements support *you* as a discussant? What are the implications for your work?

ACCESS

In her important book *Quiet,* author Susan Cain (2012) articulates the role of silence in supporting collaboration and the value of teaching introverts to participate in discourse. Not all of our students love to talk. And yet, to support their academic and lifelong success, we owe learners our unanxious expectation: they *will* speak in this class. Still, some students will be more vocal than others. In what ways might we equalize opportunities to speak? (See Figure 6.12 for the PEBC Teaching Framework for Access.)

	First Steps	Next Steps	Advancing	Peak Performance
Access	Welcome all learners to share thinking orally. Balance quiet think time, teacher talk, and learner talk.	Encourage peer-to-peer conversation and feedback. Intentionally integrate strategies to equalize voices.	Encourage all learners to participate in and listen to discussions. Maintain mutual respect by providing feedback on appropriate tone or comments.	Learners lead respectful, learning-focused discussions that include multiple perspectives.

Figure 6.12 Discourse: Access

Accessible Talk

There are many reasons learners might not feel ready to talk: fear of failure, limited language skills, cultural norms, low confidence, shyness, and more. And yet allowing enthusiastic speakers to dominate the airwaves robs the reluctant ones of much-needed opportunities to practice their oral language skills. We can prompt all learners to use their voices when we initially set the bar low: ask a straightforward question, "What is your favorite ice cream?" Allow oral rehearsal with partners through a pair and share before asking anyone to speak aloud before the whole group. Cue less willing learners ahead of time so they have opportunities to prepare with confidence, as in "When we come back together as a group, I would like to ask you to share your thinking, so please be ready."

We grow learners' confidence to speak in class when we:

* Respond positively to all speakers, honoring their ideas and saluting their courage, as in "Thank you, Adam, for bravely sharing your thinking this morning."

* Call on everyone, not just those with hands raised or bright ideas. You might try any system of drawing cards or popsicle sticks, use an app, or just keep track of who has and has not spoken yet today or this week.

* Demonstrate that you value the thinking of every learner by creating regular invitations for each to speak and have their voice heard. Frequently invite discourse.

* Model and expect wait time, and hold off energetic speakers to allow time for classmates to gather their thoughts and join in.

Protocols That Invite Participation

There are several conversation structures intentionally designed to increase engagement, grow learners' confidence, and bring in all voices. Figure 6.13 lists a couple to play with.

Structure	Purpose	Set Up	Process
Numbered Heads Together (small-group discussions followed by whole-group share-out)	Increase accountability and participation in discussion.	In small groups, learners each choose a number, say 1–4.	Provide a conversation topic to all groups. After a few minutes of discussion, call on a random number, say 2, to share out to the whole group on behalf of their group. Then, dive in with another topic or question and repeat.
Give One—Get One (paired conversations followed by whole-group share-out; ideal for replacing whole-group brainstorming)	Engage all learners and elevate less confident speakers.	Ask students to each number a piece of paper 1–10. Pose an accessible topic appropriate for brainstorming. Invite learners to put four of their own ideas next to numbers 1–4 and to leave the rest open.	Invite learners to get up, mingle, match with partners, and exchange ideas to gather six more to fill up their list. Students should record the name of who offered each idea. After learners have completed their lists, begin a whole-group share by asking a speaker to tell an idea someone else shared with them, to name the contributor, and then to call on that contributor to share an idea from someone else and so forth. Record.

Figure 6.13 Protocols That Support Participation

Wait Time

Wait time—the space between the end of a question or comment and beginning of the next—typically averages about one second. Yet researchers observing and timing classroom interactions found that even minor expansions of wait time—from one second to three—can significantly increase students' thoughtfulness and participation. Mary Budd Rowe's (1986) meta-analysis of the impact of wait time found that as a result of an increase in wait time:

- The length of student responses increases 300 to 700 percent.
- More student inferences are supported by evidence.
- Student questioning increases.
- Student-to-student exchanges increase.
- The variety of students participating increases.
- Student confidence increases.
- Failures to respond ("I don't know") decrease.
- Achievement improves.

All this with a couple of seconds of additional wait time. How do we do it?

1. Teach learners to be at ease with silence. It's OK to stop and think.

2. After posing a question or inviting comments, take a long, deep breath and count to three—or five or ten—silently in your head before calling on anyone to share.

3. If a lot of learners are ready to speak, shift from whole-group discussion to turn-and-talk so they each get air time.

> "What if silence means that people are thinking, not that they are waiting for you to rescue them? And so what if they are waiting for you to rescue them? Try keeping yourself out of the discussion by avoiding eye contact, taking notes, mapping the conversation, doodling, or counting to ten. If you must jump in, try asking a question instead of making a statement. And if you have a deep suspicion that people aren't thinking during the silence, try asking why it's so quiet."
>
> —*Elizabeth A. City (2014)*

TALK BACK

What is your experience with wait time? What do you think would happen if you increased it? Try it, and reflect on what happens.

LANGUAGE DEVELOPMENT

Some students—often those living in poverty, those who struggle with reading, some culturally and linguistically diverse learners, and English learners—have significantly smaller English vocabularies than their peers. By age three, Hart and Risley (1995, 2003) estimate, some less advantaged students have heard thirty million fewer words than their more advantaged peers. For this reason, these researchers predict, these students' vocabularies upon entry to kindergarten are, on average, half the size of those of their more advantaged counterparts; closing this gap is a huge task. When we attend intentionally to the language demands of the conversations we are striving to foster, we provide valuable language development opportunities. (See Figure 6.14 for the PEBC Teaching Framework for Language Development.)

	First Steps	Next Steps	Advancing	Peak Performance
Language Development	Expose learners to rich metacognitive and academic language.	Provide scaffolds for understanding disciplinary vocabulary, figurative language, and academic language.	Create authentic opportunities for learners to practice academic language and exercise social capital in conversation.	Learners use academic language with increasing sophistication as they participate in classroom discussions.

Figure 6.14 Discourse: Language Development

Provide Vocabulary Supports

As described in Chapter 2, language development can be at the heart of every unit design. When engaged in discourse, students benefit from additional cues to enhance and incorporate their academic language. To this end, we might:

- Post vocabulary cues and clues in the classroom.
- Review essential terms before a deep dive into discourse.
- Invite learners to keep graphic organizers with vocabulary terms in hand during discussion.
- Pair learners with limited English proficiency with peers who can translate as needed.
- Pause as necessary to clarify terms or provide just-in-time vocabulary instruction.
- Model language use.

And, as learners are speaking, we can relinquish the impulse to correct, lest we hush their confidence. "When ELLs [English language learners] are engaged in academic discussion, privilege communication over precision of language. Overcorrection or too much attention to grammatically correct language can hinder ELLs' language production and interrupt the flow of ideas. During a discussion, we want our ELLs to approximate correct and sophisticated language, not perfect it," describes Nicole Knight (2014) in her synthesis of research on supporting English learners. Bottom line: let the students talk.

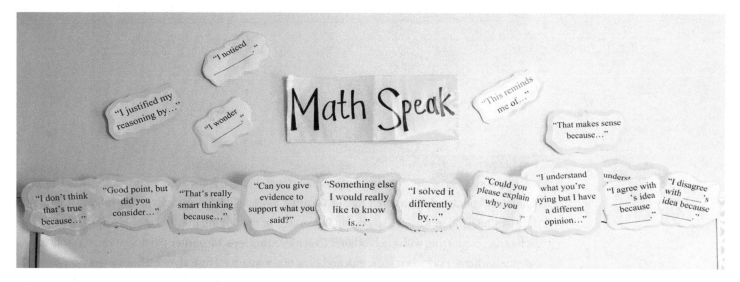

Offer Sentence Stems and Conversation Frames

As in writing, sentence stems or other prompts can help us get started sharing ideas aloud. There are a number of lists of questions and prompts already provided in this chapter. Feel welcome to grab one of them or to develop those that work best for you. Some teachers create a generic set of question and sentence frames to prompt discourse, post them in the room, tape them to the tables, glue them into journals, project them on the screen, or distribute them as traveling table tents to prompt conversation.

Sometimes a task or routine lends itself to a specific sort of discourse, which necessitates its own prompts. Ashley Bromstrup and her third graders developed their own protocol for their morning warm-up discussions, in student-led small groups, shown in Figure 6.15.

Student Leader Questions

1. Can someone read the grapple problem?
2. What are the unfamiliar or important words?
3. I need a volunteer to show their representation and explain how they solved the problem.
4. Did anyone make a mistake that they want to share?
5. Please put your journals to sleep for the calendar.

Figure 6.15 Student-Led Math Warm-Up Discussion Protocol

What regular discourse routines do you or might you incorporate? If you were to create a protocol with simple steps for student leaders to follow, what might they be?

FACILITATION

Key to the success of any discourse experience, long or short, is the stance and behavior of the facilitator. Middle school teacher Rachel Gardner asserts, "The person doing the talking is doing the learning. Students need to be doing 90 percent of the talking in the classroom, questioning each other, conferring with each other." To achieve this level of learner participation, our role is essential: what we say when we speak and how often we insert ourselves influence the flow of conversation and the agency learners experience as speakers and thinkers. We can model discourse behaviors intentionally and consistently so learners can repeatedly observe and hear what it means to engage in respectful, academic conversation. Soon students will mimic our modeling, and, with time and practice, we will have a room full of sophisticated negotiators ready to speak and listen in accountable ways. (See Figure 6.16 for the PEBC Teaching Framework for Facilitation.)

	First Steps	Next Steps	Advancing	Peak Performance
Facilitation	Listen. Facilitate learning-focused discussions.	Ask compelling questions. Model invitational language, clarifying questions, effective argument, and respectful disagreement. Monitor and document learners' talk.	Invite learners in conversation to ask questions, synthesize, test concepts and hypotheses, formulate conjectures, construct explanations, challenge reasoning, argue, and draw conclusions. Invite learners' metacognition about the evolution of their own understanding through discourse.	Learners provoke and challenge peers' thinking, and invite and welcome differing views, as well as share their own evolving perspectives.

Figure 6.16 Discourse: Facilitation

Ask

To get learners talking, we need to ask for their thoughts with open-ended, invitational questions. We can probe for deeper thinking when responses are scant. Here are some to try:

- "What do you think?"
- "Turn and talk to your partner about . . ."
- "Who would like to explain . . .?"
- "Can someone repeat what the previous person just said in your own words?"
- "Do you agree or disagree and why?"
- "Would someone like to add on?"
- "Show what you mean."
- "Say more about that."
- "How do you know?"

We can also answer questions with questions; ask instead of telling. In general, when we say less, learners say more. By leading conversations in this way, we model for learners the ways in which they can consistently invite the thinking of others.

Listen

"Attention is the rarest and purest form of generosity," said Simone Weil (1982). If we want someone to speak, we need to listen. If we want them to say more, we need to listen more deeply, ask curious questions, ply for deeper understanding. When we model listening—intentional, curious, probing listening—for learners in the contexts of conferring conversations, whole-group discussions, and everything in between, we demonstrate the value we place on listening, model listening skills, and prompt learners to incorporate these strategies into their own conversations. "Teaching," said Deborah Meier (2002), "is listening. Learning is talking."

TALK BACK

What is difficult about listening in schools? How might you overcome these challenges?

Resources for Further Study

Courtney Cazden, *Classroom Discourse: The Language of Teaching and Learning*

Suzanne Chapin, Catherine O'Connor, and Nancy Canavan Anderson: *Classroom Discussions: Using Math Talk to Help Students Learn*

Douglas Fisher, Nancy Frey, and Carol Rothenberg, *Content-Area Conversations: How to Plan Discussion-Based Lessons for Diverse Language Learners*

Michael S. Hale and Elizabeth A. City: *The Teacher's Guide to Leading Student-Centered Discussions: Talking About Texts in the Classroom*

Ilana Seidel Horn, *Motivated*

Martin Nystrand, *Opening Dialogue: Understanding the Dynamics of Language and Learning in the English Classroom*

Ron Ritchhart, Mark Church, and Karin Morrison, *Making Thinking Visible*

Jeff Zwiers, *Academic Conversations: Classroom Talk That Fosters Critical Thinking*

Invitational Language

We can lower affective filters and motivate creative thought by incorporating invitational language: using inclusive pronouns, plurals, and conditionals. For example, we might ask, "What are some of the ways we might introduce an argument?" rather than "How are you going to introduce your argument?" Consider the nuance of each phrase. Inclusivity: the first sentence poses that *we* are going to work on this together, teacher included, and the second suggests that *you*, the learner, are on your own to figure it out. Plurals: the first sentence asks for *some of the ways*, indicating that there are many plausible correct approaches, and the second sentence just asks *how*. Conditionals: *might* poses an air of possibility, a curiosity about options, suggesting we don't actually have to launch the argument in the first way you mention, but I am open to hearing any and all ideas, rather than locking you into a "guess what's in my head" teacher quiz game. This is invitational language: inviting all of us to consider the breadth of possibilities in a safe, nonjudgmental setting.

Sounds Like: Erika Schenk's AP Biology Discussion

Erika Schenk invites her students to engage in a fishbowl discussion about the influence of technology on human evolution. They have all read shared texts around this issue, as well as pursued independent research on various aspects of the topic. Before the discussion gets started, Erika reminds students of their roles in the fishbowl. "Outer circle, write down the most interesting things they say or what you wish they would have said. Inner circle, watch that you are participating, using evidence, talking in a way that shows you understand." With that, she retires to her stool at the side of the group and lets the teens dive into their conversation. A slide shows the statement, "Technology is increasing the frequency of disadvantageous traits."

Aliya begins, "What do you guys define as technology? We think of high-tech things like complex surgeries, but when I started doing research I realized tech can be way more simplistic. My article talked about when we started walking upright, the way we gave birth started to change. Humans started participating in childbirth. I don't know if you'd include technology as having humans help each other give birth . . ." She continues a bit further.

Keisha responds, "I think the pelvis changing is evolution, not technology. What I would define as technology is our use of tools and diet, which has put humans into an adaptive niche. In all environments, we can use simple tools, like for cooking, so we can adapt. We are not necessarily victims of the circumstances of our environments. Fires and small rock tools allowed us to avoid adapting to our environments." Roman adds to this, explaining what he had learned about how diets changed due to technology.

"In relation to that, how do you think that has changed our genetic frequency of disadvantageous traits?" Keisha asks. Roman responds by drawing on a previous conversation, referring to something another classmate said. The conversation continues as students share points from their own research and question each other respectfully, ranging through topics from lactose intolerance to gut bacteria to farsightedness.

"We start to see a problem when our technology is not keeping up with our disadvantageous traits, like antibiotic resistance, an increase in C-sections. Our bodies are dependent on technology. Is the technology causing the change, or are we evolving disadvantageous traits because of it?" Cole asks.

"What is the difference?" Keisha asks.

"Are we shaping technology or is technology shaping us?" Aliya elevates the question. Their teacher had said not a word throughout this entire thoughtful conversation.

Discourse FAQs

- **"What if my students won't talk?"**

  Start small. Be patient. Give them an easy topic at first, and just one partner with whom to share. Raise the bar slowly, with more difficult topics, a shift into trios. Then, add some accountability, as in "So, what did you and your group explore?" Celebrate each and every contribution. Keep modeling and practicing.

- **"What if they all want to talk at once?"**

  If learners are alive with ideas, that is a good time to shift into duos so everyone can get their thinking out and their voices heard. You might also invite learners to stop talking and do some writing when the enthusiasm brims. Turn taking and listening require practice—narrate their benefits, model, and notice and name successes.

- **"But I don't have time for this—there is too much content to cover."**

  Talking takes time. Thinking takes time. If we want learners to understand deeply, we need to devote the time. Discourse can be quick, mixed throughout a range of learning experiences. When it comes to a deep dive into discussion, choosing a generative topic helps learners really uncover important content in meaningful ways. Their engagement will propel their understanding.

Your Turn

Given all that you know and have learned about discourse, including its great potential to advance learners' agency and achievement, what do you feel inspired to try? Take a few moments to gather your thinking about each of the elements of discourse described in this chapter as you consider your next moves.

- **Learning**

- **Structure**

- **Expectations**

- **Access**

- **Language Development**

- **Facilitation**

DISCOURSE REFLECTION

- How does your current understanding of discourse compare to your prior knowledge?

- What questions are still lingering?

- Which aspects of discourse feel most natural to you?

- What new ideas for discourse might you incorporate into your work? How?

- What difference will those changes make for students?

- How will you know you have succeeded?

REFLECTION ON CHAPTER QUESTION: IN WHAT WAYS MIGHT WE SCAFFOLD PRODUCTIVE, ENGAGED ACADEMIC CONVERSATIONS?

Invitation: Consider one new element of discourse to incorporate. Share your inner dialogue: script a conversation between your instructional coach-self and your teacher-self about how you will play this out.

7 ASSESSMENT

CHAPTER QUESTION: IN WHAT WAYS MIGHT WE MONITOR AND SUPPORT PROGRESS?

ANTICIPATION QUESTIONS

• How do you know what learners know?

• What do you gather as evidence of understanding?

• In what ways do you promote learners' agency through assessment?

Tracking Progress in the Real World

After I had ankle surgery to replace three ligaments, I spent six weeks with my left foot locked down in "the boot." When it came time to start physical therapy, that calf was half the size of my right, and the quadriceps was weak with disuse. I could not balance on that leg, and could not walk far, and my ankle joint was stiff, only moving a few degrees in each direction. My goal was to get back to normal. My physical therapist asked me, "What is normal?" I described being able to walk, hike, jump, run, and go about all my regular activities without a second thought. "We will get there," he assured.

But I had to work at it: I visited him every week, and each time he asked me to stand on one leg, squat bending my stiff ankle, practice balancing on the wobbly board, and more, then sent me home with exercises to practice. As I practiced my lunges and squats, I observed that I was able to move my knee incrementally closer to the floor. When I timed myself balancing on the repaired ankle, I was able to notice the number of seconds I could manage increase. When I chased a Frisbee with my kids, I realized that I was taking alternating steps on each leg, an ordinary gait, rather than gimping along with a double hop on the good leg. I saw progress. It took a long time, but seeing the results of my efforts sustained my dedication. I wanted to improve, believed it was possible, and knew what I needed to do to continue progressing, and so I put in the required time and energy. The ongoing feedback of my own body changing motivated me to continue to work, as the guidance of my physical therapist helped me to target and pace my efforts.

REFLECTION: TRACKING PROGRESS IN THE REAL WORLD

Tell the story of a time when you tracked your own growth toward a target. What data did you gather? How did that data support your progress? What did you learn?

What: Assessment

Assessment is the process of measuring or evaluating progress toward goals. Testing can provide valuable data, but it's not the whole story. Tests do not tell us how we got here or what we might do next to continue our growth. So, authentic assessment *for* learning involves much more: ongoing, multifaceted progress monitoring by both teachers and learners to track movement toward goals. Assessment expert Richard Stiggins (2007) describes assessment for learning as an interactive and supportive process that welcomes students to understand how to chart their own course to success:

Assessment for learning begins when teachers share achievement targets with students, presenting those expectations in student-friendly language accompanied by examples of exemplary student work. Then, frequent self-assessments provide students (and teachers) with continual access to descriptive feedback in amounts they can manage effectively without being overwhelmed. Thus, students can chart their trajectory toward the transparent achievement targets their teachers have established. The students' role is to strive to understand what success looks like, to use feedback from each assessment to discover where they are now in relation to where they want to be, and to determine how to do better the next time. As students become increasingly proficient, they learn to generate their own descriptive feedback and set goals for what comes next on their journey. Teachers and students are partners in the assessment for learning process.

This focus on assessment for learning invites us to incorporate both formative and summative assessments. Summative assessments at the end of learning experiences give us data on learners' mastery that can inform future planning, but won't necessarily help us or our students address misconceptions. Formative assessments, on the other hand, provide in-the-moment feedback about progress and allow us to adjust instruction accordingly. Formative assessment has great potential to foster ownership of learning targets, responsibility for individual progress, and targeted effort.

Assessment is comprised of feedback loops linked into a cycle of teaching, learning, and demonstrating understanding. Before we introduce new content, strategies, or skills, assessment informs us of students' present knowledge and readiness, which guides us as we make plans for instruction. During the learning process, assessment serves as a thermometer measuring learners' understanding; it informs decision making about pacing, grouping, and so on. Throughout, as well as after, the learning process, good assessment measures a student's understanding and ability to apply newly acquired information, strategies, and skills in novel contexts.

Assessment is ongoing: it can include conferring conversations and exit tickets (see Chapter 4, "Workshop"), tracking of learners' participation in discussions (see Chapter 6, "Discourse"), and examination of written work on traditional tests and quizzes, online or on paper. Tools for assessment might include checklists, rubrics, rating scales, or narrative evaluation.

Assessment is best conducted in the light of day, shared openly, and discussed frequently. Learners need to know what's expected, where they stand, and how to improve. When scores and feedback are kept secret or saved until the end, they do us little good; when instead they are shared early and often, learners gain motivation and direction for growth.

Why Assessment?

As education expert John Hattie (2009) cautioned, "We should not make the mistake . . . of thinking that because students look engaged and appear to be putting forth effort they are necessarily achieving; this is one of the myths that is held in too many classrooms—busy work in classrooms does not make the difference." We need data to know that our own and our learners' efforts are producing results. To do that, we want our students to be assessment-capable learners.

Assessment-capable learners are learners who know the learning intentions and success criteria of a given experience and are ready to explain what they are learning, why they are learning it, and how they will know they have succeeded. Most importantly, they are confident they can learn, and are strategic in working hard toward their own goals. They are active, involved, and engaged in their learning and see mistakes as opportunities for growth. When we focus on developing assessment-capable learners, our whole narrative about what assessment is and why and how we use data shifts: it becomes less about the teacher rating and evaluating anyone and more about the stories the learners are telling themselves about their own progress.

Authors Fisher and Frey (2011) explain further about the importance of student involvement in assessment:

> When students do not understand the purpose of a lesson, they are unlikely to demonstrate their best effort. Without a clear purpose, students are not motivated and do not see the relevance of the content they're expected to master. When students are not assessed or do not receive assessment results (feedback), they are unsure about their performance and assume they are doing just fine. They are unlikely to make mid-course corrections in their learning processes and understanding.

REFLECTION ON RESEARCH

• What is the value of assessment?

• What is the role of learners in the assessment process?

Into the Classroom

Fourth-Grade Teacher Jamie Salterelli Confers

As every student in the class leans silently into their own independent reading, Jamie hunkers down next to one student, notebook in hand, and begins a whispered conversation. "Let me know when you get to a good stopping point. . . ." Jamie waits. When Lilah looks up, she inquires, "How are you today?"

"Good."

"Good. What are you reading these days?"

"Monday, I wasn't having fun reading the book I was reading, so I changed my mind. Now I am reading *Sisters*."

"Is this the first time you have read *Sisters*?"

"Yes."

"What are you thinking?"

"I kind of like it, but it has a lot of heat in it. The sisters are not getting along. They are always annoyed with each other. Kind of like a full house. But I really like it how, when the pages turn yellow, that is a flashback. And when the pages are normal, white, that means it's now."

"How were you able to determine that?"

"When I first started the book, it was when she was older, and then it goes to when the sisters are younger, and they are getting named and being babies."

"Wow! So, clearly you are doing lots of thinking. I hear that you are having to infer a lot. I am really intrigued with how you are determining how this text is structured. Nowhere in the text did it say, 'I am going to give you a flashback,' but you were able to use the visual clues and put those together to understand how the text is structured with flashbacks and present tense. Why do you think the author structured the book in this way?"

"I don't know. But I notice that the person who is writing the book is writing about herself as a kid, because the author's name is Rowena, and the character's name is Rowena."

"Can I ask you something else?"

"Yeah."

"If we are not sure why the author might have put the book together this way, how does understanding that this is written as flashbacks help you understand the story?"

"That's making me think. I understand that the author really likes to draw, so that is why she wrote it in the way of a comic book. The first page you open, there are pictures, which leads me to infer that she likes to draw a lot. Because I wouldn't write a comic book if I didn't like to draw."

"I am wondering if that's a question you can ponder over the remainder of this book: How does knowing that this moves between flashbacks and present tense, how is that helping you understand?"

"Understand what?"

"The story."

"The flashbacks helped me understand what was happening when she was younger because when I first looked at the book, she was talking about now, but when I look at the yellow pages, I see her as a younger kid, and it tells me the story of why she might not like her sister and brother so much. He's always crying in the middle of the night when she is trying to sleep."

"You just said a powerful thing—you are understanding when they are younger. Perhaps by understanding the characters' past . . ."

"I understand why she doesn't like her siblings anymore."

"Do you think all narratives or stories are structured like this?"

"No. This is the first book I ever read that uses yellow pages to signal that this is a flashback."

"If you feel like it's appropriate, I want to push your thinking: ponder that idea of structure. How did the author set up the narrative? Why? If she chose to put it in flashbacks, why? Or, why not? Does that feel like it would push your thinking?"

"Yeah."

"I will leave you to do that. You have given me a lot to ponder too. But first, how did this conversation help you today?"

"It helped me think about what I am reading. Before you came to talk with me, I was just reading for my own pleasure, but now I am thinking about my own questions. It made me curious about the structure."

REFLECTION

What might you infer about Jamie as a teacher and Lilah as a learner based on this conversation? In what ways is Lilah assessment capable?

How: The Elements of Assessment

Effective assessment is intimately interwoven with instruction, as is the inhalation and exhalation of a breath. As teachers, we constantly monitor, gather data, and refine our words and actions in response to learners' needs. At times, this is done quite formally with summative assessments and major project rubrics, and yet, as we saw from Jamie and Lilah's previous conversation, assessment can also wend its way through our conversations when we offer hints of awareness, ask questions that spark insight, or respond thoughtfully to learners' thinking.

There are five elements of assessment that can be refined to enhance learning for all:

- self-monitoring
- assessment design
- data collection
- data use
- feedback.

SELF-MONITORING

Supporting learners to monitor their own progress opens the door to both agency and understanding. John Hattie's research demonstrates that increasing learners' awareness of and ability to reflect on where they stand yields strong positive results: student self-reporting of grades has a very high impact, and student self-evaluation also strongly influences student achievement (2009). Self-assessment can take many forms—a moment to ponder, a conversation, a written reflection, a student-completed rubric, a formal write-up, among others. The main idea is that we convey to learners, "This learning is your responsibility. You need to pay attention to and know where you stand." We remind students to take charge of growing their own understanding, rather than allow them to passively wait for us adults to sleuth out and fill gaps or address misconceptions.

To support learner self-monitoring, we are transparent about our purpose(s), provide appropriate tools and trackers in learner-friendly language, and create opportunities for students to use them as reflection tools. (See Figure 7.1 for the PEBC Teaching Framework for Self-Monitoring.)

TALK BACK

In what ways do you or might you provide clarity of your expectations and invite learners to self-assess along the way?

	First Steps	Next Steps	Advancing	Peak Performance
Self-Monitoring	Communicate purpose for learning.	Provide success criteria for major tasks. Invite learners to self-assess.	Coconstruct descriptors of quality. Structure learners' regular self-assessment of progress toward learning goals and success criteria.	Learners set goals, self-assess, and reflect on their growing understanding.

Figure 7.1 Assessment: Self-Monitoring

Transparency

As discussed in Chapter 2, "Plan," we need to know and let our students know the learning purpose(s) of each task. This can include explaining what will be assessed and how. If there are criteria or rubrics, we can provide them up front. And if there is going to be a test, assessment experts advise us to write or revisit the test before we teach the unit to be clear in our own minds of what we are pursuing as we embark. When we and our learners know why we are doing what we are doing, when we are clear about our intentions, we set everyone up for success.

Into the Classroom

Sounds Like: Transparency

Let's listen in on eighth-grade math teacher Jessica Piwko.

Before students enter class, Jessica has already recorded the day's content objective (CO) and language objective (LO) on the whiteboard on one side of her classroom:

> **CO:** I understand and can differentiate between proportional, decreasing proportional, inverse variation, and exponential functions in real-world contexts.
>
> **LO:** I will monitor for meaning as I construct an argument to justify the chosen function.

Jessica knows that posting these objectives is not enough: she needs students to interact with the information. After leading a discussion to make sure students know the meaning of the words in the objectives, she says, "Now your job is to paraphrase this: What are we doing today?" Students offer their partners their own interpretations of the targets. Jessica then uses names drawn from a jar to call on a few students to share their and their partners' thinking to the whole group.

"We need to know different kinds of functions."

"We are going to make arguments."

"And the word *differentiate*," Jessica asks the group, "what does that mean? Tell your partner."

In this brief two-minute interaction, Jessica handily sets the tone for the lesson, providing learners time and opportunity to engage with and grapple to understand their purpose this day.

Middle school teacher Jenn Brauner takes time to communicate expectations to learners in written form as they embark on a writing project. Rather than keeping success criteria secret, she provides a handout identifying specific learning targets for the piece, as well as a clear statement of the assignment process. Figure 7.2 is one example from her classroom.

How much responsibility do we have to understand and address the human impacts of the digital revolution?

- **How does the digital revolution impact humans (socially, physically, cognitively, mentally)?**
- **Should we do anything about some of these impacts?**

Success Criteria for Your Essay

I can employ the whole writing process of plan, draft, get feedback, revise, publish to engage and inform my audience.

I can clearly present my perspective about a complex topic to **inform and engage** my audience.
- I can articulate the arguments of the topic and the one I support.
- I can explain why I support this argument.
- I can embed evidence and expertise to explain the issue and my position.
  - I can embed quotes to correctly help the flow of my piece.
  - I can cite my source correctly to credit the original thinker.
- I can share a narrative, analogies, or other writer's tricks that help my reader to care.
- I can use words, phrases, and clauses that create cohesion and clarity between the parts of my writing.
- I can capitalize, punctuate, and organize my writing to help my reader make sense of my writing.

Your final essay at a minimum should be five paragraphs, demonstrate quality work on the above learning targets, and be completed on time.

Figure 7.2 Jenn Brauner's Sample Success Criteria for an Essay

Rubrics and Trackers

Written trackers can be useful in communicating success criteria to students and can also invite learners to be agents in their own progress monitoring; they might be used for specific tasks or for unitlong or yearlong targets. Figures 7.3 and 7.4 are two examples of self-assessment, self-report tools. Figure 7.3 was designed by elementary teachers for promoting sophistication of learners' engineering project designs across the year and used as a project guide for a variety of tasks in their STEM lab. Figure 7.4 is the first page of a tracker developed by high school math teacher Tracey Shaw; she distributes a packet like this to her students at the start of each unit and asks them throughout to pause and monitor their own progress toward the learning targets, including notes and evidence in the space provided.

	1	2	3	4
		All of 1, plus . . .	All of 2, plus . . .	All of 3, plus . . .
I can ask questions and define a problem.	I have a question.	My question is testable.	My question invites me to solve a problem with engineering.	My question explores new topics in engineering.
I can research a problem to gain background knowledge.	I gather information about my topic.	I use reliable sources for my research.	I use internet and print sources. I cite my sources.	I synthesize my research into a written overview of the topic.
I can create a plan to address my problem.	I have a plan.	My plan is written legibly, includes materials list and design sketch.	My plan includes details of materials needed, dimensions of my project, and a timeline for design work.	My plan is so specific and precise that anyone could follow it.
I can create a prototype/model.	I build a model.	My model follows my plan.	I use my time efficiently. I use my materials wisely.	I use unique materials purposefully.
I can test my project, collect, analyze, and interpret my data.	I test my project.	I document each test in an organized table.	I analyze my test data.	I draw conclusions from my data to help me revise my project.

Figure 7.3 Engineering Design Rubric

Unit 3A Topics: Exponential Functions ~ Structures and Modeling

Name: _____

Guiding Questions
- How can patterns help us solve problems?
- How does it grow? (Linearly, exponentially, geometrically, arithmetically, etc.)

Big Ideas
- Structure allows us to recognize how a function will behave (grow, translate, etc.), giving us greater efficiency and accuracy as a mathematician. [CCSS A.CED.2]
- We can explore patterns in sequences to determine whether the relationship is changing by a common difference (arithmetic/linear), common factor (geometric/exponential), or neither to write equations, graph, or predict additional values.
- Real-world situations can be modeled with linear, quadratic, or exponential functions. This allows us to analyze them to better understand, make accurate predictions, and justify our conclusions. [CCSS S.ID.7]
- Systems of equations allow us to compare two or more related quantities to describe, interpret, and make conclusions about the situation. [CCSS A.REI.5, 6, 10, 12]

Vocabulary
Arithmetic sequence and common difference
Geometric sequence and common ratio
Horizontal asymptote ($y = \#$)
Additive vs. multiplicative pattern
Base and exponent
Rate of change (slope vs. growth factor)
Translations: vertical and horizontal shift

Self-Scores: **4** = Expert [10]; **3** = I get it [8]; **2** = I kind of get it [6]; **1** = I'm lost [4]

Learning Target #	Learning Target	Debriefing: Synthesize your thinking around the learning target. (Include examples, pictures, things to remember, steps, etc.)	Self-Scores/Results
3A.1	**Structure of exponential functions:** I can analyze the structure of an exponential function: $y = a \cdot b^x + k$ and state key features about how it behaves [i.e., $f(x) = 5 \cdot 2^x + 1$, base is 2 (growth factor), 5 is the start value, vertical shift up 1, etc.].		
3A.2	**Graphing exponential functions:** I can graph an exponential function.		
3A.9	**Properties of exponents:** I can use the properties of exponents to simplify and evaluate expressions.		

Figure 7.4 Tracey Shaw's First Page of a Unit Self-Tracker

REFLECTION

• What do the two tools in Figure 7.3 and Figure 7.4 have in common? How do they differ?

• What new ideas do you have for conveying your expectations for learning to your students?

ASSESSMENT DESIGN

What will understanding look and sound like? This is the question I ask myself whenever I develop a learning experience. Assessment design is integral to unit and lesson planning. Grant Wiggins (2002), coauthor of *Understanding by Design*, cautions us against the twin sins of coverage-based and activity-based teaching, and describes the importance of assessment design in our intentional planning:

> We call it backward design. Instead of jumping to the activities—"Oh, I could have kids do this, oh, that'd be cool"—you say, "Well, wait a minute." Before you decide exactly what you're going to do with them, if you achieve your objective, what does it look like? What's the evidence that they got it? What's the evidence that they can now do it, whatever the 'it' is? So you have to think about how it's going to end up, what it's going to look like. And then that ripples back into your design, what activities will get you there. What teaching moves will get you there?

In my early years of teaching, Wiggins and McTighe's (2005) approach to backward design got me away from doing a bunch of stuff about, say, plants, and helped me to identify what it was that I really wanted my students to comprehend, and then focus my efforts in that direction. Many standards documents have progressed from a list of topics to a collection of performance assessments, providing models of what we can target in our work; for example, the Common Core State Standards for Literacy ask that third-grade readers "describe characters in a story (e.g., their traits, motivations, or feelings) and explain how their actions contribute to the sequence of events" (National Governors Association 2010). With these targets in mind, we can consider the building blocks toward those ends and create checkpoints along the way, in the form of formative assessments.

When we have in mind what understanding looks and sounds like, we can carefully craft formative assessments as well as rich tasks that allow learners to exhibit progress toward targets as they engage with those tasks. (See Figure 7.5 for the PEBC Teaching Framework for Assessment Design.)

	First Steps	Next Steps	Advancing	Peak Performance
Assessment Design	Plan informal and formal assessments of process and content goals.	Integrate multiple forms of assessment, including performance assessments. Plan backward from a summative assessment aligned with objectives and standards before teaching the unit.	Provide authentic, engaging, and purposeful opportunities for learners to demonstrate understanding. Plan to observe for specific learner behaviors that demonstrate understanding.	Learners exhibit progress toward mastery of standards in multiple meaningful ways.

Figure 7.5 Assessment: Assessment Design

Formative Assessment Strategies

Formative assessment gives us and our students data about where they individually or collectively stand, and is placed before, within, or between learning experiences or more formal assessment tasks. A good formative assessment task is also a learning experience in and of itself!

Formative assessment can be done individually or in small or large groups. When we invite students to complete formative assessment tasks independently, we gain understanding of what each grasps and can record alone. When students work in groups, we create opportunities for shared construction of knowledge but gain less insight on what any individual student knows and can do.

Figure 7.6 lists some formats and ideas for formative assessment—kinesthetic, written, visual, aural, and graphic. The reflection invitations at the end of each chapter in this book present more examples of formative assessment tasks. As you consider these ideas, add your thinking in the right-hand column: Have you tried this? If yes, how did it go? If no, how and when might you use this strategy? How might you adjust it? What else might you add to this list of ideas?

	How?	Example	Notes
Kinesthetic			
Fist of Five	Using zero to five fingers, learners rate their readiness or comprehension.	"Show me on the fingers of one hand how ready you feel to get started independently."	
Magnets	After preparing each learner's name on a magnet on a board, invite students to move their magnet in response to a question.	"How ready do you feel for the quiz on Friday? Put your magnet in the appropriate box: totally, kind of, not at all."	
Thermometers	Using the width of the room as a thermometer, invite learners to position themselves between two parallel walls to represent their level of understanding.	"If this wall is zero and this wall is one hundred, where would you stand to rate how confident you are with inferring an author's purpose?"	
Thumbs Up/ Sideways/ Down	Silently, learners self-assess with thumbs pointed up for confirmation of understanding, thumbs pointed sideways to indicate a partial understanding, and thumbs down for next to no understanding. Thumbs can also point anywhere in between.	"With your thumb, rate your understanding of how to write an argument."	
Written			
Concept Map	Welcome learners to create visual maps of how unit vocabulary and concepts interrelate.	"Show the relationship between the following terms: *democracy, election, candidate, voting, electoral college, constituent . . .*"	
Exit Ticket	At the end of a learning experience, ask learners to demonstrate understanding by solving a problem, answering a question, or relaying their grasp of the concept.	"Who is your favorite character so far in this text and why?" (See Figure 7.7.)	
Essential Question (see Chapter 2, Plan)	Invite students to lean out from learning activities and respond to the essential question of the unit at intervals.	"Take a few minutes to revisit our essential question, 'How do scientists make accurate predictions?' What do you know now?"	

Figure 7.6 Formative Assessment Palooza

	How?	Example	Notes
Written			
Survey	Online or on paper, gather data from learners about how they perceive their own progress.	"What is the most interesting thing we have learned so far about China? What are you still wondering? What would you like to explore more deeply?"	
Visual			
Draw Content	Students create maps, diagrams, cartoons, pictures, or other representations of the main ideas.	"Draw and label a bee's interaction with a flower." (See Figures 7.8 and 7.9.)	
Emojis	Learners choose from an array of emojis and select the one that best represents how they feel about their learning, and they describe why.	"Which emoji best represents your experience as a problem solver today?"	
Tableau	In partners or small groups, students create a human sculpture representing the concept or characters of study.	"With your group, create a freeze-frame image to demonstrate how Atticus Finch feels about social justice in *To Kill a Mockingbird*."	
Visual Metaphors	In small groups, students visually represent metaphors that show how topics interrelate.	"Sketch a metaphor for the relationship between the North and South in the Civil War."	
Aural			
Conferring Conversations (see section on data collection later in this chapter)	Teachers speak with individuals or small groups about their thinking and understanding during work time.	"What do you understand so far?"	

Figure 7.6 *continued*

continues

	How?	Example	Notes
Aural (continued)			
Discussion of Essential Question	As small groups or a whole class, students connect their current learning with the essential question.	"We have been exploring this question over time. Let's zoom back and ask ourselves, 'What do we think now about equality and genetics?'"	
Presentation	Learners present their work by reading aloud or explaining to peers, paired with questioning (see below).	"Who might like to share their thinking about the checkerboard problem?"	
Reflective Discussion	Students share and explore what they understand now about process, content, or themselves as learners with partners or in small groups.	"Turn and tell your partner what you learned about determining importance as a reader today. How did that strategy support your understanding?"	
Questioning	After learners present their writing, solutions, or thinking, all peers are responsible for thinking of a question to pose to evoke deeper thinking.	"What questions do you all have for Tyler about his map?"	
Graphic Organizers			
Checklists	On a list of tasks or targets within a larger project or unit, students indicate what they have completed and what is yet to be accomplished.	Next to each goal, provide space for learners to check "not yet/started/completed."	
K-W-L	On a three-column chart, learners record what they know, what they want to know, and (later) what they learned.	"Before we start talking about the Amazons of Dahomey, what do you know? What are you wondering or curious to find out?"	
Self-Tracker	On a table listing learning targets and with an open scale for levels of progress, students pause at intervals to rate their understanding.	"How confident do you feel in your understanding of magnetism?"	

Figure 7.6 *continued*

	How?	Example	Notes

Graphic Organizers (continued)

	How?	Example	Notes
Synthesizer	On a page they can refer back to throughout the unit, students record what additional information they have gained about the topic, adding to their prior knowledge along the way.	"What do you know now about operations with positive and negative numbers?"	
Tree Map	Students use the main idea as the trunk, and draw a branch for each supporting concept and a twig for every related detail.	"Create a tree map to gather your understanding about the Russian Revolution."	
Venn Diagram	A Venn diagram with two or more circles offers space for learners to record similarities and differences between characters, concepts, places, ideas.	"Represent the similarities and differences between meiosis and mitosis in this Venn diagram."	

Figure 7.6 *continued*

Exit Ticket – 5.2   Name Jalen Proctor

1) How did you monitor for meaning today to help you identify the type of function represented?
   I monitored for meaning by using backround knowledge and creating a table and graph by using data from the text.

2) What did you learn about yourself as a mathematician today? Explain.
   I learned that if I use what I already know and take the time to draw a graph, it would be way more easyer to solve the problem

Figure 7.7 Sixth-Grade Student's Exit Ticket

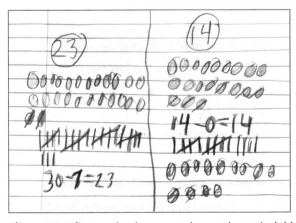

Figure 7.9 A first grader documents her mathematical thinking.

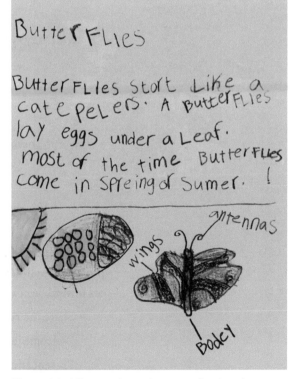

Figure 7.8 A first-grade student records what she learned from the text.

Some of the formats in Figure 7.6 or others you develop may be unfamiliar to learners, and so students will benefit from instructions and parallel examples before being asked to demonstrate what they know. A parallel example shows learners how to use the format (a Venn diagram, say), but is about another topic—say, bicycles instead of cars—and so models the process without giving away the content. Modeling the formative assessment activity reduces confusion about the format posed and supports learners' ability to demonstrate their understanding.

Rubrics

When planning assessment of an in-depth project, we consider which elements of process, product, and presentation we'd like to attend to and reflect them in our rubrics or task descriptions. For example, Figure 7.10 is a rubric for argument writing written by a cross-curricular group of sixth- to twelfth-grade teachers in Denver's North High School feeder system, which they use in content-area classes to illuminate consistent expectations for academic writing across the curriculum.

REFLECTION

- What do you notice about the structure of the rubric for argument writing in Figure 7.10 and the engineering design rubric in Figure 7.3? What do you wonder?

- In what ways are your rubrics similar? Different?

- How might you refine yours moving forward?

It is no use to build a great rubric and then keep it a secret until kids are done with the project. A well-designed rubric is like a map to success. Here are some ways we can orient learners toward our expectations:

- Share the rubric or task description at the outset of the project.
- Welcome learners to annotate the rubric and share what they notice and wonder.
- Present and discuss exemplars of this or similar projects.
- Invite learners to practice using the rubric to evaluate one or more sample projects.
- Talk about speed bumps to success that we have observed in past years' students and brainstorm strategies for overcoming them.

		1	2	3	4	Score/ Comments
			All of 1, plus . . .	*All of 2, plus . . .*	*All of 3, plus . . .*	
Content	**Claim**		Work states claim.	Claim is clear and related to topic.	Claim makes clear argument in academic language.	
	Evidence	Work includes data.	Factual evidence is present.	Evidence provided is factual and connects to claim.	Ample evidence is provided to support claim.	
	Reasoning		Reasoning is present.	Reasoning connects evidence to claim.	Reasoning is clear and convincing.	
Vocabulary			Some technical vocabulary is used.	Most of the expected content-related vocabulary is used.	Accurate academic vocabulary is used throughout.	
Structure		Work includes sections appropriate to the content.	Work is organized according to a formal style. Title and subtitles (if applicable) are used.	Paragraphs include introductory sentences. Work has a clear introduction, body, and conclusion.	Work flows logically throughout.	
Mechanics		Work is written.	Work is comprehensible.	Work is free from errors that obscure meaning.	Work is publication ready.	
Comments:						**Total:**

Figure 7.10 Argument Writing Rubric

DATA COLLECTION

We are all collecting data all the time: reading body language, overhearing conversations, watching social patterns. During formative assessment, we can gather data simply by watching signals and listening in to learners' conversations as they complete any task, as well as gather and examine completed student work. (See Figure 7.11 for the PEBC Teaching Framework for Data Collection.)

	First Steps	Next Steps	Advancing	Peak Performance
Data Collection	Ask learners whether they understand. Listen to and learn about learners' academic and socioemotional needs.	Seek evidence of understanding by observing and listening to learners during work time.	Confer with learners to name, understand, support, respond to, and document thinking. Gather a variety of artifacts as evidence of understanding.	Learners self-assess regularly and accurately and document their own growth.

Figure 7.11 Assessment: Data Collection

We seek to gather a body of evidence, to triangulate, to ensure that we see the whole picture of where each learner stands. This evidence might include written work, observed behaviors, heard comments, and conversations. Throughout learning time, as you confer (see Chapter 4) or notice learners at work, watch and listen for evidence of the learning focus. What will you look for? Figure 7.12 shows some ideas; add your own.

	Listen For	Look For	And
Understanding	• Explanations • Justifications	• Accurate descriptions or answers • Ability to transfer to novel settings	
Agency	• Confidence of speech • Problem-solving language	• Gathering materials efficiently • Using time wisely	
Process Skills	• Thinking strategies • Invitational language	• Effective group collaboration • Conflict resolution as needed	
Presentation	• Well-organized thoughts • Clarity of explanation	• Precise written work • Creative displays	

Figure 7.12 Things to Listen and Look For

DATA USE

At a recent conference, I met a former teacher who now owns a company providing web-based data management software for teachers. He described his product: "After each assessment, teachers input their students' data, and then that becomes part of each learner's record that can be analyzed." He pulled up an array of tables and graphic representations showing individual, class-wide, and grade-level achievement.

A listening teacher asked, "Why don't you just put the assessments all online? And then we would not have to use our time for data entry."

This wise former teacher explained, "We believe it is critical that teachers are looking at student work, that we need to see their paper-and-pencil products to really understand what they can do. Then, teachers can put that information into our online grade book, but teachers' eyes on student work is not something we want to remove from the teaching and learning cycle." This man knew that to teach well, we have to know our students well, and that to do so we need to observe their progress every step of the way. This takes time and organization. (See Figure 7.13 for the PEBC Teaching Framework for Data Use.)

	First Steps	Next Steps	Advancing	Peak Performance
Data Use (also see Chapter 2, Plan)	Use data for grading.	Use data to assess learners' progress, design or adjust instruction, invite learners to revise, and make decisions about resources and groupings.	Triangulate a variety of formal and informal assessments, including conferring records, to assess learners' understanding, and guide planning and instruction. Assess impact of instruction on achievement; revise plans accordingly.	Learners use data to set goals and monitor growth.

Figure 7.13 Assessment: Data Use

Organization

We need to know our learners; this takes time. Analyzing formative assessment data need not take a great deal of time, though: with pulse checks like the kinesthetic activities described in Figure 7.6, we can quickly see where the group stands. When listening in to conversations, we can keep tally of who is making sense and who needs additional time or support; we can sort exit tickets into piles: "got it" and "not yet," and we can respond accordingly. All of this collected evidence might be recorded in notes, on checklists, in grade books, or on classroom maps. Don't wait! When we let our evidence pile up, it can become cumbersome, so having a system of organization and sticking with it can really pay off. (See Figure 7.14.)

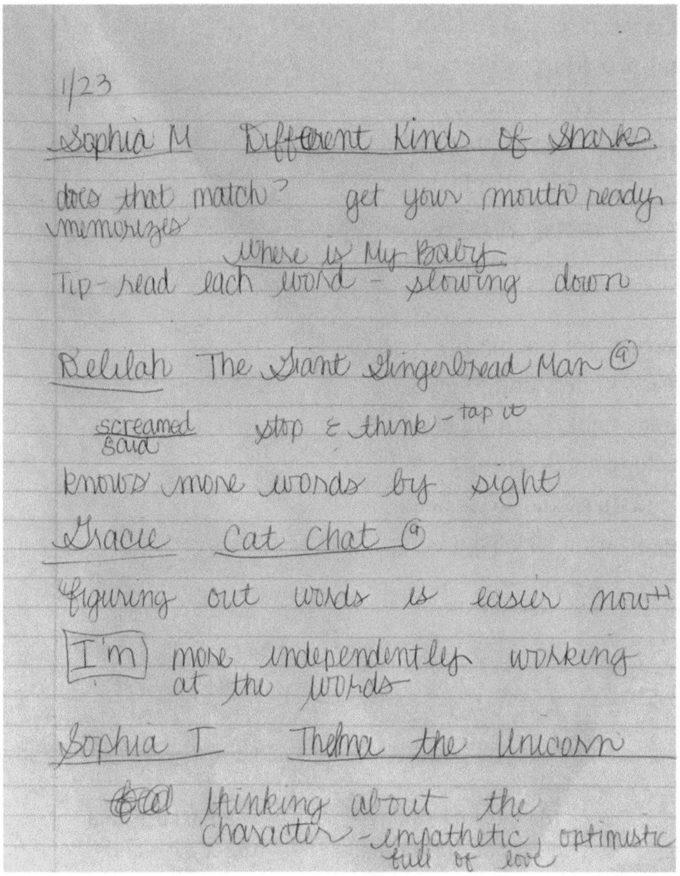

1/23
Sophia M Different Kinds of Sharks
does that match? get your mouth ready
memorizes
Where is My Baby
Tip- read each word - slowing down
Delilah The Giant Gingerbread Man (9)
screamed
said
stop & think - tap it
knows more words by sight
Gracie Cat Chat (9)
figuring out words is easier now++
I'm more independently working at the words
Sophia I Thelma the Unicorn
thinking about the character - empathetic, optimistic, full of love

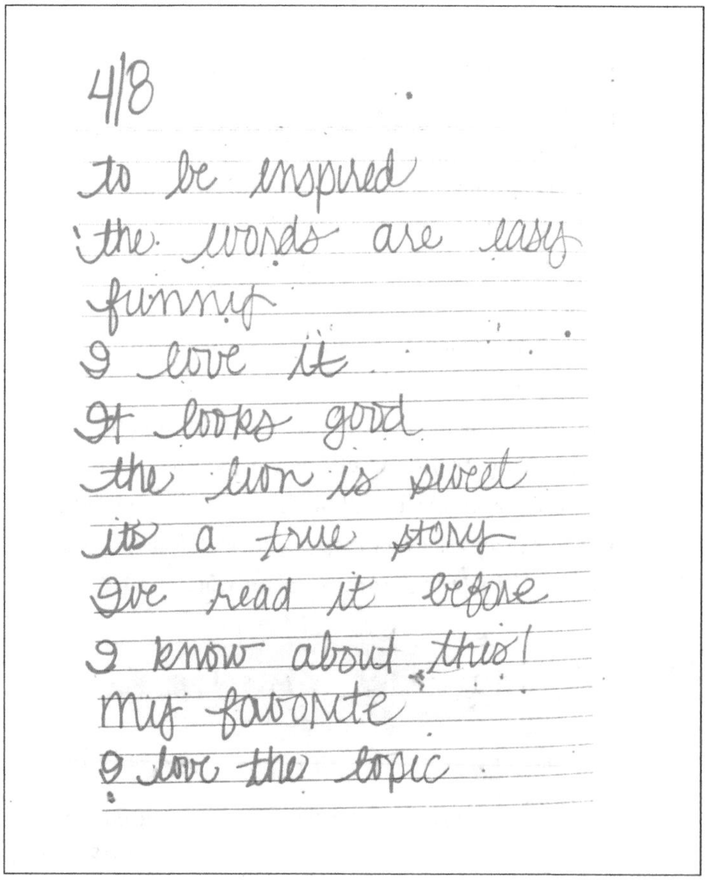

4/8
to be inspired
the words are easy
funny
I love it
It looks good
the lion is sweet
its a true story
Ive read it before
I know about this!
my favorite
I love the topic

Figure 7.14 First-grade teacher Susan McIver documents her conferring conversations by date and student name in a binder (left) and records notes about students' comments during reading discussion in her spiral notebook (right).

Responsiveness

Once learners (and their teachers) know where they stand, the next question becomes "So, what are you going to do about that?" Teacher Jeff Lewis describes the conditions that promote self-assessment and learners' wise decision making in response to that data. "I think when students are able to act on informal self-assessment, it is because there is a safety around learning from our mistakes. Students know that we are all growing, that we are a community of learners, and we support each other. So, when you are sitting down to start your work in math and realize you are stuck, you can decide, 'Yeah, I am going to go back to the carpet and join that group to get some more ideas,' there is a safety in doing that. No one is going to make a big deal about it." This is the ultimate goal of assessment for agency: learners taking action to self-monitor and self-advocate as they progress. We support them to this end when we consistently narrate their key role as actors on the stage of their own educations.

FEEDBACK

Feedback is critical to learning, and yet needs to be presented gingerly. Brain research suggests that when we feel threatened, our frontal cortex shuts down, and we enact a fight-or-flight response: this is not a learning space. To share data in ways that celebrate growth and promote effort, we can be mindful of our tone, timing, and delivery, as well as the content of our feedback. Authors Marcus Buckingham and Ashley Goodall (2019), whose article "The Feedback Fallacy" appeared in a recent edition of *Harvard Business Review*, described, "Focusing people on their shortcomings or gaps doesn't enable learning. It impairs it." Rather, we—and our students—are all best served when we catch learners at their best, and when we identify, analyze, and celebrate productive behavior or an impressive product.

Carol Ann Tomlinson (2014) explains, "I see formative assessment as an ongoing exchange between a teacher and his or her students designed to help students grow as vigorously as possible and to help teachers contribute to that growth as fully as possible." Formative feedback provides timely, supportive, and specific information and might include verification of answers, discussion of examples, analysis of worked problems or completed work, and conversations about effective processes and approaches. (See Figure 7.15 for the PEBC Teaching Framework for Feedback.)

	First Steps	Next Steps	Advancing	Peak Performance
Feedback	Provide feedback about task completion.	Provide descriptive, accurate, and timely feedback about thinking, process, and/or content. Structure peer review of works in progress and work completed. Give feedback that propels learning and growth.	Notice and name productive learning behaviors and how they lead to understanding. Create multiple opportunities for learners to give feedback to one another, as well as to their teacher, about their own progress. Teach learners to give feedback that propels learning and growth.	Learners seek, expect, and welcome feedback on their progress. Learners provide effective feedback to one another and their teacher, as well as honestly assess themselves.

Figure 7.15 Assessment: Feedback

Structures for Feedback

We provide feedback informally throughout the flow of our days in our conversations and interactions with learners. How we respond to their thinking sets the tone for their interactions with one another as well as the learning culture in our classrooms, as described in Chapter 3, "Community." Feedback can flow intentionally in many directions: teacher to learner, learner to teacher, learner to learner, learner to self. Figure 7.16 shows a few feedback formats.

Teacher to Learner	Learner to Teacher	Learner to Learner	Learner to Self
• Conferring conversations • Written comments on work • Oral responses to presentations	• Conferring conversations • Reflection writing • Survey responses • Discussion • Exit tickets	• Response to peer sharing • Peer review of draft products • Peer feedback to collaborative partners • Collaborative assessment conferences	• Self-edits on written work • Self-assessment with a rubric • Letter to self

Figure 7.16 Feedback Options

Sentence Frames for Feedback

Marcus Buckingham and Ashley Goodall (2019) state: "Telling people how we think they should improve actually hinders learning." We best promote growth when we notice and name what stood out to us and made the greatest impact. When supporting learners in providing peer feedback, we can teach them to be productive and kind. In addition to agreeing or disagreeing and stating reasons why, we might try some of these sentence frames for feedback. Which appeal to you?

- "I appreciate how . . ."
- "You really got my attention when . . ."
- "The part that makes the most sense . . ."
- "Because of . . . , I am thinking . . ."
- "I wonder why . . ."

We can also teach learners to avoid "gotcha" questions or thinly veiled coaching such as "Why didn't you . . . ?" or "What if you . . . ?" and instead provide more ownership of advice, as in "If it were me, I might . . ."

Summative Feedback

In addition to formative feedback, learners also need to know at the completion of a learning experience, project, or formal assessment how they did. When students understand the targets and put forth their best effort, they deserve to hear from us promptly about their results. This summative feedback might take the form of a score, a grade, an assessment on a rubric, a conference, a narrative evaluation, or some combination of the above and can be most impactful when learners have an opportunity to respond. We might invite them to:

- discuss results with a peer or teacher
- rework missed problems
- revise their final project

- write a note to their teacher about what went well, and in what ways they might improve
- write a letter to their future self about what they need to remember from this learning experience.

TALK BACK

What feedback would you provide on these methods for providing feedback?

Resources for Further Study

Kim Bailey and Chris Jakicic, *Common Formative Assessment*

John Hattie, *Visible Learning for Teachers: Maximizing Impact on Learning*

Jay McTighe and Grant Wiggins, *Understanding by Design*

Graham Nuthall, *The Hidden Lives of Learners*

Valerie Shute, *Focus on Formative Feedback*

Richard Stiggins et al., *Classroom Assessment for Student Learning*

Assessment FAQs

- **"What about the online and standardized assessments required by our district?"**

  Standardized assessments are one tool to measure learners' progress, but don't stop there! The more effort we make to understand students' strengths and needs, to remain vigilant to their progress, the better our lesson plans become.

- **"How do I teach my students to give one another quality feedback, not just 'good job'?"**

  We can model high-quality feedback, as in "The way you connected the map to the timeline really helped me understand how the events were related." This comment, offered right as a learner shares her project, explains what we appreciated and why, and points the way to her future successes, connecting visual representations. Also, we can teach students to nudge one another: when someone says, "Good job," they can respond with "What was good about it?"

- **"Where is the time supposed to come from to do all this assessing?"**

  Assessment can be seamlessly woven throughout the fabric of our days and units. It does not need to be another thing to add, but can be part and parcel of the work learners do. Every day, when learners are engaged with texts, problems, or discussion, we can invite self-monitoring and gather data. In our planning, we can create regular points for learners to respond within the routine of our workshops; assessment never stops.

Your Turn

Considering everything discussed previously, take time to look ahead to your next unit with an eye on assessment. Consider:

- In what ways will you invite self-monitoring?
- What assessments will you integrate?
- What data will you and your students collect? How will it be used?
- In what ways will you provide feedback?

These questions, applied to any unit, can support you in developing an assessment plan that focuses on learners' thinking.

REFLECTION

- How does your current understanding of assessment compare to your prior knowledge?

- What questions are still lingering?

- Which aspects of assessment feel most natural to you?

- Which aspects might you want to refine in your work? How?

- What changes do you feel inspired to make in your assessment practices?

- What difference will those changes make for students?

• How will you know you have succeeded?

REFLECTION ON CHAPTER QUESTION: IN WHAT WAYS MIGHT WE MONITOR AND SUPPORT PROGRESS?

Invitation: From the list in this chapter, choose a formative assessment format that is new to you, and use that structure to record your thinking here about the content of this chapter.

Conclusion

When we design a workshop learning experience, we look at the work of work time and ask ourselves, what is it that learners truly need to know or understand in order to get a foothold and be prepared to grapple with this task? There may appear to be a great many things we ought to teach before releasing students to independence, and yet a well-crafted minilesson targets one or more skills, strategies, ideas, or concepts that will be the linchpins of learners' success. We keep it brief. We bite our tongue, and save our breath, even when there is more we might add, and we let learners get to work, knowing we may circle back later and sprinkle in some other possibilities, perspectives, or tools.

That's what this book represents, a mere minilesson. In these pages, I have aspired to offer you the best of what I know now about cultivating agency and understanding for all students. My intention is that this serves as just enough to propel you forward into a phenomenal career-long work time grappling with this responsibility. Now, it is your turn to experiment, expand, and make this pedagogy your own.

This book and the Teaching Framework it's built upon represent a moment in time when PEBC stepped back to put a stake in the ground, to share with you what we have figured out so far about instruction that authentically inspires engagement, ownership, and achievement for each and every student. There is more to learn and more to share along these lines, and I invite you to continue this exploration in service of your best hopes for learners.

REFLECTION

• Which strand of the Teaching Framework offers you the greatest leverage? Why?

• If you were to add a seventh strand, what would it be and why?

- What do you want to remember most from your experience working with this text?

- What strategies will you use to help yourself to remember, implement, and reflect on your learning?

Appendix
PEBC Teaching Framework

This Framework represents over three decades of research and practice in classrooms across the country in pursuit of teaching each and every student for agency and understanding. Reflective, humble, and striving teachers have led the way in pioneering the instructional approaches described here. It's not magic, and it's not secret: the strands of this Framework are powerful tools for actualizing phenomenal instruction every day.

The Framework is designed not as a teacher evaluation rubric but rather as a tool for professional growth. Please use it as such: be honest and gentle with your own self-assessment. Study this Framework to consider next steps in your own development; seek ideas from this text, the recommended resource lists, other sources, the insights of your colleagues, and your own good judgment as you strive forward.

In terms of its structure, this Framework, like the other rubrics in this book, is designed additively. That is, the column to the left starts by identifying first steps a teacher might take in implementing that particular element. The next column builds on with next steps, and so forth. The rightmost column answers the question, "To what end for students?" and describes observable behaviors and dispositions that will result from effective implementation of this element. These descriptions have been honed across classrooms, grade levels, and content areas and seek to describe what is possible for every learner.

Know that this tool was created by teachers for teachers, and that it is, as are we all, a work in progress.

PLAN

ELEMENTS	Level of Proficiency			
	First Steps (1)	**Next Steps (2)** (all of 1, plus . . .)	**Advancing (3)** (all of 2, plus . . .)	**Peak Performance (4)** (all of 3, plus...)
Purpose				
Clarity (also see Assessment)	Attend to standards and standardized assessments. Design assessment(s).	Prioritize a small number of important content and process standards. Design demonstrations of understanding and success criteria aligned with learning intentions.	Align targets, tasks, and assessments with essential questions and enduring understandings; communicate these clearly with learners. Identify evidence of learners' understanding that can be gathered before, during, and after the unit of study.	Learners demonstrate understanding, can articulate their own growth toward targets, and advocate for their learning needs.
Life-Worthiness	Seek connections between content and life outside the classroom.	Establish relevance of current learning.	Engage with content that has meaning beyond the classroom and will support learners as scholars, citizens, and humans.	Learners know the relationship between their learning and their lives at large.
Content and Process	Be familiar with the content and standards.	Connect facts, events, and phenomena to overarching principles; provide a conceptual framework for the discipline. Pair process (practices) and content standards.	Model, think aloud, demonstrate, and invite learners to experience the process standards integral to this area of study.	Learners come to know about the discipline through processes authentic to experts in the discipline. Learners understand, remember and apply their learning.

continues

ELEMENTS	Level of Proficiency			
	First Steps (1)	Next Steps (2) (all of 1, plus . . .)	Advancing (3) (all of 2, plus . . .)	Peak Performance (4) (all of 3, plus . . .)
People				
Context	Be aware of learners' cultures, interests, and language backgrounds, as well as prior knowledge.	Select or refine content and materials to connect to learners' knowledge and heritage, individually and collectively.	Build on learners' language skills, cultural backgrounds, interests, and readiness in planning differentiated instruction.	Learners can explain the relevance of their learning in their own cultural contexts and beyond.
Responsiveness	Consider learners' prior assessment data.	Gather formative assessment data throughout planning and instruction.	Use data to hone priorities for instruction and adjust as needed. Plan differentiated instruction with flexible groupings and scaffolds, based on data.	Learners self-assess, set and refine goals, and reflect on their growing understanding.
Inquiry	Pose invitational, open-ended questions. Model a stance of curiosity and interest.	Invite authentic questions. Offer choice and variety. Anticipate adjustments to resources and targets in response to learners' interests, needs, and understanding.	Provide time, space, and structure for exploring topics of interest, sharing learning, and the unexpected.	Learners demonstrate curiosity, autonomy, and agency by asking their own questions and investigating beyond the content provided.

ELEMENTS	Level of Proficiency			
	First Steps (1)	Next Steps (2) (all of 1, plus . . .)	Advancing (3) (all of 2, plus . . .)	Peak Performance (4) (all of 3, plus . . .)
Process				
Learning Experiences	Prepare learning activities.	Design cognitively challenging tasks that invite learners to explore important content through discipline-authentic processes.	Engage learners with open-ended, differentiated challenges that invite struggle in service of conceptual understanding. Create opportunities for learners to authentically "uncover" and synthesize key ideas.	Learners understand the discipline, both as a body of knowledge and a process of making meaning. Learners understand, remember, and reapply their learning.
Language Development	Use academic language.	Identify language objectives and key vocabulary for each unit. Plan to integrate intentional and frequent academic language instruction and practice.	Design academic language supports that deepen learners' conceptual understanding.	Learners use the language of the discipline to describe their understanding.
Resources	Offer resources.	Leverage selected resources to differentiate instruction. Match resources, including technology, to learners' needs.	Provide an abundance of varied texts, imagery, media, realia, and manipulatives to support thinking and understanding. Integrate technology as a tool to increase rigor, depth, access, and opportunity.	Learners explore and make connections between information from multiple sources (some of which they self-select) in varied ways.

COMMUNITY

ELEMENTS	Level of Proficiency			
	First Steps (1)	Next Steps (2) (all of 1, plus . . .)	Advancing (3) (all of 2, plus . . .)	Peak Performance (4) (all of 3, plus . . .)
Productive Dispositions	Acknowledge each and every learner. Refer to learners as *readers, writers, mathematicians, scientists,* etc. Describe and model growth mindset.	Notice, name, and acknowledge the assets of culturally and linguistically diverse learners. Model and encourage empathy and perspective bending. Celebrate effort. Share own mistakes and self-corrections.	Include and celebrate learners of all backgrounds and abilities. Teach self-advocacy, goal setting, and self-regulation. Encourage perseverance; honor mistakes as learning experiences.	Learners demonstrate respect for and curiosity about people and cultures different from their own. Learners persevere, self-advocate, and encourage peers.
Environment	Display resources, strategies, norms, and content. Make learning materials available.	Arrange furniture to invite collaboration and accommodate learners' needs. Organize materials for ease of learner access. Post thinking on anchor charts.	Create an aesthetically pleasing, thoughtful, and thought-provoking environment. Display a variety of work representing diverse strategies and perspectives.	Learners independently use the environment—including materials, displayed work, and spaces for collaboration—as a resource for their learning.
Relationships	Learn and accurately pronounce learners' names. Appreciate differences between home cultures and school culture.	Devote time regularly to relationship building with and among students. Communicate with families about beliefs and purpose.	Know about learners' lives outside the classroom. Develop ongoing connections between home and school.	Learners belong to and care for the learning community. Families are engaged in supporting learners' success.

ELEMENTS	Level of Proficiency			
	First Steps (1)	Next Steps (2) (all of 1, plus . . .)	Advancing (3) (all of 2, plus . . .)	Peak Performance (4) (all of 3, plus . . .
Norms (also see Workshop)	Refer to shared values, such as honesty, integrity, and responsibility. Establish behavior expectations.	Model and discuss shared values. Notice and name behaviors congruent with expectations. Invite learners to make decisions.	Weave intentional conversations about shared values into academic work. Cocreate and invite reflection on class agreements. Welcome learners' leadership in upholding agreements.	Learners exhibit integrity, agency, and kindness. Learners hold peers accountable for scholarly behavior.
Ownership	Listen. Welcome learners' ideas.	Recognize learners' thinking and understanding through paraphrasing and probing. Demonstrate the expectation that all are teachers and learners by using plural pronouns *we* and *our*.	Acknowledge, attribute, and record learners' ideas and refer to them throughout studies. Create explicit links between what learners say, do, and understand and instructional next steps.	Learners own their role in the intellectual life of the group, referring to and celebrating peers' thinking. Learners' questions and ideas influence teaching and learning.
Collaboration (also see Workshop)	Provide opportunities for learners to work together. Model conflict resolution.	Use multiple grouping strategies, including choice. Support learners' social problem-solving.	Invite regular reflection on learners' efficacy with interdependence. Strategically balance individual and collaborative work.	Learners make wise choices about when to work independently and interdependently. Learners collaborate inclusively, flexibly, and effectively.

WORKSHOP

ELEMENTS	Level of Proficiency			
	First Steps (1)	**Next Steps (2)** (all of 1, plus . . .)	**Advancing (3)** (all of 2, plus . . .)	**Peak Performance (4)** (all of 3, plus . . .)
Independence	Create daily opportunities for learners' independence and collaboration.	Match resources, supports, and time to work with complexity of task(s) and individual needs.	Engage learners in authentic work of the discipline for the majority of learning time.	Learners lead meaning making throughout learning time.
Rituals and Routines	Experiment with routine and structure.	Enact a daily routine to guide workshop. Prioritize learner work time.	Learners understand and independently follow rituals to efficiently transition through workshop. Workshop elements sequenced effectively, flexibly.	Learners own and operate the workshop in the absence of their teacher.
Opening	Hook learners' interest.	Activate and build background knowledge.	Engage learners' minds in the work of the day; create a "need to know."	Learners feel curious and compelled to explore.
Minilesson (Crafting)	Communicate purpose for learning. Provide directions.	Efficiently demonstrate processes integral to learners' independence. Model precise academic language that facilitates learners' discourse.	Teacher or learners think aloud, model, or demonstrate one or more specific thinking strategies in service of metacognition. Flexibly time minilesson in response to learners' needs.	Learners actively listen and set purpose for learning. Learners know why and how to persevere during work time.

ELEMENTS	Level of Proficiency			
	First Steps (1)	Next Steps (2) (all of 1, plus . . .)	Advancing (3) (all of 2, plus . . .)	Peak Performance (4) (all of 3, plus . . .)
Work Time (Composing) (also see Community)	Structure time so that the majority is devoted to learners' independent and collaborative work. Redirect as needed.	Invite learners to read, write, solve, talk, create and/ or think, then document their understanding. Integrate independent, paired, and group work as appropriate.	Offer choice among various levels of challenge aligned with the learning goals and resources. Create opportunities for learners to work and share with a variety of peers.	Learners use work time efficiently for purposeful and meaningful learning authentic to the discipline.
Awareness and Response (also see Assessment)	Watch and listen to learners. Check in with individuals and small groups to reengage them in the task as needed.	Provide clear expectations and appropriate supports to ensure that learners use time wisely. Notice and name strategic thinking to propel learning and engagement. Provide general feedback to learners at the end of the workshop.	Respond to patterns and trends in learners' thinking by extending challenges, and adjusting available scaffolds, including invitational groups, as needed. Catch and release learners for timely, intentional instruction that deepens understanding or enhances efficiency.	Learners are able to provide feedback about their progress and needs. Learners make efficient and wise choices about their task, use of resources, pursuit of scaffolds, and selection of collaboration partners.
Conferring	Circulate during work time. Monitor and record learners' growth.	Listen in on individual or collaborative work to formatively assess. Ask learners questions about their progress. Individualize instruction as needed.	Notice and name attributes of high-quality thinking and engagement. Research learners' thinking and understanding by asking questions that promote insight and metacognition. Cocreate goals and next steps.	Learners confer with peers. Learners own progress toward their goals.

continues

ELEMENTS	Level of Proficiency			
	First Steps (1)	Next Steps (2) (all of 1, plus . . .)	Advancing (3) (all of 2, plus . . .)	Peak Performance (4) (all of 3, plus . . .)
Sharing and Reflection (also see Assessment)	Set aside daily time for reflection.	Invite learners to share work and thinking. Revisit purpose as lesson closes.	Structure varying opportunities for learners to synthesize their learning. Invite reflection on process and content learning goals, as well as learners' own growth.	Learners integrate and contextualize learning experiences to remember and reapply. Learners deepen awareness of themselves as learners.

THINKING STRATEGIES

ELEMENTS	Level of Proficiency			
	First Steps (1)	Next Steps (2) (all of 1, plus . . .)	Advancing (3) (all of 2, plus . . .)	Peak Performance (4) (all of 3, plus . . .)
Metacognition • Draw on background knowledge. • Ask questions. • Infer. • Develop sensory images. • Determine importance. • Synthesize. • Monitor for meaning.	Honor all thinking. Notice and name strategies used to make meaning.	Create time for thinking, dwelling with ideas; highlight understanding as the purpose of thinking. Describe own experiences of thinking that led to understanding. Notice and name learners' progress using the language of thinking strategies.	Narrate the evolution of individuals' and the group's thinking and learning. Engage learners in conversations about how and why thinking strategies support their understanding. Celebrate insight, as well as growth and revision.	Learners notice and name how thinking strategies support their journey toward understanding. Learners use thinking strategies to persevere in the face of challenge or confusion.
Intention	Expect learners to use one or more thinking strategies. Communicate the need for and value of thinking.	Set goals for learners' acquisition of thinking strategies. Match thinking strategies to learning experiences.	Leverage understanding with thinking strategies. Weave thinking strategy instruction consistently over time into content learning experiences.	Learners honor thinking, as demonstrated by careful listening, articulate speech, and clear written communication.
Tasks (also see Plan)	Welcome learners to share their own ideas about content.	Provide rich tasks and diverse texts that spark learners to respond.	Intentionally layer ideas and learning experiences that invite learners to deepen and refine conceptual understanding.	Learners make meaning over time and take action to apply their understanding.

continues

THINKING STRATEGIES (continued)

ELEMENTS	Level of Proficiency			
	First Steps (1)	**Next Steps (2)** (all of 1, plus . . .)	**Advancing (3)** (all of 2, plus . . .)	**Peak Performance (4)** (all of 3, plus . . .)
Gradual Release of Responsibility	Post the thinking strategies in the room. Refer to the thinking strategies. Describe strategies and their use.	Describe thinking strategies as transferable tools for meaning making. Model thinking strategies during minilessons and while conferring.	Create and scaffold intentional and varied opportunities for learners to authentically apply thinking strategies as tools for comprehension. Appreciate learners' innate knowledge of thinking strategies as tools for living.	Learners use thinking strategies authentically, flexibly, and independently in a variety of genres and across disciplines in service of understanding.
Speaking and Listening (also see Discourse)	Invite conversations about thinking.	Provide explicit vocabulary instruction to amplify learners' use of thinking strategies and academic language.	As needed, provide sentence stems, protocols, and conversation structures to facilitate meaningful discourse about thinking.	Learners socially construct knowledge through purposeful and meaningful conversations.
Documentation	Provide structures for learners to document thinking. Post individual and group thinking in the classroom.	Model and invite learners to record thinking in multiple formats. Match method of holding thinking to the text or task.	Demonstrate how to reference and re-apply "held" thinking. Create ongoing need and use for learners to access their recorded thinking.	Learners independently select appropriate structures to hold their thinking, and then use those intentionally.
Reflection (also see Workshop)	Model reflection about strategy use.	Structure reflection about how thinking strategies help learners understand.	Establish routines of self-monitoring that support learners' ongoing awareness of thinking strategies as tools for understanding.	Learners naturally consider, "How is this thinking helping me to understand?" and "What strategies work best for me to independently create meaning?"

DISCOURSE

ELEMENTS	Level of Proficiency			
	First Steps (1)	Next Steps (2) (all of 1, plus . . .)	Advancing (3) (all of 2, plus . . .)	Peak Performance (4) (all of 3, plus . . .)
Learning (also see Plan)	Focus discussions around making meaning of standards-based content.	Present important concepts, challenges, or paradoxes that invite rigorous thinking and conversation.	Use discussion to build enduring understanding of complex ideas. Structure opportunities for learners to provide and discuss claims, evidence, and reasoning.	Learners capitalize on the perspectives of their peers to explore depth and complexity and make meaning as experts in the discipline.
Structure	Plan time for discussion.	Create time for learners to independently generate ideas and questions before or during discussion. Use a variety of discussion formats regularly.	Invite partners and small groups to construct meaning before engaging in whole-class discussions. Purposefully select protocols, thinking routines, and linguistic frames to guide group conversation and promote participation by all.	Learners take ownership of the structure and content of engaged, academic conversations in service of understanding.
Expectations	Invite discussion. Expect learners to deepen understanding through conversation.	Cocreate and post agreements that describe participation in discourse. Uphold agreements. Asks learners to reflect during or after discussion on both content and process.	Model effective speaking, active listening, pausing, probing, and paraphrasing. Model and practice accountable talk.	Learners invest in the success of each discussion and hold peers accountable for upholding norms of productive discourse.

continues

ELEMENTS	Level of Proficiency			
	First Steps (1)	**Next Steps (2)** (all of 1, plus . . .)	**Advancing (3)** (all of 2, plus . . .)	**Peak Performance (4)** (all of 3, plus . . .)
Access	Welcome all learners to share thinking orally. Balance quiet think time, teacher talk, and learner talk.	Encourage peer-to-peer conversation and feedback. Intentionally integrate strategies to equalize voices.	Encourage all learners to participate in and listen to discussions. Maintain mutual respect by providing feedback on appropriate tone or comments.	Learners lead respectful, learning-focused discussions that include multiple perspectives.
Language Development	Expose learners to rich metacognitive and academic language.	Provide scaffolds for understanding disciplinary vocabulary, text structures, figurative language, and academic language.	Create authentic opportunities for learners to practice academic language and exercise social capital in conversation.	Learners use academic language with increasing sophistication as they participate in classroom discussions.
Facilitation	Listen. Facilitate learning-focused discussions.	Ask compelling questions. Model invitational language, clarifying questions, effective argument, and respectful disagreement. Monitor and document learners' talk.	Invite learners in conversation to ask questions, synthesize, test concepts and hypotheses, formulate conjectures, construct explanations, challenge reasoning, argue, and draw conclusions. Invite learners' metacognition about the evolution of their own understanding through discourse.	Learners provoke and challenge peers' thinking, and invite and welcome differing views, as well as share their own evolving perspectives.

ASSESSMENT

ELEMENTS	Level of Proficiency			
	First Steps (1)	Next Steps (2) (all of 1, plus . . .)	Advancing (3) (all of 2, plus . . .)	Peak Performance (4) (all of 3, plus . . .)
Self-Monitoring	Communicate purpose for learning.	Provide success criteria for major tasks. Invite learners to self-assess.	Coconstruct descriptors of quality. Structure learners' regular self-assessment of progress toward learning goals and success criteria.	Learners set goals, self-assess, and reflect on their growing understanding.
Assessment Design	Plan informal and formal assessments of process and content goals.	Integrate multiple forms of assessment, including performance assessments. Plan backward from a summative assessment aligned with objectives and standards before teaching the unit.	Provide authentic, engaging, and purposeful opportunities for learners to demonstrate understanding. Plan to observe for specific learner behaviors that demonstrate understanding.	Learners exhibit progress toward mastery of standards in multiple meaningful ways.
Data Collection	Ask learners whether they understand. Listen to and learn about learners' academic and socioemotional needs.	Seek evidence of understanding by observing and listening to learners during work time.	Confer with learners to name, understand, support, respond to, and document thinking. Gather a variety of artifacts as evidence of understanding.	Learners self-assess regularly and accurately and document their own growth.

continues

ELEMENTS	Level of Proficiency			
	First Steps (1)	**Next Steps (2)** (all of 1, plus . . .)	**Advancing (3)** (all of 2, plus . . .)	**Peak Performance (4)** (all of 3, plus . . .)
Data Use (also see Plan)	Use data for grading.	Use data to assess learners' progress, design or adjust instruction, invite learners to revise, and make decisions about resources and groupings.	Triangulate a variety of formal and informal assessments, including conferring records, to assess learners' understanding, and guide planning and instruction. Assess impact of instruction on achievement; revise plans accordingly.	Learners use data to set goals and monitor growth.
Feedback	Provide feedback about task completion.	Provide descriptive, accurate, and timely feedback about thinking, process, and/or content. Structure peer review of works in progress and work completed. Give feedback that propels learning and growth.	Notice and name productive learning behaviors and how they lead to understanding. Create multiple opportunities for learners to give feedback to one another, as well as and to their teacher, about their own progress. Teach learners to give feedback that propels learning and growth.	Learners seek, expect, and welcome feedback on their progress. Learners provide effective feedback to one another and their teacher, as well as honestly assess themselves.

References

Allen, Janet. 1999. *Words, Words, Words*. Portland, ME: Stenhouse.

Allen, Patrick. 2009. *Conferring: The Keystone of Readers' Workshop*. Portland, ME: Stenhouse.

Almarode, John T. 2017. "Teacher Clarity Is to Collective Teacher Efficacy As . . ." *Corwin Connect*, October 17. https://corwin-connect.com/2017/10/teacher-clarity-collective-teacher-efficacy.

Anderson, Carl. 2000. *How's It Going? A Practical Guide to Conferring with Student Writers*. Portsmouth, NH: Heinemann.

Anderson, Lauren, and David Krathwohl. 2001. *A Taxonomy for Learning, Teaching, and Assessing: A Revision of Bloom's Taxonomy of Educational Objectives*. Abridged ed. New York: Longman.

Aspen Institute National Commission on Social, Emotional, and Academic Development. 2018. *From a Nation at Risk to a Nation at Hope*. Washington, DC: Aspen Institute. http://nationathope.org.

Atwell, Nancie. 1998. *In the Middle: New Understanding About Writing, Reading, and Learning*. 2nd ed. Portsmouth, NH: Heinemann.

August, Diane. 2003. *Supporting the Development of English Literacy in English Language Learners*. Baltimore, MD: Center for Research on the Education of Students Placed at Risk.

Bailey, Kim, and Chris Jakicic. 2011. *Common Formative Assessment*. Bloomington, IN: Solution Tree.

Bandura, Albert. 2001. "Social Cognitive Theory: An Agentic Perspective." *Annual Review of Psychology* 52: 1–26.

Beck, Isabel L., Margaret G. McKeown, and Linda Kucan. 2002. *Bringing Words to Life: Robust Vocabulary Instruction*. New York: Guilford Press.

Beilock, Sian L., Elizabeth A. Gunderson, Gerardo Ramirez, and Susan C. Levine. 2010. "Female Teachers' Math Anxiety Affects Girls' Math Achievement." *PNAS* 107 (5): 1860–63. https://doi.org/10.1073/pnas.0910967107.

Belle, Crystal. 2019. "What Is Social Justice Education Anyway?" *Education Week*, February 20. www.edweek.org/ew/articles/2019/01/23/what-is-social-justice-education-anyway.html.

Bennett, Samantha. 2007. *That Workshop Book*. Portsmouth, NH: Heinemann.

Berger, Ron. 2003. *An Ethic of Excellence*. Portsmouth, NH: Heinemann.

Bloom, Benjamin S. 1956. *Taxonomy of Educational Objectives, Handbook I: The Cognitive Domain*. New York: David McKay Co. Inc.

Boston, Melissa D., Frederick Dillon, Margaret S. Smith, and Stephen Miller. 2017. *Taking Action: Implementing Effective Mathematics Teaching Practices in Grades 9–12*. Reston, VA: National Council of Teachers of Mathematics.

Buckingham, Marcus, and Ashley Goodall. 2019. "The Feedback Fallacy." *Harvard Business Review*, March/April. https://hbr.org/2019/03/the-feedback-fallacy.

Cain, Susan. 2012. *Quiet: The Power of Introverts in a World That Can't Stop Talking*. New York: Crown Publishing Group.

Carey, Bjorn. 2013. "Language Gap Between Rich and Poor Children Begins in Infancy, Stanford Psychologists Find." *Stanford News*, September 25. https://news.stanford.edu/news/2013/september/toddler-language-gap-091213.html.

Cazden, Courtney. 1988. *Classroom Discourse: The Language of Teaching and Learning*. Portsmouth, NH: Heinemann.

Center on the Developing Child at Harvard University. 2015. "Supportive Relationships and Active Skill-Building Strengthen the Foundations of Resilience." Working Paper No. 13. https://developingchild.harvard.edu/resources/supportive-relationships-and-active-skill-building-strengthen-the-foundations-of-resilience.

Chamot, Anna U., and J. M. O'Malley. "The Cognitive Academic Language Learning Approach: A Model for Linguistically Diverse Classrooms." *The Elementary School Journal* 96 (3): 259–73.

Chapin, Suzanne, Catherine O'Connor, and Nancy Canavan Anderson. 2003. *Classroom Discussions: Using Math Talk to Help Students Learn*. Sausalito, CA: Math Solutions.

City, Elizabeth A. 2014. "Talking to Learn." *Educational Leadership* 72 (3): 10–16. http://www.ascd.org/publications/educational-leadership/nov14/vol72/num03/Talking-to-Learn.aspx.

Cloud, Nancy, Fred Genesee, and Else Hamayan. 2009. *Literacy Instruction for English Language Learners: A Teacher's Guide to Research-Based Practices*. Portsmouth, NH: Heinemann.

Colorado Department of Education. 2010. Colorado Education Statistics. http://www.cde.state.co.us/index_stats.htm.

Conrad, Lori, Missy Matthews, Cheryl Zimmerman, and Patrick Allen. 2008. *Put Thinking to the Test*. Portland, ME: Stenhouse.

Contemporary Educational Psychology. 1983. 8 (3): 205–345 (entire issue). www.sciencedirect.com/journal/contemporary-educational-psychology/vol/8/issue/3.

Cummins, Jim. 1983. "Language Proficiency and Academic Achievement." In *Issues in Language Testing Research*, edited by J. W. Oller Jr., 108–29. Rowley, MA: Newbury House.

Cunningham, Wendy, and Paula Villasenor. 2016. *Employer Voices, Employer Demands, and Implications for Public Skills Development Policy: Connecting the Labor and Education Sectors*. Policy Research Working Paper No. 7582. Washington, DC: World Bank.

Dancis, Jerome. 2010. "Alternate Learning Environment Helps Students Excel in Calculus: A Pedagogical Analysis." University of Maryland, College Park. http://www-users.math.umd.edu/~jnd/Treisman.txt.

Daniels, Harvey "Smokey." 2017. *The Curious Classroom*. Portsmouth, NH: Heinemann.

de Jong, Esther, and Candace A. Harper. 2005. "Preparing Mainstream Teachers for English-Language Learners: Is Being a Good Teacher Good Enough?" *Teacher Education Quarterly* 32 (2): 101–24. https://files.eric.ed.gov/fulltext/EJ795308.pdf.

Delpit, Lisa. 2012. *"Multiplication Is for White People": Raising Expectations for Other People's Children*. New York: The New Press.

Duke, Nell, and P. D. Pearson. 2002. "Effective Practices for Developing Reading Comprehension." In *What Research Has to Say About Reading Instruction*, 3rd ed., edited by A. E. Farstrup and S. J. Samuels. Newark, DE: International Reading Association.

Duke, Nell, P. Pearson, Stephanie Strachan, and Alison Billman. 2011. "Essential Elements of Fostering and Teaching Reading Comprehension: In *What Research Has to Say About Reading Instruction*, 4th ed., edited by A. E. Farstrup and S. J. Samuels, 51–93. Newark, DE: International Reading Association.

Duncan-Andrade, J., and E. Morrell. 2008. *The Art of Critical Pedagogy: Possibilities for Moving from Theory to Practice in Urban Schools*. New York: Peter Lang.

Dweck, Carol. 2006. *Mindset: The New Psychology of Success*. New York: Random House.

Echevarría, Jana, MaryEllen Vogt, and Deborah J. Short. 2008. *Making Content Comprehensible for English Learners: The SIOP Model*. 3rd ed. Boston: Allyn & Bacon.

Ermeling, Brad, James Hiebert, and Ron Gallimore. 2015. "Beyond Growth Mindset: Creating Classroom Opportunities for Meaningful Struggle." *Education Week Teacher*, February 19. www.edweek .org/tm/articles/2015/12/07/beyond-growth-mindset-creating-classroom-opportunities-for.html.

Fisher, Douglas, and Nancy Frey. 2011. *The Purposeful Classroom: How to Structure Lessons with Learning Goals in Mind.* Alexandria, VA: Association for Supervision and Curriculum Development (ASCD).

Fisher, Douglas, Nancy Frey, and Carol Rothenberg. 2008. *Content-Area Conversations: How to Plan Discussion-Based Lessons for Diverse Language Learners.* Alexandria, VA: Association for Supervision and Curriculum Development (ASCD).

Fitzgerald, Jill. 1995. "English-as-a-Second-Language Learners' Cognitive Reading Processes: A Review of Research in the United States." *Review of Educational Research* 65 (2): 145. doi:10.2307/1170711.

Fosnot, Catherine. 2016. *Conferring with Young Mathematicians at Work.* New London, CT: New Perspectives on Learning.

Freeman, Yvonne S., and David E. Freeman. 2009. *Academic Language for English Language Learners and Struggling Readers: How to Help Students Succeed Across Content Areas.* Portsmouth, NH: Heinemann.

Freire, Paulo. 1970. *Pedagogy of the Oppressed.* New York: Seabury Press.

George, Steph. 2018. "Turn & Talk with Ellin Keene, Tom Newkirk, and Kathy Collins." *Heinemann Blog,* October 18. http://blog.heinemann.com/turn-talk-with-ellin-keene-tom-newkirk-and-kathy -collins.

González, Norma, Luis C. Moll, and Cathy Amanti. 2005. *Funds of Knowledge: Theorizing Practices in Households, Communities and Classrooms.* Mahwah, NJ: Lawrence Erlbaum.

Gopal, Priyamvada. 2017. "Yes, We Must Decolonise: Our Teaching Has to Go Beyond Elite White Men." *The Guardian,* October 27. www.theguardian.com/commentisfree/2017/oct/27/decolonise-elite -white-men-decolonising-cambridge-university-english-curriculum-literature.

Gratz, Alan. 2017. *Refugee.* New York: Scholastic.

Hadaway, N. L., S. M. Vardell, and T. A. Young. 2001. "Scaffolding Oral Language Development Through Poetry for Students Learning English." *The Reading Teacher* 54 (8): 796–806.

Hale, Michael S., and Elizabeth A. City. 2006. *The Teacher's Guide to Leading Student-Centered Discussions: Talking About Texts in the Classroom.* Thousand Oaks, CA: Corwin.

Hammond, Zaretta. 2015. *Culturally Responsive Teaching and the Brain: Promoting Authentic Engagement and Rigor Among Culturally and Linguistically Diverse Students.* Thousand Oaks, CA: Corwin.

Hart, Betty, and Todd Risley. 1995. *Meaningful Differences in the Everyday Experience of Young American Children.* Baltimore, MD: Paul H. Brookes Publishing Company.

———. 2003. "The Early Catastrophe: The 30 Million Word Gap." *American Educator* 27 (1): 4–9.

Harvey, Stephanie, and Anne Goudvis, 2000. *Strategies That Work.* Portland, ME: Stenhouse.

Hattie, John. 2009. *Visible Learning: A Synthesis of Over 800 Meta-Analyses Relating to Achievement.* New York: Routledge.

———. 2012. *Visible Learning for Teachers: Maximizing Impact on Learning.* New York: Routledge.

Hiebert, James. 1997. *Making Sense: Teaching and Learning Mathematics with Understanding.* Portsmouth, NH: Heinemann.

Hill, Jane D., and Kathleen M. Flynn. 2006. *Classroom Instruction That Works for English Language Learners.* Alexandria, VA: Association for Supervision and Curriculum Development (ASCD).

Hoffer, Wendy Ward. 2009. *Science as Thinking.* Portsmouth, NH: Heinemann.

———. 2012. *Minds on Mathematics.* Portsmouth, NH: Heinemann.

———. 2016. *Developing Literate Mathematicians.* Reston, VA: National Council of Teachers of Mathematics (NCTM).

hooks, bell. 1994. *Teaching to Transgress: Education as the Practice of Freedom.* New York: Routledge.

Horn, Ilana Seidel. 2017. *Motivated: Designing Math Classrooms Where Students Want to Join In.* Portsmouth, NH: Heinemann.

Hoy, Wayne K., C. J. Tarter, and Anita Woolfolk Hoy. 2006. "Academic Optimism of Schools: A Force for Student Achievement." *American Educational Research Journal* 43 (3): 425–46.

Huff, Gisèle. 2019. "Wither Education: Are We Preparing Our Children for the Twenty-First Century?" *Flypaper.* fordhaminstitute.org/national/commentary/wither-education-are-we-preparing-our -children-twenty-first-century.

Hutchinson, David. 2016. *Great Groups: Creating and Leading Effective Groups.* Thousand Oaks, CA: Sage.

Hyde, Arthur. 2006. *Comprehending Math: Adapting Reading Strategies to Teach Mathematics, K–6.* Portsmouth, NH: Heinemann.

———. 2014. *Comprehending Problem Solving.* Portsmouth, NH: Heinemann.

Hyde, Arthur, Susan Friedlander, Lynn Pittner, and Cheryl Heck. 2009. *Understanding Middle School Math: Cool Problems to Get Students Thinking and Connecting.* Portsmouth, NH: Heinemann.

Johnston, Peter. 2004. *Choice Words: How Our Language Affects Students' Learning.* Portland, ME: Stenhouse.

———. 2012. *Opening Minds.* Portland, ME: Stenhouse.

Keene, Ellin Oliver. 2008. *To Understand.* Portsmouth, NH: Heinemann.

Keene, Ellin Oliver, and Susan Zimmermann. 2007. *Mosaic of Thought: The Power of Comprehension Strategy Instruction.* 2nd ed. Portsmouth, NH: Heinemann.

Keene, Ellin Oliver, Susan Zimmermann, Debbie Miller, Samantha Bennett, Leslie Blauman, Chryse Hutchins, Stephanie Harvey, Anne Goudvis, Brad Buhrow, Gina Cervetti, Marjorie Larner, Cris Tovani, Nancy L. Commins, Anne Upczak Garcia, Tanny McGregor, P. David Pearson, and Harvey "Smokey" Daniels. 2011. *Comprehension Going Forward: Where We Are and What's Next.* Portsmouth, NH: Heinemann.

Kempton, Sue. 2007. *The Literate Kindergarten: Where Wonder and Discovery Thrive.* Portsmouth, NH: Heinemann.

King, Martin Luther. 1947. "The Purpose of Education." *The Maroon Tiger.* Atlanta: Morehouse College. https://kinginstitute.stanford.edu/king-papers/documents/purpose-education.

Klaus-Quinlan, Moker, and Sally Nathansen-Mejia. 2010. *Bridging Words and Worlds: Effective Instruction for Culturally & Linguistically Diverse Learners.* Denver, CO: PEBC.

Klemenčič, Manja. 2014. "What Is Student Agency? An Ontological Exploration in the Context of Research on Student Engagement." In *Student Engagement in Europe: Society, Higher Education and Student Governance,* edited by R. Primozič, 11–29. Council of Europe Higher Education Series No. 20. Strasbourg: Council of Europe Publishing.

Knight, Nicole. 2014. "Why Are Academic Discussions So Important for Our ELLs?" *The Teaching Channel,* October 24. https://www.teachingchannel.org/blog/2014/10/24/academic-discussions -and-english-language-learners-ousd/.

Kohn, Alfie. 1996. *Beyond Discipline.* Alexandria, VA: Association for Supervision and Curriculum Development (ASCD).

Krashen, Stephen. n.d. "General Principles for Teaching ELL Students." https://studylib.net/doc/7517581 /general-principles-for-teaching-ell-students.

Langer, Judith, and Arthur Applebee. 1986. "Reading and Writing Instruction: Toward a Theory of Teaching and Learning." *Review of Research in Education* 13: 171–94.

Lasky, Kathryn. 1994. *The Librarian Who Measured the Earth.* Hong Kong: South China Printing Company.

REFERENCES

Lerch, Carol, Andrea Bilics, and Binta Colley. 2006. "Using Reflection to Develop Higher Order Processes." Paper presented at the Annual Meeting of the American Educational Research Association, April. https://files.eric.ed.gov/fulltext/ED491643.pdf.

Liben, David, and P. David Pearson. 2018. Published April 3, 2013. Adjusted January 2, 2018. "The Progression of Reading Comprehension." https://achievethecore.org/page/1195/the-progression -of-reading-comprehension.

Marzano, Robert, and Debra Pickering. 2005. *Building Academic Vocabulary: Teachers' Manual.* Alexandria, VA: Association for Supervision and Curriculum Development (ASCD).

McTighe, Jay, and Elliott Seif. 2014. "Teaching for Understanding: A Meaningful Education for 21st Century Learners." *Teachers Matter* 2014 (Spring): 15–17. https://www.jaymctighe.com/wp -content/uploads/2011/04/Teaching-for-Understanding.pdf.

McTighe, Jay, and Grant Wiggins. 2004. *Understanding by Design.* Alexandria, VA: Association for Supervision and Curriculum Development (ASCD).

———. 2012. "From Common Core Standards to Curriculum: Five Big Ideas." http://grantwiggins.files. wordpress.com/2012/09/mctighe_wiggins_final_common_core _standards.pdf.

Meier, Deborah. 2002. *The Power of Their Ideas: Lessons for America from a Small School in Harlem.* Boston: Beacon Press.

Michael Jr. 2015. "Know Your Why." YouTube video. https://www.youtube.com/watch?v=1ytFB8TrkTo.

Miller, Debbie. 2002. *Reading with Meaning.* Portland, ME: Stenhouse.

———. 2018. *What's the Best That Could Happen?* Portsmouth, NH: Heinemann.

Montgomery, Sy. 2018. *Inky's Amazing Escape.* New York: Simon & Schuster.

Munson, Jen. 2018. *In the Moment: Conferring in the Elementary Math Classroom.* Portsmouth, NH: Heinemann.

Murray, Donald. 1987. *Write to Learn.* New York: Holt, Rinehart, and Winston.

National Governors Association Center for Best Practices, Council of Chief State School Officers. 2010. *Common Core State Standards.* Washington, DC: National Governors Association Center for Best Practices, Council of Chief State School Officers.

National Research Council. 2000. *How People Learn: Brain, Mind, Experience, and School.* Washington, DC: National Academies Press.

———. 2012. *Educating for Life and Work: Developing Transferrable Knowledge and Skills for the Twentieth Century.* Washington, DC: National Academies Press.

National Scientific Council on the Developing Child. 2015. "Supportive Relationships and Active Skill- Building Strengthen the Foundations of Resilience." Working Paper 15. Boston: Harvard University Center on the Developing Child. https://46y5eh11fhgw3ve3ytpwxt9r-wpengine .netdna-ssl.com/wp-content/uploads/2015/05/The-Science-of-Resilience2.pdf.

Newkirk, Thomas. 2011. *The Art of Slow Reading.* Portsmouth, NH: Heinemann.

NGSS Lead States. 2013. *Next Generation Science Standards: for States, by States.* Washington, DC: The National Academies Press.

Nuthall, Graham. 2007. *The Hidden Lives of Learners.* Wellington, New Zealand: NZCER Press.

Nystrand, Martin. 2012. *Opening Dialogue: Understanding the Dynamics of Language and Learning in the English Classroom.* New York: Teachers College Press.

Olson, Carol Booth, and Robert Land. 2007. "A Cognitive Strategies Approach to Reading and Writing Instruction for English Language Learners in Secondary School." *Research in the Teaching of English* 41 (3): 269–303. http://www.nwp.org/cs/public/print/resource/2385.

Organization for Economic Cooperation and Development (OECD). 2015. Program for International Student Assessment (PISA). International Data Explorer. https://nces.ed.gov/surveys/pisa/idepisa/.

Ovando, Carlos J., Virginia P. Collier, and Mary C. Combs. 2003. *Bilingual & ESL Classrooms: Teaching in Multicultural Contexts.* 3rd ed. Boston: McGraw Hill.

Paton, Alan. 1948. *Cry, the Beloved Country.* New York: Charles Scribner's Sons.

Pearson, P. David. 2007. "An Endangered Species Act for Literacy Education." *Journal of Literacy Research* 39 (2): 145–62. https://doi.org/10.1080/10862960701331878.

Pearson, P. David, and Margaret C. Gallagher. 1983. "The Instruction of Reading Comprehension." *Contemporary Educational Psychology* 8: 317–44.

Pearson, P. David, and James V. Hoffman. 2011. "Principles of Effective Reading Instruction." In *Rebuilding the Foundation: Effective Reading Instruction for 21st Century Literacy*, edited by T. V. Rasinski, 9–40. Bloomington, IN: Solution Tree Press.

Pearson, P. David, Laura R. Roehler, Janice A. Dole, and Gerald G. Duffy. 1992. "Developing Expertise in Reading Comprehension." In *What Research Has to Say About Reading Instruction*, edited by J. Samuels and A. Farstrup, 145–99. Newark, DE: International Reading Association.

Peterson, Ralph. 1992. *Life in a Crowded Place.* Portsmouth, NH: Heinemann.

Phillips, Barbara E. 2018. "Take a Praise Walk!" *Educational Leadership* 76 (3). http://www.ascd.org/publications/educational-leadership/nov18/vol76/num03/Take-a-Praise-Walk!.aspx.

Plaut, Suzanne, ed. 2009. *The Right to Literacy in Secondary Schools: Creating a Culture of Thinking.* New York: Teachers College Press.

Pransky, Ken. 2008. *Beneath the Surface: The Hidden Realities of Teaching Culturally and Linguistically Diverse Young Learners: K–6.* Portsmouth, NH: Heinemann.

Public Education & Business Coalition. n.d. *Thinking Strategies for Learners.* https://www.pebc.org/wp-content/uploads/publications/thinking-strategies.pdf.

Puentedura, Ruben R. 2013. "SAMR: Moving from Enhancement to Transformation." *Ruben R. Puentedura's Weblog,* May 29. http://www.hippasus.com/rrpweblog/archives/000095.html.

Quate, Stevi, and John McDermott. 2010. *Clock Watchers: Six Steps to Motivating and Engaging Disengaged Students Across Content Areas.* Portsmouth, NH: Heinemann.

Reed, Brecken, and Jennifer Railsback. 2003. *Strategies and Resources for Mainstream Teachers of English Language Learners.* Portland, OR: Northwest Regional Educational Laboratory. https://educationnorthwest.org/sites/default/files/ell.pdf.

Reinhart, Steven. 2000. "Never Say Anything a Kid Can Say!" *Mathematics Teaching in the Middle School* 5 (8): 478–83.

Resnick, Lauren, Christa Asterhan, and Sherice Clarke. 2018. "Accountable Talk: Instructional Dialogue That Builds the Mind." *Educational Practices Series* 29. International Academy of Education and International Bureau of Education.

Resnick, Lauren B., Sarah Michaels, and M.C. O'Connor. 2010. "How (Well-Structured) Talk Builds the Mind." In *Innovations in Educational Psychology: Perspectives on Learning, Teaching, and Human Development*, edited by D. D. Preiss and R. J. Sternberg, 163–94. New York: Springer.

Riley, Heather, and Youki Terada. 2019. "Bringing the Science of Learning into Classrooms." *Edutopia,* January 14. www.edutopia.org/article/bringing-science-learning-classrooms.

Ritchhart, Ron. 2002. *Intellectual Character: What It Is, Why It Matters, and How to Get It.* San Francisco: Jossey-Bass.

———. 2015. *Creating Cultures of Thinking: The 8 Forces We Must Master to Truly Transform Our Schools.* San Francisco: Jossey-Bass.

Ritchhart, Ron, Mark Church, and Karin Morrison. 2011. *Making Thinking Visible: How to Promote Engagement, Understanding, and Independence for All Learners.* San Francisco: Jossey-Bass.

Rosenthal, Robert, and Lenore Jacobson. 1968. *Pygmalion in the Classroom: Teacher Expectation and Pupils' Intellectual Development.* New York: Holt, Rinehart & Winston.

Rowe, Mary Budd. 1986. "Wait Time: Slowing Down May Be a Way of Speeding Up!" *Journal of Teacher Education* 37 (1): 43–50. https://doi.org/10.1177/002248718603700110.

Saul, Wendy. 2002. *Science Workshop.* Portsmouth, NH: Heinemann.

Schmoker, Michael. 1999. *Results: The Key to Continuous School Improvement.* Alexandria, VA: Association for Supervision and Curriculum Development (ASCD).

Schwartz, Katrina. 2016. "How 'Productive Failure' in Math Class Helps Make Lessons Stick," *Mind/Shift*, April 19. www.kqed.org/mindshift/44726/how-productive-failure-for-students-can-help-lessons-stick.

Serravallo, Jennifer, and Gravity Goldberg. 2007. *Conferring with Readers.* Portsmouth, NH: Heinemann.

Shetterly, Margot Lee. 2016. *Hidden Figures.* Young readers' ed. New York: HarperCollins Publishers.

Shute, Valerie. 2008. *Focus on Formative Feedback.* Princeton, NJ: Educational Testing Service. https://www.ets.org/Media/Research/pdf/RR-07-11.pdf.

Stein, Mary K., and Suzanne Lane. 1996. "Instructional Tasks and the Development of Student Capacity to Think and Reason: An Analysis of the Relationship Between Teaching and Learning in a Reform Mathematics Project." *Educational Research and Evaluation* 2 (1): 50–80.

Stiggins, Richard. 1996. *Student Centered Classroom Assessment.* 2nd ed. Upper Saddle River, NJ: Prentice Hall.

———. 2005. *An Introduction to Assessment for Student Learning.* Upper Saddle River, NJ: Prentice Hall.

———. 2007. "Assessment Through the Students' Eyes." *Educational Leadership* 64 (8): 22–26. http://www.ascd.org/publications/educational-leadership/may07/vol64/num08/Assessment-Through-the-Student%27s-Eyes.aspx.

Stiggins, Richard, Judith A. Arter, Jan Chappuis, and Stephen Chappuis. 2004. *Classroom Assessment for Student Learning.* New York: Assessment Training Institute.

Telegraph staff. 2013. "Mothers Asked Nearly 300 Questions a Day, Study Finds." *The Telegraph*, March 28. www.telegraph.co.uk/news/uknews/9959026/Mothers-asked-nearly-300-questions-a-day-study-finds.html.

Tovani, Cris. 2000. *I Read It, but I Don't Get It.* Portland, ME: Stenhouse.

———. 2004. *Do I Really Have to Teach Reading?* Portland, ME: Stenhouse.

———. 2011. *So What Do They Really Know?* Portland, ME: Stenhouse.

Tovani, Cris, and Elizabeth Birr Moje. 2017. *No More Teaching as Telling.* Portsmouth, NH: Heinemann.

Turnaround for Children. 2018. "Key Findings and Implications of the Science of Learning and Development." http://www.turnaroundusa.org/wp-content/uploads/2018/02/Key-Findings-and-Implications-of-the-Science-of-Learning-Development.pdf.

Uribe, M., and S. Nathenson-Mejía. 2008. *Literacy Essentials for English Language Learners: Successful Transitions.* New York: Teachers College Press.

U.S. Department of Education, Institute of Education Sciences. National Center for Educational Statistics, National Assessment of Educational Progress (NAEP), various years (1992–2013) Mathematics and Reading Assessments. Washington, DC: U.S. Department of Education.

U.S. Department of Energy. 2017. "Ionizing Radiation Dose Ranges." https://www.remm.nlm.gov/DOE_PosterShowingRadiationDoses_Part2.pdf.

Vygotsky, L. S. 1978. *Mind in Society: Development of Higher Psychological Processes.* Boston: Harvard University Press.

Washington, Denzel, dir. 2008. *The Great Debaters.* DVD. New York: The Weinstein Company.

Webb, Norman L. 1997. *Criteria for Alignment of Expectations and Assessments in Mathematics and Science Education* (Council of Chief State School Officers and National Institute for Science Education Research Monograph No. 6). Madison: University of Wisconsin, Wisconsin Center for Education Research.

——. 1999. *Alignment Study in Language Arts, Mathematics, Science, and Social Studies of State Standards and Assessments for Four States.* Washington, DC: Council of Chief State School Officers.

——. 2005. *Alignment, Depth of Knowledge, and Change.* Paper presented at the annual meeting of the Florida Educational Research Association, Miami, FL.

Weil, Simone, to Joë Bousquet, April 13, 1942. 1982. (Original quote: L'attention est la forme la plus rare et la plus pure de la générosité.) In *Correspondance*, 18. Lausanne, Switzerland: Editions l'Age d'Homme.

Wiggins, Grant. 2002. "Grant Wiggins: Defining Assessment." *Edutopia*, January 21. https://www.edutopia.org/grant-wiggins-assessment.

Wiggins, Grant, and Jay McTighe. 2005. *Understanding by Design.* 2nd ed. Upper Saddle River, NJ: Prentice Hall.

Wiliam, Dylan. 2018. *Creating the Schools Our Children Need.* West Palm Beach, FL: Learning Sciences International.

Zakrzewski, Vicki. 2017. "How to Help Students Believe in Themselves." The Greater Good Science Center at the University of California, Berkeley. https://greatergood.berkeley.edu/article/item/how_to_help_students_believe_in_themselves.

Zwiers, Jeff. 2006. "Integrating Academic Language, Thinking, and Content: Learning Scaffolds for Non-Native Speakers in the Middle Grades." *Journal of English for Academic Purposes* 5: 317–32.

——. 2011. *Academic Conversations: Classroom Talk That Fosters Critical Thinking.* Portland, ME: Stenhouse.

——. 2014. *Building Academic Language: Meeting Common Core Standards Across Disciplines.* San Francisco: Jossey-Bass.

——. 2019. *The Communication Effect.* Thousand Oaks, CA: SAGE Publications.